Introduction

In recent years, increasing recognition of the importance of drama in education has led to pressure for a more complete understanding of its nature and functions. What drama is and how it influences children's learning and development are fundamental concerns which require study and clarification in terms of the curriculum. Equally important are the practical implications for teachers, since they have the task of assessing needs, appraising possibilities and deciding upon approaches, strategies and methods.

It is perhaps not surprising that they sometimes feel uncertain when considering the place of drama within the five to eleven age range and their own role within it. For while drama is often closely related to children's wider learning, developmental needs and growing maturity, it may not always be clearly differentiated as an independent curricular activity. Yet between five and eleven children move from the dramatic possibilities inherent in many play situations towards an awareness of role and role relationships, and an increased capacity to create, explore and understand within dramatic situations. Here they can take on dramatic roles and encounter new situations, while at the same time building up the necessary skills. The potential educational contribution is therefore considerable, but it needs to be matched by teachers' confidence and understanding if it is to be effectively realised and not undervalued. Often they need help and would welcome clarification on matters like organisation, structure, methods and assessment. Without this, a positive and constructive use of drama is improbable.

It was in response to these needs that the Drama Sub-Committee of the Schools Council proposed a one-year exploratory study which would consider the place of drama within the curriculum for younger pupils. As a result of the survey, it was hoped to clarify aspects of provision, staffing and organisation, analyse teachers' views on the contribution of drama to children's education and identify their problems.

Initially, forty schools were selected for the survey and this sample included infant, first, primary, junior and middle schools. As far as possible they were geographically and socially representative. However, they did not represent a random sample but were drawn from schools with an interest in drama submitted by local authorities. It was felt that in this way the limited resources of the project would be used to fuller effect. Nevertheless, a balance was maintained between . schools with a stronger drama commitment and those where drama was being introduced, or was sustained by only one or two staff members. Indeed, during the year, concern for ensuring a more complete picture led to more schools being visited so that the final total was fifty-seven.

Some observational guidance came from L.E.A. response to a survey request for an outline of specific concerns which might be examined during the project. These included drama as an integrative agent and the influence of role variety on learning, as well as more sharply focused aspects like the qualities of drama encouraged by literature. However, a major concern was the relationship between drama and language. How could teachers realise the potential of drama to help build and extend children's language confidence and abilities? What are the ways in which the language resources of individual and group meet the challenges of personality, role and dramatic situation, where children discuss, reflect, express or appraise and, if appropriate, express in writing? This seemed a particularly important area, especially in view of the Bullock Report observation which drew attention to the shortfall in drama practice here. Consequently, the survey has attempted to take a constructive look at the drama-language relationship within a context of teacher comment and approaches.

Overall, the survey schools strongly believed in the educational value of drama. Through it children are offered new experiences, or given the opportunity to compare experiences, in a process bringing fuller awareness and understanding of themselves, and their relationships with other people. In doing so, it contributes to personality development, but does so within a group environment. Importantly, through the opportunities provided for children to build up and explore a variety of situations, to extend the "here and now", it fosters fundamental learning involving many curricular areas. Emphasised too is childrens natural approach to drama and the intrinsic strength of interest and motivation that can make it such a powerful educational force. Against such a backcloth many goals are formulated in terms of a whole range of skills and capacities. Teachers refer to encouraging language, expression and communication, organising information, solving problems, formulating and testing hypotheses. They stress the development of social understanding and an ability to work constructively in groups, while at a physical level they seek to maximise powers of response and feeling, linking these to group ideas and relationships.

The content of the report reflects specific needs voiced by teachers. They frequently asked if comments on drama, its achievements and problems, could be set within a framework of illustrated practice. These requests relate to another strong desire, to know what other teachers were seeking through drama and their varied approaches. Inevitably, meeting these requests has meant making the survey report longer than originally intended. Nevertheless, perhaps it will better serve both informational and dissemination functions by sharing insights, problems and methods more fully.

Throughout the survey schools were generous in terms of time and readiness to discuss relevant issues. They were willing to share ideas and be frank about both theoretical and practical difficulties.

Contents

Looking at drama

A young five year old boy wearing a black peaked sailor's hat built his ship using wooden blocks, and with his friend as crew moved out of harbour. Presently he returned in some excitement holding a bag of gold he had recovered from the seabed. Was it easy to recover the gold? Yes, he had simply to pick it out of the water. But wasn't it deep out there away from the harbour? Wouldn't it be difficult to bring the gold up? The captain paused for a second or two, then looked a little impatient as he replied, "It's only pretend you know," but returned thoughtfully to his ship. Subsequently his next haul was not so easily found and turned out to be "different gold"

This example of dramatic play was recorded to illustrate the natural drama world of most young children. However, it is a story with a broader meaning – looking for drama also produces different kinds of that particular gold and its values are not always fully recognised.

It is often difficult for teachers to determine where drama begins and ends in school, and this is especially true if younger children are being considered. So many curricular activities involve the natural capacity of children to take on dramatic roles and encounter dramatically new situations and possibilities of self. Paradoxically, this is why drama can sometimes be elusive.

The goals sought through drama

On the whole, most schools included in the survey did not fall into any neatly defined categories of drama type, yet frequently teachers in schools serving different ages and areas outlined similar goals even though approaches varied.

In one middle school, for example, the following goals were included:

(a)   To enable the children to experience something which is beneficial to the "self" – some exploration of their own abilities and personalities from which they will emerge with a deeper knowledge of themselves as individuals.

(b)   To help develop a self-imposed discipline.

(c)   To encourage co-operation with, and understanding of, other people, thus providing valuable social training.

(d)   To provide another area of school activity in which the children may develop their own ideas, imagination and creative abilities.

(e)   To improve children's speech and their ability to express themselves verbally with confidence and clarity.

(f)   To provide a stimulating way of examining various branches of our cultural heritage – poetry, prose, plays, music. . . .

(g)   To equip the children with knowledge and skills which are considered basic and desirable for future learning.

(h)   To provide another way of examining and learning about other subjects – English (of course), History, R.E. . . .

(i)   To encourage integration between this and other "blocks" (e.g. Related Studies, Art and Craft) and sometimes, as in the case of a "production" become a focal point for an all-out effort involving most of the school.

A primary school had similar goals:

(a)   To improve ability to work together as a group.

(b)   To achieve an understanding of self and others.

(c)   To build up confidence, initiative and decision making abilities.

(d)   To extend language skills and promote language awareness.

(e)   To give experience of many different situations and circumstances.

(f)   To promote children's imagination, feeling and thought.

(g)   To stimulate many curricular activities, particularly reading, writing, research, art and craft.

(h)   To allow children to explore moral issues.

Although these two statements typify how different schools recognise similar values and goals, there is often a marked variation in how far a school expresses or applies such beliefs. Usually, certain areas considered important by the teachers concerned, will determine what is attempted at the practical level and as a result differences in emphasis are common. Sometimes teachers are unsure whether they should regard drama more as subject than method, or wonder if it can be both learning tool and creative art form. Their own viewpoint influences what goals they believe can be achieved. However, several teachers who have worked over a period to build up their own strengths in the drama field emphasised how they see it essentially as a process which combines forms and skills with a mode of enquiry, discipline and learning.

What should be emphasised, is how some teachers see drama as a means of approaching many different educational purposes. It not only provides experience but also creates the opportunities which allow children to explore many possibilities within supportive frameworks. Through adopted roles and situations they can begin to understand how people, life, attitudes and knowledge are bound up together in feeling–thinking relationships. If the teacher's role is to create learning opportunities and challenges for children, then drama may be a very potent medium bringing together their creative and imaginative powers, knowledge and skills.

Nevertheless, the fact that drama has varied functions and offers a range of educational possibilities carries important implications. To understand and use it effectively in education, we require a conception of drama which recognises its nature and scope. This is where the survey reveals a pressing need; many of the important elements outlined later are often not recognised or understood, a situation which partly explains why drama practice and achievements are not always encouraging. The main concern here is how effectively teachers can see the scope and necessity for involving children in relevant and challenging situations. Situations which really engage feeling, thinking and imaginative powers, where language is considered, material is sensible and wider curricular possibilities are explored. In some schools drama limps along with teachers unsure and admitting to doubts about their own understanding of possibilities – getting by perhaps on the strength of "recipe knowledge", based chiefly upon their own past drama experiences.

Of course, much depends here on a school's own educational environment, goals and organisation. Where schools or teachers stress the development of expressive and communicative powers, the encouragement of speculation and trial, planning, discussion and group effort, then drama is more likely to be found which matches or creates these challenges. Where curriculum links are fostered, drama is often seen to draw more effectively on a wide range of material and in return provide its own integrative force, binding together material, dramatic interaction and its outcomes.

In other words, drama exercises its functions throughout the survey schools in proportion to individual objectives and opportunities provided. One crucial factor then completes the picture; how far teachers' own skills and insights match the challenges offered by their respective schools. Of course, it is not suggested that enterprising and fruitful drama needs ideal conditions before it can make a worthwhile contribution to children's education. Many teachers worked effectively in an environment they created within their classroom walls. But in these circumstances, the overall tasks involved may be more difficult unless there is sufficient support from headteachers who recognise the value of drama enterprises.

Reference

Drama as Education – D. Heathcote.
(Children and Drama. Ed. N. McCaslin, Pub. David Mackay, New York 1975.)

Drama from 5 to 11

The next three sections outline drama approaches observed during the survey, and discuss issues significant to children and teachers. The first task is to examine what forms of drama children meet between five and eleven years – the content, themes and structures encouraged, and how far these reflect children's developing interests and abilities. In effect, we are concerned with opportunity, challenge, what is appropriate and the quality of experience when children engage in dramatic ventures at different age or development levels, and whether it is possible to generalise about drama progression. Many teachers, including a number with considerable expertise in the field, admitted some uncertainty here, having found no firm frame of reference that would allow more convincing judgements to be made on what they were offering children as a drama diet. Consequently, there are wide variations in the kinds and levels of work attempted, the reasons for undertaking or encouraging it and how children benefit. Of course, teaching conditions and organisation also vary, together with views on how drama relates to the curriculum.

Dramatic play

Insight into and commitment to what dramatic play achieves in education is usually more apparent in infant schools. Infant children generally have adequate play facilities though there is great variation between schools, ranging from a Wendy House with domestic bits and pieces, to large well equipped rooms or areas. Several schools make their more extensive facilities available to all children by locating them in "public areas" or allocating time between classes on a rota basis. Materials also vary but many of the most effective ways into play come through inexpensive odds and ends; large cardboard boxes, old cloth lengths, hats and dresses, tyres, wood pieces etc. Interesting themes are often developed by children with the minimum of equipment and one group of boys needed no more than a single construction worker's helmet and a few wood pieces to begin an absorbing play sequence. However, some schools also emphasise the provision of more specialised items for encouraging varied role and thematic approaches such as "hospital" play.

The amount of time young children spend on dramatic play is difficult to determine accurately, but it is more likely to be evident at five years than later. By seven or eight years the picture has changed somewhat and variations in play provision and encouragement are very apparent, so that all children do not enjoy continuing opportunities or show developing play qualities to the same extent. What are the reasons for this?

1   The different extents to which teachers recognise that dramatic play performs important functions at ages greater than five or six so that their commitment to play provision is strong.

2   How the school organises its teaching and the degree of curricular flexibility available either enhances or restricts play opportunities.

3   Different social environments which affect children's attitudes and capacities in play situations.

4   Different degrees of teacher insight and expertise which can affect stimulation and enrichment.

These next examples illustrate the varying contexts that may be observed and suggest differing developmental levels, though these are not always coincident with age.

S.P.A. Infants School

A group of five year old children, two boys and two girls, played in a Wendy House which contained cooker, table, chairs, cot, tea-set, and other domestic utensils. One girl sat holding a doll, dressing it and making "mothering" noises, while her companion stood by and commented occasionally. The boys were baking and setting out cups and saucers for tea, with one acting as "mother" giving instructions. All that happened and was spoken reflected imitation of roles, activities and language interaction drawn from a domestic background.

Village First School

A large creature was constructed from cardboard boxes by first year infants and, after discussion, was tethered to a table because it was fierce. It became a source of interest and concern for the children who decided that it required feeding at intervals and this was done by keepers who would discuss what to give and how much. Over a period the creature stimulated many other play activities, leading children into discussion, art and writing (children's oral language being written in a large class book by their teacher).

Urban Infants School

Five year old boys spread P.E. hoops and blocks on the floor to create another planet which they then explored as space travellers from a "Skytrek" craft. They worked fairly independently but nevertheless kept within a broad plan of agreement and used technical terms like astronaut, module and link-up in their language exchanges. Movement showed an awareness of the space environment chosen and their teacher commented afterwards on the obvious influence here of television programmes. They managed to sustain the activity for some time through co-operative endeavour and suggestion.

Urban Primary School

A group of seven year old children established a giant's castle using assorted large cardboard boxes and then enjoyed a series of short adventures in which the giant was taunted. Discussion centred on who should act as giant next and the content of various action sequences with most children making a contribution. A number of imaginative possibilities were suggested and explored, including a ghost sequence intended to frighten the giant from his castle. Two children exerted an obvious influence on the remainder of the group and there seemed to be tacit agreement between them on who would lead at different times.

S.P.A. Primary School

Second and third year juniors were allowed to develop dramatic play activities based upon their own interests. One group of boys arranged chairs and rostra blocks to form a ship and then proceeded to load this with food supplies. From their conversation it was apparent that the ship was in New York harbour and they were to sail across the Atlantic Ocean to Britain. Crew members worked convincingly in language and mime during the voyage until the radar spotted an enemy warship. They were fired upon and despite frantic pumping operations had to abandon ship and take to the lifeboat, rowing energetically to keep warm. Finally, exhausted and cold, they were rescued by helicopter.

Urban Primary School

Fourth year junior children created a life-sized bathysphere and large fish models as part of a sea project. Inside they set up chairs and desks to create a working environment and added control panels, alarm switches and driving instructions. Children were keen to work inside the model and identified themselves with crew members going through operational activities that involved them in varied undersea adventures. Some of these they subsequently recorded in writing and illustrations.

What is accomplished through play?

These examples illustrate the many situations and possibilities dramatic play provides as children's "here and now" is extended through their capacity to represent people, things, places and events. Through their own choices and decisions they are able to free themselves from present constraints and enter their own worlds, whether these concern giants or castles, picnics and bus trips to the seaside, mothers at home or doctors tending the sick in hospital. Because what is created in these situations reflects children drawing on past experiences and recombining them in a make-believe environment, they not only exercise imagination but use it to explore themselves, others and the known world. Here they discover what they are as well as what they are not. This is what makes a rich background of experience so necessary for extending possibilities and providing the essential raw material for building up play. The capacity to alter an environment, shape it into something new and work actively within it, must depend largely upon how perceptively children observe and draw from a wide range of experiences. As they succeed in developing this ability so the complexity of what they can deal with in play increases.

Any dramatic play situation provides a frame of reference within which children must order their activities for the process to be meaningful and satisfying. This requires selective application of relevant experience and knowledge to fit the demands of assumed roles and the situation itself. Again, the importance of enriched background is emphasised so that children can draw comparisons, select what appears appropriate and increasingly appraise role performance and thematic content. When the young astronauts ventured into space they obviously drew heavily upon television and films, which helped to provide a vocabulary, role stance and an awareness of what the situation required and they used these selectively in their play sequence.

One important indicator of development is how far roles and themes reflect conceptual levels, which are deepened by the dramatic activity.

By experiencing particular roles, varying aspects of human make-up
are perceived which helps to strengthen an awareness that different
sets of responses are available. Similarly, children's thinking abilities
gain when words become substitutes for things and are progressively
explored. The five year old bus driver, commenting on being able to
go on because imaginary traffic lights showed green, is journeying in
powers of thought as well as in dramatic play. Later he will find drama
one means to achieve fuller understanding of abstractions like
friendship, justice or obligation, as he encounters them and explores
their meaning with his classmates. Attitudes to thinking may also be
affected through dramatic play and a developing realisation that
many different possibilities exist within situations and themes. If this is
achieved then planning, "open-mindedness" and invention begin to
characterise children's ideas and appraisals.

Dramatic play brings together the individual experiences and
resources of those involved and allows them all to share in a common
enterprise underpinned by what each contributes – a vital
contribution to fuller learning, for what is developed draws from the
common stock and in return feeds the minds and feeling of individuals
forming the group. But the sharing of dramatic play adds other
ingredients to make learning more effective, by moving children from
egocentric tendencies towards developing co-operative, social skills
without which group activity would break down. Because play
normally has such a strong motivational force and is so satisfying,
children learn tolerance, mutual help, trust and that give and take
which enables group planning and decisions to be undertaken and
played through. Younger children find it difficult to speak objectively
about social aspects, but where juniors have the opportunity to
develope their own dramatic play they are usually more fluent in
expressing social interdependence. Here one group of second and third
year juniors from an S.P.A. school make some pertinent comments.

> We usually toss up to see who plays what, it's fairer that way. If
> someone doesn't agree with something we talk about it to sort it out.

> We nearly always talk a lot about how it should go at the start.

> If anybody is stupid, they're thrown out of it.

> Yes, you have to act like the person and do what the play needs.

> We don't like people being killed because then they're out of it and
> that always causes arguments.

We usually have a kind of leader but if you're too bossy you get thrown out.

Sometimes it's one person's ideas, then somebody else's.

Comments like these show how children adapt to group demands and develop social co-operation based upon self-discipline that is voluntarily imposed because the joint activity is enjoyable. They also illustrate how, within the group, each individual is accorded a recognised place but is expected to conform to certain norms or standards of behaviour. This is not a "free for all" situation; participants are expected to apply themselves to situations and roles so that their contribution is acceptable.

All these functions of dramatic play help to confirm for the child his own creative power, developing a sense of himself as an active agent in his own world. However, this depends upon developing the capacity for make-believe and conceptions of what is possible in a play situation and not all children show this development to the same extent.

Sometimes other problems are associated here; an unwillingness to enter new situations involving unsuitable roles, an apparent reluctance or inability to co-operate in making play possible and difficulty with its management. In addition, children may possess weak language resources which make it difficult for them to develop dramatic themes. So instead of achieving play which extends understanding, they are constrained by the dominance of objects, or else engage in actions which lack spontaneity and purpose.

These characteristics contrast strongly with those already outlined, where most children tended to develop co-operative methods of solving problems and formulate their roles through discussion and compromise, reaching a stage where they were able to begin forward planning and elaborate roles and themes. The examples of play given earlier show something of these contrasts with five year old children and they highlight some problems which may occur throughout the infant years.

When difficulties are discussed in schools it is usually social or ethnic backgrounds which are stressed as probable causes, in terms of the adverse effect of deprivation or authoritarian upbringing on children's attitudes to situations. The challenge in these circumstances centres upon how far supportive structures should be provided in schools so that children are presented with play opportunities which retain essential freedom and spontaneity, but endeavour to involve some degree of systematic exploration and development, perhaps with careful adult supervision. In this sense, structured themes can provide opportunities for all children.

The survey indicates that teachers often meet problems in appraising play quality and knowing what kind of structures would be most productive. There seems to be a need to raise more questions of the following kind:

1 *Themes and roles.* The kinds and degree of development. Does the play develop? Is there growing understanding of the factors involved in the dramatised social situation? What is the range and depth of relationships? Do the other children react to them in role?

2 *Behaviour of children.* Do leaders emerge? How well do they deal with problem-solving activities? Do they co-operate and share, or compete? Can they accept different rules, different interpretations etc. in their play?

3 *Language.* What sort of language and how does it function in the play? Does it progress from imitation of adult speech to imaginative make-believe? How much is for play management, explanation and discussion? (This important area is considered later.)

Three further aspects of dramatic play were raised by teachers.

1 Its value as preparation for other learning situations. Here dramatic play can give younger children a basis for understanding other complex processes they will meet later. Often, for example, a story read to them stimulates play and relates it to the book, or they will play at reading in varied situations. Play can also lead into subsequent discussion which encourages a level of oracy and understanding desirable as pre-reading experience. Wider learning applications are possible, deriving from strengthened make-believe capacities; thinking up a story to write, grasping how a bushman lives, or entering into story, history or R.E. situations, all depend upon a power to construct imaginatively. A number of teachers commented on how children's imaginative writing developed in association with, and as a result of, dramatic experience. Moreover, many problems require imaginative projection in order to act upon the material and arrive at a solution.

2 For some children dramatic play permits "letting off steam". Children respond emotionally to pressures and frustrations and these

may be played out within a dramatic context. Among the trial situations and responses possible, are those which allow them to go beyond what is socially acceptable, not becoming uncontrolled but perhaps releasing tensions. Within the same dramatic process, of course, is the means to initiate children into role-reversal situations where they see another's viewpoint, develop empathy and thus create the means for agreement and resolution of conflict.

3   Dramatic play continues after the infant years and most children maintain their interest in make-believe activities right through from five to eleven. Drama, of course, builds upon this continuing response to imaginative challenge, but some schools also allow children time to develop their own play ventures. Reasons vary for including free dramatic play as a curricular activity after the infant years; sometimes it reflects a concern for children who have not developed satisfactorily, or it simply represents a school's belief that older children still need a free play environment to some degree. For dramatic play to flourish, teachers need to be confident in their understanding that it has value for children.

Moving from play to drama

Most teachers agree that when they refer to drama rather than play, what they have in mind are situations where the elements of play remain unchanged but approaches are often more structured and involve planning within varied frameworks. Specific goals may be sought, skills strengthened, particular themes worked through and different dramatic forms encouraged.

Alternatively, drama may originate in a more or less spontaneous response to many school situations and experiences, where it serves the concerns of the moment. In these circumstances, extended dramatic exploration may still follow, but often the activity primarily functions as incidental stimulation.

Spontaneous drama in schools

The survey schools provide some useful illustrations to indicate how pervasive this latter function may be. A project on "Our Senses" took six year old children into work associated with smells and animals' noses. They used a poem "Being a Nose" as the basis for action in which they mimed reactions to smells while words were recited. Later they listened to the story of a Mr. Uppity, were caught up in the mood, and finished by "passing on a smile and then a frown". Story telling provided many opportunities for incidental dramatisation, along with the number rhymes and activities intrinsic to work in mathematics; soldiers marched, birds flew and fish were caught, as mime and language helped to consolidate children's mathematical understanding. After scale work on large sea mammals, older infants created the various creatures in movement by allocating an appropriate number of children for each one and so experienced in this form the knowledge they were dealing with.

Other infants had a "magic paintbox" for painting things that "came alive". "There is no limit to what we can explore this way" was their teachers comment and a colleague added "Very often this kind of work is something personal between you and the children, it comes from a bond and sensing opportunities".

The same process was observed in junior-aged classes. Puppets created in craft led to drama activities – ranging from short two-way conversations with finger characters to more extended interaction using modelled figures. Children, learning how their own valley was formed, used music and movement to recreate earthquakes, glacial action and the elements. An actual earthquake reported in the news and discussed as a matter of immediate interest, led to the establishment of a "stricken village" and concern for how survivors would cope with their problems. The lower form of a middle school studying factory conditions established a workshop atmosphere in classroom with roles, machine noises and movement, "not for long-term drama but just to get the feel of things and create an atmosphere".

It is difficult to assess how far this kind of activity is general throughout the five to eleven age range but many teachers recall using drama in similar ways. Not surprisingly, perhaps, the tendency seems stronger where they work with younger age groups and accompanying play situations provide an environment likely to encourage "make-believe" challenges. As children move through the age range, however, the awareness of possibilities and their exploitation again depends upon teachers encouraging dramatic forms and their own insight into the value of particular circumstances. It does seem, however, that we often miss opportunities here, especially with the older age groups.

Drama as a more regular part of the curriculum

These examples of "incidental" drama and the learning they foster
indicate how useful such approaches may be, but they do not provide
a comprehensive picture. For this, we must look at work observed in
schools which have some commitment to drama and include it as part
of their normal curricular activity. Consequently, the illustrations
have been drawn from a range of schools and approaches so that
attention can be focused upon the experiences provided for children
between five and eleven years. Underlying these observations will be
the questions – what are schools seeking through drama, and is there a
discernable pattern of drama development during the primary years of
education?

Example 1

A small First School, surrounded by fields and serving an established
mining community. Though the area is now attracting commuters, a
colliery village atmosphere still prevails and the school is supported by
strong parental interest. The building itself is less than twenty years
old and has a pleasant hall and separate classrooms. Doorways to these
rooms are sometimes transformed so that they become entrances to
caves, dens, wigwams etc. Children remain in the school until they are
nine.

The headmistress emphasises how drama arises naturally from many
different school activities and leads effectively into varied areas of
learning. She stresses flexibility as a teacher strength and believes that
the secret of good drama is tied up with teaching philosophy and
approach; and the ability and confidence to drop the daily plan and
take advantage of opportunities as they arise. Only by venturing
themselves will teachers grow in confidence and gain insight into how
children respond to different dramatic challenges. An example from
lower infants illustrates how the class teacher provided an
environment for drama which began to develop form, shape and early
dramatic consciousness.

The Bogglybog World: The idea for the Bogglybogs grew out of making
papier mâché masks for Christmas. As work on the masks progressed,
it was suggested that they could be utilized in some form as part of a
Christmas show which was being put together by the older children.
Due to the unusual character of the masks, which fell into none of the
normal categories, i.e. goblins, ghosts etc., it was decided to let the
children devise a name of their own and thus were born the
Bogglybogs.

At this point, the class teacher recognised that here was potential material for drama, so she set out to help the children create their world of Bogglybogs. With this as a starting point, the idea grew into a theme encompassing drama, discussion, painting, music and creative language, which appeared to develop through the following five stages.

1   The creation of the Den.
2   Discussion sessions.
3   The gathering of material for the class book "All about Bogglybogs".
4   Development of stories and songs.
5   Further creative work through paintings, mobiles etc.

1   *The creation of the Bogglybogs Den:* The beginning was the door. This was transformed into the entrance to the Bogglybogs Den. The shape of the door was altered by a large sheet of brown paper formed into an arch, painted and decorated with leaves and flowers by the children. A mask was hung in the middle of the door and the words "Bogglybogs Den" were added. Conversation took place throughout. The children became increasingly aware that this was their territory and proceeded to guard it – all members of staff (except their teacher), children and visitors were denied entry to the Den until they said the magic words "Open Sesame".

2   *Discussion sessions:* It was during discussions with the children that the structure and life of Bogglybog society was established. They devised a key which enabled them to change in and out of role at will; "Abrakadabra" changed them from children to Bogglybogs and "Rozanna" from Bogglybogs to children. It was found that children could change individually, in groups or as a class and were capable of maintaining their role for quite long periods. With the help of their teacher some Bogglybog characteristics were recorded and included:

Bogglybogs live in a Den
You get in the den by saying "Open Sesame", then the Bogglybogs will not eat you up.
Bogglybogs are friends with fairies and wizards.
They sit around on rooftops but they cannot be seen because they are invisible. People know they are because they sometimes make a noise.
Bogglybogs have mammies, daddies, brothers, sisters, grandmas, nannas and tiny babies.
They feed the babies on tables. They paint the tables flat on paper and feed the paper to the babies.

Bogglybogs sing songs and tell stories.
They can magic themselves twenty miles up into the sky.
They have knives and sharpen them with their noses and on stones.
Their noses do not wear away but stones do.

3 *Other creative work:* The Bogglybog theme encouraged creative
ideas expressed through drawing, painting, writing and construction.
Chants, songs, poetry and stories provided additional and integral
language experience and the Den continued to be developed over a
period of seven weeks. The class teacher commented, "The normal
structure of the working day continues although the children can slip
in and out of their drama as they or I desire. There is great interest in
the theme and a desire to embellish it. Each piece of creative work
promotes discussion as the children justify its assimilation into their
drama world."

A number of useful indicators are provided by this example. First, it
needs to be stressed how young infants will respond at their own level
to a challenging dramatic environment, which offers them scope and
opportunity for active participation. One of the major problems here
is providing an appropriate theme, but when teachers are prepared to
accept children's interests and ideas they can often establish a
productive drama base.

Second, there are extended language possibilities when group
discussion and role enactment takes place. The class teacher observed
how talking and listening had contributed to children's readiness to
tackle situations. Children reached a stage where they let each other
talk, whereas at the outset this discipline was not strong.

Third, there was the beginnings of greater dramatic awareness as they
responded to role and became involved in group reactions. Finally,
they had discovered and developed more of the social disciplines
necessary for dramatic building. In doing so they had not been
regimented or coerced, but extended their play to explore more widely
and co-operatively.

Example 2

A primary school in an urban metropolitan area surrounded by
modern housing and serving a socially mixed intake. The building is
fairly new with cheerful teaching areas and a good hall. Organisation
is on a unit basis with three units, divided horizontally by age, for the
whole school. Considerable stress is placed upon dramatic play with
younger children and it is acknowledged that the learning and

creative possibilities explored there are also potentially available in later drama. At present, however, the school is building up its drama strengths, and movement approaches are chiefly used to extend experience until a basis for further development is secured. Meanwhile the staff is examining in detail the curricular goals and key priorities. This lesson involved about thirty infants from unit one for half an hour.

Children moved freely to the changing rhythms of a bongo drum before going on to vigorous movements. From there they were asked to imagine a sunny day and a trip to the sea-side. The sensations and qualities of the beach were explored; sifting sand, splashing in the sea, listening to the wind and waves. Effective noises were provided by a wire brush moved over the bongo drum. A mood of relaxation was induced by the teacher clapping two sticks together. Was it someone walking? Yes, a horse. Where was it going? What did it see? A simple story was built up and then improvised in movement. The horse met an old man who wanted to ride him. They talked, then there was a chase before the horse finally returned to his stable, tired and hungry.

Some useful discussion took place during and after the lesson as children were challenged to define words used in their story; proud and unusual being two that induced much effort. "It had purple feet, that's why it was unusual" volunteered one boy. The class teacher remarked later that she sought a variety of experiences for younger infants within one lesson and thought the establishment of mood important. Even in a movement lesson a listening quality was important, and could be developed both in terms of response to aural stimuli and participation through discussion. She regarded the encouragement of more imaginative "stories" as being one effective way to improve dramatic content as children matured and thought they were ready during their second school year to begin simple group work.

There is a security within a movement situation for both children and teacher and this is important. Yet in many cases the question must be asked – does the work undertaken by children really provide an effective spur and challenge to developing abilities? Is there sufficient scope for fully maintaining a process in which children help to create their drama, make and implement decisions, interact with feeling and thought and later reflect upon events and outcomes? Schools vary in their attitudes here and some argue that a movement approach for infants is a surer way to establish dramatic quality later, when confidence, imagination and physical sensitivity have been nourished. Nevertheless, the survey observations suggest that more careful thought needs to be given when we consider what dramatic experiences are appropriate for drama development. In all approaches the *quality* of experience provided for children should be a crucial factor and teachers themselves need to be confident in the assessment of their drama enterprises and what is being achieved.

Example 3

A large infants' school in a semi-rural setting although it serves a fairly extensive urban area of pleasant housing. Nevertheless, industry is not far away and the intake was socially mixed. The school is modern with separate teaching areas and a hall of good proportions. Its commitment to drama was evident in the large space-like creature which guarded the main entrance and, together with a colourful display of writing and art, originated in drama-related activities. Curricular organisation is based upon age groups and class teaching, with drama established as an integrative force drawing together many areas of learning. Because the tradition is strong, children work confidently within varied dramatic structures and share in building up a joint enterprise. The work here represents a theme developed over several weeks by approximately thirty older infants.

The drama theme was "Pirates" and evolved after the summer holidays from general project work on the sea. Many stories and poems were read, including some with pirate incidents which led to "incidental" dramatisation, while art work showed a variety of pirate faces and stimulated imaginative mime. Oral adventures took children and pirates to imaginative destinations searching for treasure, sailing to strange islands, meeting strange creatures, falling into quick sand and being rescued. As the class teacher remarked, it was difficult to determine where drama began and ended in all this activity, but it was certainly there, motivating children strongly.

Eventually a decision was taken that the pirates would meet a creature with special qualities. One challenge was to invent a name but each of the five groups in the classroom wished to invent their own group creature. Finally discussion decided that mathematical shapes in the room should form the basis of the creatures and children were asked to draw their creation, write down any outstanding characteristics it might have and finally give it a name. Final group choices were: Boxsy (cuboid shape), Pom Pom (cube), Federick (cylinder), Flees (sphere), Blip (cone).

Children then took on the characteristics of these creatures and explored reactions within the classroom. Subsequently children's own rhythmic music helped to establish movement patterns and involved a good deal of trial and error.

Boxsy	Body bend forward, clapping three times and jerk up with mouth clicks
Pom Pom	Block of children, tramping movement to slow soft drum beat
Federick	A line of children, shuffling to mouth popping noises and taps on sticks
Flees	On all fours, moving side to side, and using shaker sounds
Blip	Zig zag path with children in line to mouth noises and Indian bell.

A special island was to be visited on which these creatures lived, ruled by a mysterious woman who guarded hidden treasure. Drama action took the pirates in their boat to the island and they argued about its eeriness and whether to land. Eventually, they explored the island furtively, hiding behind rocks when the creatures appeared. Later, however, one of the gang discovered the mysterious woman's treasure and brought his gang to see it.

A variety of outcomes were stimulated by the drama and included models of the invented creatures, art work, music making, poetry and expressive writing. All the children compiled an individual book in which they recorded drama adventures, or used them as the basis for further story writing. Six year old Jane wrote:

> *An Adventure :* I am a monster in the drama. The pirates are frightened. They are hiding behind a rock. Their gold is behind another rock. The pirates had a boat and all of them came. Then they saw Ian and it was horrible because he has a fierce face. But then he went away. Pom Pom was stuck in the sinking sand, and Federick, but they got up and weren't stuck again.

In this work, language is actively engaged as children discuss, suggest, write and decide within their drama framework. The importance of decision making is stressed throughout. The emphasis is on available choices and group consensus, in a process which involves experiment

23

and adaptation. This is a joint enterprise depending on tolerance and acceptance of other ideas; but there is opportunity to later reflect as individuals, record thoughts and extend them creatively into story or art. The enactment itself is a blend of voice, sounds, music, mime, movement and language interaction. The pattern of the work suggests that children are developing a consciousness of what is possible in drama where imaginative involvement feeds and is fed by constructive attitudes, skills and knowledge.

The capacity of infant children to develop a group identity in drama is shown in this next example where the interaction also reveals growing dramatic maturity. The drama concerned a group of people taking opposing views. All had suffered loss of freedom under the power of a computerized machine. As a result one group blamed "the god" for their suffering, while the other group were equally suspicious of the disillusioned people. Eventually, a "court" was held to sort things out with teacher in role as judge, her main aim being to establish a suitable atmosphere and illustrate appropriate language and behaviour. A "dinosaur's foot" became the symbolic truth decider.

Judge	I have been sent to you people. I am very wise. I will pass judgement in this court today and this (shows dinosaur's foot) will help me to know who is telling the truth. When one person speaks the rest of the court will be silent. The leaders will call upon those they wish to speak. The foot will point to the side who will speak first.
Martin	Well, it was one of Patrick's men.
Judge	Which man?
Martin	I don't know. It was one of their men. He's not there now, he's got away. I don't know his name.
Judge	What do you say to this accusation?
Patrick (the god)	I say I sent the computer but I sent it to look after the people. I thought it was supposed to capture us. I think I built it right but something went wrong (*Foot decides he tells the truth*).
Peter	I think its the guard who's on the computer's side.
Judge	Have you not heard the "god" say he built the machine. Do you accept this? The dinosaur's foot has

	discovered the truth. Do you still believe it was a guard.
Peter	Yes.
Helen	That man's wrong. We didn't do anything. We just helped to build this machine.
Judge	She tells the truth. Do you accept the judgement of this court?
Martin	I have something to say. I think if we had some people in that group and we were more joined together, it would be better.
Patrick	I disagree with it. Anything, a war could break out. One side might be wanting a war.
Martin	We don't want a war. We haven't got many men. I can build great machines. He can an' all, but I could go further and be better than him, but I wouldn't want to. I want . . . I want to learn more about machines. I don't want war.
Patrick	I think I'll have to have a vote to see who wants war and who doesn't. That's how we'll sort it out.

However, war was averted and the leaders shook hands.

The class teacher commented on the quality of listening, the interaction of personalities and language flow evident in the work where, through growing sympathy and honest exchange, they met at a point of agreement and friendship. The court was one example of the many situations provided by drama for enriching and extending infant experience. It gave insight into formal procedures, justification and defence in an atmosphere of slow pace and deliberate language. She recognised the problem when children were shy and reluctant to express opinions in front of the class, but this did not mean abandoning challenging drama approaches, since drama allows the teacher to construct situations in which all children talk and anticipate; sometimes work in pairs or small groups is appropriate but suitable activities are often suggested by the context of the work itself and issues stemming from it.

Development between 5 and 8 years

The examples outlined illustrate how drama approaches vary widely in the early years which make any definitive statement of drama progression very difficult to formulate. Within the same school and between different schools teachers' opinions on where, why and how they should be guiding children's dramatic ventures reflect differing conceptions of drama and its functions. Very often they refer to the same elements – imaginative nourishment, group co-operation, language development, bodily control and sensitivity, feeling and thinking etc. but variations exist between priorities and the structures provided for development. Development in these circumstances depends on the patterns being built up by the teachers and the children concerned, which elements are strengthened, when this should be attempted and how it is achieved.

This is the crux of many teachers' problems; there is no simple way to outline drama development or progression in straightforward terms. A blend of factors is always involved. What can be firmly stated, however, is that they all concern children's capacity to "become someone else" and do things in a variety of roles and situations. By strengthening and enriching this capacity, through appropriate opportunities and challenges, we foster development of both children and drama.

The material we use is fundamentally important here. Observations of play show how soon after five years children begin to look outward and develop new interests. It seems sensible for schools to relate what is offered in drama to these developing interests, so that children are offered a relevant challenge. This is often a difficult task for the teacher. In one of the survey schools a six year old class was introduced to *The Emperor's New Clothes* by their teacher and later she asked them to dramatise the story. The material represented a venture for both children and teacher for she had doubts whether the central concern – how a king was hoaxed – would be understood in the course of one drama lesson and at their stage of development. Her approach broke down the story into small individual and group incidents, some of which included:

1   You're the king looking in your wardrobe for something to wear. Take out the clothes and try them on.

2   Examine the material. Feel how soft it is.

3   Show me what a robber looks like when he's out to steal.

4   You have a bag of nothing. Invisible cloth but you make it seem heavy.

5 Find a partner, one be robber, the other king. Show the king your material. Talk about it.

6 You're in families. Decide where you live and who with. What you're doing before the procession comes.

Children enjoyed these activities but at this point roles for the story were allocated and it was enacted through mime and interaction. Afterwards the class teacher commented on how the latter part of the lesson had taken the children too quickly into an over-challenging situation. Her assumption that the conceptual and dramatic level required might prove too demanding without a slower evolution that built upon children's experience and capacities was right, but there had been much of value in the lesson and it succeeded particularly where the children experienced each character and aspect of the story, allowing spontaneous response and individual exploration. The group situations too allowed flexibility and gave the children an opportunity to work out details together using language in role or for discussion and decision making.

In one infants' school a "programme" for development outlined this sequence of approaches.

1 Listening to sounds and responding.

2 Using sound, music and movement to stretch imagination.

3 Individual dramatic activities followed by co-operative group work using group or class themes.

4 Emphasis on language situations in groups.

5 Situations involving more complex issues, perhaps fantasy or reality, more thinking and discovering for themselves.

Of course, this leaves unanswered the question – what is considered suitable material? Though it does indicate how infant schools are looking more closely at the need for an intellectual challenge in drama by maturing minds. To think and discover for yourself in a dramatic context implies stimulating material to work upon and the sources are many. Some teachers find what they need in story, history and scripture, others in objects, pictures, music or improvisation built round class ideas and interests.

Teachers are sometimes concerned over the place of fantasy and reality in drama as children move upwards through the infant age group. They wonder how far they should allow preoccupation with fantasy events and issues to determine drama content and shape, and when it is appropriate for children to be moved on towards recognition of reality and acceptance of it in their drama. In effect, this implies that within an imaginative framework, events, people and relationships are subject to agreed ground rules; decisions have to be honoured, consequences faced and responsibility accepted. Drama then becomes a world in which experience is consistent though varied. Some fantasy in infant drama is upheld because of interest and motivation, but examples of work have shown how children can be guided towards real concerns within a framework. The need for children to accept reality is emphasised by many survey schools, though agreement on *when* this should happen is not general. Ultimately, of course, the problem brings teachers up against the relationship of children to their experiences in drama. What are they doing there? What are they getting from it? Are they deepening their level of involvement, feeling and thinking?

The complement of appropriate material for drama and another important indication of development seems to be children's increasing ability to work within more challenging dramatic structures. Here dramatic and social maturation are mutually enriching – drama increases the need for children to work together and, in return, drama itself gains from children's developing group awareness, sense of responsibility and commitment. Because drama is a social experience, the nature and quality of the sharing imply some degree of social and dramatic opportunity to be a group and grow as a group, as well as enjoy personal satisfaction.

So, when the five year old infants became "friendly or fierce animals" each in its "family" and assumed distinctive group characteristics (though at their own level of understanding) their activity represented an early stage in a social and dramatic journey. Perhaps those children dealing with the problem of their village water supply and showing ability to make joint decisions indicates a further point on the journey (see pages 183–9). Of course, children come to school at varying stages of understanding and degrees of social responsiveness. While the majority adapt readily to social demands, others retain strong egocentric tendencies until they are six or even seven. Consequently, bringing young children together in group drama activities requires a framework offering security and confidence and one that can cope with differences as well as provide opportunities for creative endeavour. But most older infants are capable of reaching the stage where they actively help to build and shape their drama, discuss events and issues within it and respond to the challenge of having problems to solve. This capacity seems to be developed most where drama allows children a share of responsibility. It is a process marked by trust, exercise of choice, opportunity to try out ideas and the chance to make mistakes in safety.

Teachers at one survey school believed that younger children achieve more through drama in vertically grouped classes. One teacher remarked "I've taught reception infants and they would never have managed such co-ordination and group awareness without the presence and support of older children". In these classes young children do seem to enjoy sharing the tensions and climax of dramatic action, though their interest is action-oriented and normally they take little part in discussion. Initially they require guidance and this affects teachers' methods. Material and approaches must be appropriate for all ages and abilities while more support from the teacher in role is required to sustain commitment and understanding. Discussions need to be kept short or concentration wavers and involvement weakens. Nevertheless, by the end of their first year they have usually merged effectively within the class group and become capable of helping to shape their drama and contribute ideas. Drama disciplines have been absorbed and they respond to dramatic atmosphere and challenge more positively. It was also observed that some seven year olds with limited ability remain at a five year old level and find security in mixed age range drama situations.

Most older infants develop in a number of important ways. There is growing interest in the drama itself and a greater desire to participate in both discussion and decision making. Because there are fewer older children in vertical group classes, they tend to become the natural leaders and accept drama responsibilities which offer more scope and challenge. All age groups were certainly active during the vertical group drama observed though two main characteristics distinguished the younger children: a ready acceptance of older children's ideas and relative quietness in discussion, and an obvious difference in commitment compared to older classmates. At the same time it was very evident that drama had established confidence and leadership among the older children who were familiar with dramatic activity which offered opportunity to discuss and contribute suggestions.

A further sign of children's growing dramatic maturity in general was observed in their response to role when drama activities allowed scope for its development. Teacher comment, on the whole, supported a view that opportunities for children to assume varied roles and engage in situations which encourage role awareness, modified feeling and thinking, become increasingly important and possible as children move towards seven years. However, their ability to develop deeper understanding of character and cope with more complex relationships depends upon how effectively they come up against both real and imagined circumstances. Drama can provide so many situations to make this possible and allow the trying-out of an individual's self against others. At first this is an uncertain business but uncertainty originating in either lack of experience or confidence gives way eventually, for most children, to greater sensitivity and insight. They enlarge their response to each other through movement, mime, or language and work more constructively within situations where role expectancy and exploration become significant.

Teachers sometimes refer to the problem of role stereotypes or "cartoon characters" in infant drama. A witch, for example, or an Indian can lead to difficulties in imaginative interpretation. This view is supported by work observed in schools, especially where children are asked to assume dramatic roles which lie outside their present capacities. Character nuance is difficult for young children to appreciate, but the level of understanding with which they relate and react to characters in their drama will be increasingly enhanced by the knowledge and insight found there. As they mature, development is more obvious but still supported and partly determined by feeling and thinking, stimulated by both situation and roles. Seven year old Indian braves releasing a captive settler against the wishes of their medicine man, but on the orders of their chief, were asked afterwards why they defied the former. They considered for a moment then replied that though the medicine man could "turn you into a buffalo and have you eaten" he was not as powerful as the chief. If it came to a clash between them, the braves would support their chief because "we picked him and all the braves would be against anyone else". Since he spoke for the whole tribe, his authority was greater than the magic and fear of the medicine man. Who children are in drama and what they do there can be marked by maturing reflective processes even with seven year old infants. Certainly they develop a knowledge of understanding so that a king now really does begin to show attributes of kingship. "When they realise they have role power it becomes a case of trying it out and relishing the dramatic possibilities." Children also accept teacher as a drama participant rather than "teacher".

What children achieve in drama between the ages of five and eleven cannot be divorced from school objectives and learning policies. Promising work that leads into and supports developments essential for more complete growth often takes place where drama is regarded as means to an end, without losing its creative integrity. It is enriched by many activities and in turn provides situations where imagination is nourished, problems are posed and solutions found. As one teacher said "They love anything that has a problem in it".

Drama related activities may assume increasing dramatic relevance to children and they can recognise their need and purpose. "They seem to enjoy it much more; the older children especially will work hard at writing lists of requirements for drama, or anything else concerned with it, and will go to books for information when they have the chance."

Development between 8 and 11 years

Where children have experienced the kinds of drama examined in previous pages, they should come into the junior or middle school years with some degree of dramatic and social maturity. Their teachers emphasise that drama is now moving towards a point where children may have more effective control and resources, "sieving and drawing from their own experience and beginning to monitor themselves in role". By this age, children experienced in drama can exploit its possibilities in many situations "provided the atmosphere is right and the theme has interest". The following criteria seem to characterise this stage of development.

1   A more conscious entering of the drama world and appreciation of its possibilities.

2   Greater awareness of relationships and role, yet perhaps not seeing "shades of grey" in roles encountered.

3   Growing ability to sort out and organise ideas at their own level.

4   More careful appraisal of their individual and group work.

5   Deeper interest in teasing out issues and threads of argument.

6   A working basis of social, linguistic and movement skills.

7   Ability to concentrate and apply themselves to specific tasks.

8   Improved learning skills; finding, reading, selecting and co-ordinating relevant material.

9   Sensory awareness.

In practice, however, progress is not so straightforward. Children are influenced by social environmental factors and their capacities to work in drama vary, while different schools have their own approaches and emphasise particular strengths in many cases. The result is that children may transfer between schools where differences in approach and emphasis cause loss of dramatic impetus or necessitate adjustments to new forms and traditions. Fortunately children are fairly resilient to these changes. Observations suggest that junior approaches tend to concentrate chiefly on movement themes, supplemented by drama exercises or games in the early years. More language-conscious approaches with events and issues to be explored are usually developed towards ten or eleven. However, as with the infants schools, an extensive range of approaches characterises drama activities; sometimes movement is the basis for all work, or movement combined with language in varying ways, while several schools chiefly emphasise language-based improvisations.

Examples of Drama in Practice

Example *1*

During the survey, several metropolitan boroughs were visited and this large junior school was situated in one of them. It is a modern Open Plan building with well-equipped teaching areas and a spacious hall. The children mainly come from a mature post-war housing estate and many of their parents work in the car manufacturing industry. Organisation within the school is based upon year groups, each with its own teaching team responsible for work undertaken. Curricular approaches stress the integrated nature of learning and this is reflected in regular thematic work. Their drama has been effectively established largely through the efforts of teacher/advisers and the enthusiasm of the school's headmistress who says: "I can't see that children don't need drama. To me it would be just like saying that they can learn division or any other process in mathematics without needing to understand. They're people and it's so necessary for them to say 'What if...' in all kinds of situations, to feel and think through the issues." Because the dramatic work in this school originates mainly from the projects of each year group there is mutual feed-back and each strengthens the other. Drama is not viewed as a separate activity but is related to discussion, reading, writing and making. Every year group is given drama experience and the school tries to ensure that this appeals to all ability levels and allows each child to participate fully. A prime objective is involvement where expression, communication, imagination and social awareness use both body and mind to create challenging situations.

Development includes:

1   Ability to work sensibly as an individual, or part of a group.

2   Establishment of co-operation, understanding and trust. Children learning to appreciate how a group functions both in drama itself and in planning or discussion.

3   Increasing use of drama as a teaching and learning tool to explore issues, co-ordinate experience.

4   Growing ability in physical and language skills.

5   Improving children's confidence.

6   Moving towards more active dramatic appreciation and understanding.

Lesson 1   First Year Juniors: Children sat quietly and listened while their teacher introduced the lesson theme. Something magic was going to happen. When she struck the tambourine they would shrink. But they had to "do something" themselves for this to happen – their own magic signal. This happened and they discussed how things would appear to them and the problems to be faced. Where would they live? What would they eat? Who would be their enemies? Some of the ideas are given here.

	I'd make friends with a mouse.
	Live in a doll's house.
	Eat crumbs.
	Live with owls – but what if they ate me.
	You could live in a teapot.
Teacher	Would that be any good?
	Yes, you could make a ladder to go down the spout and have the hole in the lid for a chimney.
Teacher	Let's listen to each others ideas.
	I'd carve furniture out of cheese.
	I'd use match boxes to make things I needed.

	Make a home in a radiator with sticks.
	A cheese house – cut it out to live in.
Teacher	Who would you be afraid of?
	People's feet, they could crush us.
	Rain – we could be washed away.
	And raindrops. They would be big.
	Yes, like boulders falling on us.

After discussion children moved around and mimed the actions of small people in varied situations of their own choice, closely observed by the teacher who encouraged them with ideas and comments. Then they chose a partner and were asked to sit and discuss an adventure that both could become involved in and these were enacted using mime and language. Afterwards they recounted what had happened and the lesson ended.

The class teacher assessed their activities on several dimensions. They had been involved, concentration was good, ideas and thinking were evident in both mime and language with some degree of feeling also apparent and also important, they had enjoyed the work.

Lesson 2   Third Year Children : The teacher here prefers a structure which will allow a large group to be involved in some way even though smaller group work may be necessary. However, she stresses that the needs of children determine the kind of challenge they should be offered. Project work on "The Sea" had led to the reading of related literature and the *Marie Celeste* mystery along with *Flannan Isle* provided a base for creating their own sea mystery in drama. After brief discussion on boats and fishing, children met their working partner, and took their boat out to sea in a movement sequence that also involved language.

Further discussion followed, concerning the possibility of finding a mystery vessel with an unconscious survivor on board. Children were invited to form groups of four to discuss what they would find and what could have happened. Their task was then to take a boat out, enact a sequence and work through group suggestions. This was done and a variety of interesting group work followed showing considerable originality and initiative. For the next phase of the lesson a fishing community was established to which unconscious survivors were

34

brought while others struggled there themselves, shocked and hungry. The teacher's questions sought reactions.

They'd not know what had really happened.

Their thirst would make them a bit mad.

They'd be seeing things – having hallucinations.

And nightmares.

The final challenge was concerned with how this community would react to television reporters and camermen demanding to see survivors. Was it fair to interview a shocked person? In the event, they formed a convincing group showing maturity and sympathetic insight as they argued cogently to protect their charges against inquisitive questioning.

Afterwards the teacher emphasised her concern to create open-ended situations and allow children opportunity to develop drama using their own ideas. At some stage in a lesson she tried to bring children into a group situation where they had to grapple with underlying issues as well as surface events. This meant allowing scope for initiative, building on children's developing ability to think and plan in a co-operative atmosphere. She saw her role essentially as a guide and resource – "like a mountain leader on an expedition".

While a global view of one school's approach illustrates how a pattern for development in drama work can be established effectively, other schools with their own drama traditions often follow different paths and provide varying challenges. These examples from year groups across the age range emphasise the variation.

Example 2

An S.P.A. primary school situated on the outskirts of a large industrial conurbation. This is a mature building, celebrating its centenary but with a good-sized hall in addition to the separate classrooms. Drama is viewed as important by the head master who is fortunate in having a well-qualified deputy to undertake work across the age range. But it has other values as a strong motivating agent and potential integrative force. In their particular situation they find its capacity to bring children into creative working relationships especially useful, together with the reflective qualities it may engender. These aspects are reflected in drama and its related discussions which give children scope for appraisal and decision making. Organisation allows drama to be flexible so that the hall periods or classroom activities suit needs and demands. The teacher concerned believes that activities in the early years should emphasise imaginative development, but must also offer increasing scope for children to strengthen skills and begin shaping their own work. Steps on the way would include:

1 Necessary social, physical and language skills.

2 Development of a "story line" or structure.

3 Children recognising possibilities and exploiting these.

4 Achievement of reflection and awareness.

5 Power to "stand still" and consider; evaluate the realities of the situation and find solutions to problems.

Lesson I   First Year Juniors: At the commencement of the lesson children found their own space and worked individually on refining hand movements, shaking, twisting etc. They were then invited to hold an imaginary paintbrush "sharp as a needle" and paint an outside scene on a small stamp-sized piece of paper. This was done with concentration and care so that when they were invited to talk about their pictures much detail was forthcoming. The scenes were mainly rural and included mountains, houses and cliffs.

The next stage entailed using a bigger canvas and "painting" on a larger scale. Afterwards they were invited to close their eyes and "look" at what was there. More oral description followed.

A third stage took children to a wall and an even larger scale creation. This time actions were represented, cycling, ice-skating, the movement of a train etc. Partners were chosen and they described their paintings to each other in words, gestures and sounds.

They were invited to choose which picture to go into and explore. This led to lively activity and language interaction between children, with the class teacher moving round to guess who and what were involved. Finally, a second choice was allowed and a different picture chosen.

The class teacher saw the activity successfully attaining his goals; a variety and refinement of movement, language interaction and improved concentration. These represented necessary steps towards further objectives where children could confidently shape their own drama activity and reflect within it. It was not a pattern of work to be adhered to throughout four years but basic skills and attitudes were being developed in addition to an extension of imaginative capacities.

Lesson 2   Upper juniors in a forty-five minute session developing their version of the Children's Crusade. The lesson began with children moving rostra blocks to the purposes of their drama. They did this sensibly and thoughtfully, discussing among themselves the most effective arrangement.

The task completed, they sat near their teacher who questioned them on what had been accomplished in the drama so far, their own roles and what should be attempted during that lesson. They wished to experience certain aspects of the crusade again.

At first this involved reacting to the "holy man" organising the mission and it required a large crowd scene with families and friends grouped round a central point. Children quickly became involved and contributed to the ensuing discussion in which many questions were asked. How can you prove the sea will open? What's so special about you? What about food for a journey like that? Why should we win when the others didn't?

It was agreed that they would join the crusade and reassemble in the square after collecting their belongings. Here the teacher in role as a cynical bystander intervened and provoked further discussion: "If fully grown men fail what can you do?" Reaction was rather boisterous but the teacher, still in role, controlled the situation by questioning individual children. This approach caused the remainder to listen attentively while question and answer proceeded. Eventually, the children marched away singing *Onward Christian Soldiers*.

Now a new situation was established. It had been decided that cold and hungry children would become quarrelsome and disillusioned. Some might believe it better to turn back and abandon their mission. So children developed a "camp fire" scene with quiet and effective interchange of views against a backcloth of hunger and fatigue. People will call us cowards you know. But it's three thousand miles. And we have no water at all. Shall we say a prayer? Finally, they attempted to beg food from strangers, a development which obliged them to explain and justify their situation, fears, hopes and intentions. Both feeling and language qualities were evident in the nuance of tone and content of argument.

Discussion closed the lesson with teacher and children appraising their work. They thought some ideas were faulty or needed more attention and listening quality should be improved. One boy commented "It's sometimes quite hard to get your thinking right so what you say is sensible". Afterwards the teacher confirmed his satisfaction with how these children were maturing. They were becoming increasingly aware of those qualities which sustained purposeful drama and could now build up situations so that to challenge was constructive and they enjoyed the drama experience.

Example 3

This school is a modern Open Plan building and serves an outlying suburb of a large industrial city. Organisation is based upon year groups with drama an established part of the curriculum.

In discussing approaches, teachers emphasise the degree of trust existing between children and themselves. "This relationship is a key aspect. They need to feel confident in themselves and be able to handle themselves as real and dramatic people. We want them to be sure of language and movement gained through practice in helping to develop situations. In this way they have been used to decision making right from the start – way back at infant level." Drama is seen as motivating and enriching experience in the school context, with great learning potential that links with much other work, so that individual and social strengths are developed from a motivating activity in which the whole of life and living can be represented and explored. The work examined here was built up over several weeks but general school policy ensures that a balance of activities is maintained and overall development considered. Younger children are seen to require more immediate and successful response and are perhaps not yet ready for deeper characterisation. Therefore approaches for them emphasise movement and the use of space. Often movement "has story wrapped up in it" and is concerned with fantasy; being small and trapped in a tree, experiencing life as another creature; exploring a world of gnomes and trolls. Some teachers say that a fantasy stage is necessary for most children as they establish a dramatic vocabulary based on movement and language skills. This encourages concentration, together with ability to handle feeling and thought in a dramatic context. At the third and fourth year junior levels, historical or literary themes may provide useful material, supplemented by aspects of children's own social life and environment.

A group project on Vikings was the origin of drama in this example. Among a wall display which included writing, illustrations, shields and spears, one large warrior provoked particular interest and discussion leading to dramatic involvement. Preliminary activities led to an extended theme and their work was observed at a mid-way point in its development.

Discussion came first; children recalled with their teacher details of work done in previous lessons, particularly how they had recreated a Viking ship in movement and decided to raid. Then each found an individual space and took up a "concentration position" sitting cross-legged with folded arms and eyes closed. Their teacher quietly asked them to create imaginatively and they did so with commitment and absorption. Build a Viking warrior, his dress, his weapons. Build his family. What does he like or dislike? Give yourself a name, the person you will be.

> "I can do this because they have begun to think who they actually are. Who am I? Why am I here? Where did I come from? Who are my family? In class they have found out and incorporated the information into their own character."

Immediately after this the children recreated their ship prior to the raid. It involved skilful and sensitive movement construction with groups forming prow, sides and stern; warrior oarsmen, chief, time-beater and lookout all had their place while other children simulated wave action and provided a sense of speed. An island was reached and the "ship" was transformed into raiding Vikings but it quickly became apparent that the raiders had no agreed plan.

Chief	Did we start too quickly?
Teacher	Is there a better lead in? How would you prepare.
Boy	We'd talk together first

The class gathered round their chief for discussion and suggestions began to emerge.

Boy	I don't think we should look as organised as this.
Girl	I don't think we'd be like this. We wouldn't know we were going.
Teacher	How would you tell them? Think about who you are.
Chief	I would have a council.

In this way the children came together for discussion and provided suggestions or comments. They talked sensibly in small groups and together as a community, taking decisions on where they were going, what they would take with them and possible action when they landed. Their ship was relaunched and a better-planned raid followed involving battle in movement, ransacking, and the chief's death. At once, all other activity ceased as he was solemnly carried back to the ship, together with other wounded warriors and anxious conversations took place. One severely wounded man opted to be left behind and thus posed another problem. "They have the confidence to take this on themselves which is due to their continuous experience in drama earlier. They don't need direction anymore, they'll embellish as they go on. At first they were cardboard cut-outs but as we've talked and read they've filled out and are developing in character. They can shape drama now and can begin to see how it works. Here they're realising that it's not always the person still standing on their feet who is the more dramatic force."

A further discussion between teacher and children followed:

Teacher	I liked the impromptu way you reacted to your leader and commented as you went along. When you died your hand went up and waved: you wanted people back on the ship. We'll need to think about space there so you can be seen more.
Girl	Would it be better to have people to fight?
Girl	How would we manage that?
Girl	Like at the theatre, killing people but they're not really killed.
Boy	Would it be better to have the ship chalked out?
Boy	Yes, it would stop us going into the side when we're fighting.
Boy	It's difficult to lift the chief and carry him to the boat.
Teacher	Have you thought how much space you'd lose if you drew the boat?
Boy	Yes, I suppose.
Boy	Should we write our ideas down?
Teacher	If you want to and we'll use them later.

The discussion is interesting in its blend of drama content and theoretical technique. It marks a development which comes when children are given opportunity to shape and plan by talking together. At this stage the class was asked to focus thought upon the attacked settlement. What sort of people were these islanders? How did they live? Gradually a picture of life was built up and formed the basis for an exploratory enactment. Roles were chosen so that each knew who he was and occupations gave some purpose and shape to the establishment of a peaceful fishing community. Each determined where he lived and, beginning at daybreak, went through routine activities in mime and conversation that, however, quickly revealed a need for further information and more definite purpose. This was recognised by both teacher and children in a concluding discussion and they agreed that a coherent community required factual background concerned with people, their conditions and work tasks. For dramatic development they were asked also to decide how and when the Vikings would attack. "I like them to be able to look at things from another angle but go into a person's make-up far enough to understand. I want them to be able to handle all kinds of roles and relationships, handle situations and themselves. There's such a lot of enjoyment in this for them, but so much development too."

Some implications for teachers

These examples illustrate the variety of approaches and achievements in schools. They reinforce comments made earlier that satisfactory dramatic development hinges upon the provision of sufficiently challenging material and structures. This represents a problem for some teachers and schools, especially when exercises and games are over-emphasised or heavily-directed and constricted. Awareness of possibilities is also crucially important so both teacher and children can build up dramatic strengths together. If drama is to flourish educationally, then it seems important that all concerned should establish a "vision of excellence" and this can only be achieved in practice through informed awareness and experiment by both teacher and children.

Achievements in drama throughout the age range varied as widely as approaches and it was not uncommon for children of similar age to be found working at different levels depending on ability, environment and school. Sometimes adverse circumstances were particularly apparent, especially in mixed ethnic classes attending urban schools.

Here movement-based approaches often provided one effective means of involving children in drama activities and developing imaginative insight and social skills. Yet even here it is not possible to generalise, since challenging drama situations of other kinds were also found in similar schools and much depended upon teacher insight and enthusiasm, the school itself and how far drama was recognised as having educational value.

Some useful indicators taken from examples help to provide a basis for observing development, but they can only be regarded as pointing towards possibilities and need consideration within the context of a school, its goals, and its children. They do not attempt to outline a developmental programme; but comment on certain aspects of drama between five and eleven which seem to build on those characteristics considered earlier. Where a school has particular difficulties there will be variations in the patterns of work attempted and achieved, though the basic elements inevitably remain the same.

One of the most significant indicators is children's growing consciousness that drama represents a means to explore events, issues and relationships. They become more aware of the process itself and the demands made upon their feelings and thinking power as people in a joint enterprise.

Even when a group of lower juniors assumed the roles of Guy Fawkes, executioners and crowd, to explore why he should be burned, their teacher commented: "Perhaps because they were in a situation where the thing became real you could detect a lot of whirring and grindings going on there as they tried to justify and searched for reasons. They worked really hard."

Often more complex or subtle issues derived from drama concerns, require thoughtful response – exemplified when Viking invaders demanding monastery treasures (page 192) were shown a piece of bone symbolising the holy relic and entered into discussion on what represents treasure to different people. In the same drama, threat to a peaceful settlement's existence evoked strong reaction through argument and illustrated how with experience and increasing maturity children's thinking became energised by feeling. When teachers refer to "depth" in drama this is usually what is meant; sufficient involvement and concern to stimulate response from children as participants with something at stake, so that feeling, thinking and expression have a frame of reference. Obviously, children's own level of development and abilities play an important part in determining particular responses in drama and what we can expect, but because it offers so many ways to extend children's thinking and feeling about self, others and the world outside, they can work "above themselves". We need to begin by getting children inside a situation physically, intellectually and emotionally and then encourage the drama process to stretch all concerned.

In all drama, children's own experience is brought in to synthesise with dramatic events and consolidates or extends understanding. As they grow older the ability to compare consciously what happens in drama against real life (or with other drama or literature) increases. The work of nine year old juniors offers an interesting illustration here; in looking at how it would be possible to use an old warrior as human bait for ridding themselves of Grendel the monster (page 94), they encountered objections based upon their own experience and used analogies to illuminate and clarify an imaginative concern.

One infant's school commented on how its seven year old children were becoming role conscious in drama and trying out role possibilities. Given drama experiences that build on this throughout the eight to eleven age span, children begin to move away from the earlier "masks" tried on briefly and discarded, towards an interest in character so that people's motivations and reactions not only interest them but also influence levels of feeling and thought in drama. The nuances of character make-up are more apparent, allowing for greater discernment in role playing and increasing critical appraisal of actions. When third year fishing villagers were confronted by a television crew wishing to interview survivors from a shipping disaster (page 34), they responded with indignant but reasoned argument, clearly reflecting their relationship as protective hosts safeguarding helpless guests and revealing some insight into how the role of public reporter assumes threatening dimensions. It is this interaction between viewpoints and attitudes represented by dramatic roles which often heightens awareness and response so that where role challenge is absent in a teacher's approaches, one means of deepening feeling and thought is also lost.

Older children in particular often seem to appreciate opportunities to explore and consolidate role through extended themes.

Some insight into how third year juniors saw the role of one in authority comes through from discussion and indicates a maturing consciousness ready to be exercised in drama.

It would be hard, you've never been that. You would have to find
something good to say.

You'd have to try to be fair.

It wouldn't be nice to punish people.

And you wouldn't have to take sides.

Hard not to take sides though.

It would be hard to make decisions. You wouldn't want to
disappoint anyone. Wish you could help both.

I'd go by what the person had done to other people if I had to
punish him.

And you'd have to judge if it's fair or not.

It would be harder being a person like that, you'd have to try to get
ideas.

It's easier to be a not real person because you can make up your
ideas what they do. With a real person you have to think what.

One class teacher commented that sometimes she encouraged children
to slow their drama down and think more fully about it. Their ability
to achieve this marks a move from the action-oriented drama of
younger juniors who are often keen on "seeing it through" towards a
greater interest in people and events. At about ten or eleven (or even
earlier) many children will probe into motivation and implication
when their attention is caught. They seem to enjoy savouring issues of
importance to them and considering them more fully. Some of the
drama observed encourages this trend, chiefly where drama material
and structures provide concerns of interest to children and allows them
to explore these. But many other drama approaches extend and build
on the same development when they involve children in useful
discussions derived from drama. In this way learning opportunities are
made available for teachers and their pupils to exploit. Children as
Pharaoh's slaves (page 121) discovered his treachery within a drama
context and extended their thoughts in discussion, afterwards, they
knew better what treachery is like. Similarly, obligation was explored
through a Thegn's commitment (page 190) and therefore was better
understood. So drama presents the abstract world in concrete
situations from which children take account according to their abilities
and opportunities.

44

Drama observed in schools differed considerably in how far it allowed children to be tentative, going this way or that as events and interests directed. Most teachers influenced the working structure of their children but some were rigid and gave little scope to vary pre-set programmes. Teachers justified some of these activities on the basis that certain skills were being extended, confidence required strengthening and tight structures were necessary in certain conditions. This is very true and only the practitioner on the spot can be fully aware of children's needs and plan approaches accordingly. Yet we cannot disregard how much is added to the drama process when they are allowed to contribute ideas and make the activity more their own. At no time is this more apparent than when children are moving through the junior age range and their growing reflective abilities produce relevant and often exciting suggestions to take drama forward. In a small village school nine year old juniors read *Stig of the Dump* and asked to build drama around it. So a Stig community was established and they were given the task of using their ideas to create a pattern of primitive life. They resolved how they were governed. How they moved blocks of stone. How they built shelters. The means to create and build fire. How to hunt their prey. When a "rival tribe" came at night to steal food the first Stig reaction was to kill them, but then they were asked to think more about the matter and concluded that they would make useful slaves. Their headmaster observed: "Stimulation and direction are important but we use a loose framework. Children quickly get the idea of developing and they have all sorts of ideas. So the teacher must make himself redundant at times but be available and sensitive to needs."

Essentially, what we are doing here is urging teachers to recognise that children are able to work effectively as a group, co-operating, planning, trying out and criticising within drama activities. They become very aware that this is a social experience requiring certain disciplines to be successful, especially the ability to discuss sensibly and productively.

The readiness of a group to understand why an idea may be dropped or changed is a further indication that they are maturing in social and dramatic terms. Control of drama as a learning tool for teachers to use is strengthened as children's commitment and willingness to apply themselves builds up from the reality of tasks attempted. Most older juniors regard thinking about their drama as almost as important and satisfying as actually doing it, a characteristic responsible for the involved procedures devised by one group for a Pharaoh's selection and by another for their Saxon pagan ritual.

At the same time group abilities to accept and deal with the unexpected in drama is also important. This always represents a challenge, whether requiring response to a major event or to the unexpectedness of words during interaction. When the nine year old king was being criticised for his inability to kill Grendel, he suddenly announced that he would be king no longer. Suddenly the group attitudes, opinions, and intentions were thrown into a melting pot and had to be refashioned spontaneously. The ten year old wounded Viking (page 40) volunteering to be left near the raided village presented his classmates with an unexpected dramatic and moral problem. Children can enjoy coping in these circumstances when they have developed the skills, confidence and dramatic awareness to do so.

Two areas of development crucial to drama throughout the age range are movement and language. Language is examined more closely later but many teachers emphasise a combination of the two when planning their drama work, so that skills and abilities in each are exercised. The examples discussed so far show how strongly movement features in drama generally and illustrate children's growing skills of action as they mature.

One teacher working in a difficult area expressed her thoughts this way. "I can draw a group together and deepen what we are about with movement; it's a positive action which somehow helps to clarify and deepen the experience a child is going through. It's another way or experiencing the same kind of ideas that might come through language, but some are not skilled with words and are happy to experience with their bodies. They get a feeling for the situation which can be then put more easily in words as a result."

Where children have confidence and movement experience they can succeed in bringing imaginative ideas and a sense of collective feeling to their drama, enriching the total process. The third and fourth year juniors who were launched into dramatic exploration by the creation in movement of a Viking longboat (page 39) and subsequently expressed a group poignancy in the way a dead chief was brought home, showed not only well developed movement skills but also an awareness of their aims. This seems important if movement is not to remain at a level of skill practice or expressive activity for its own sake, fundamental as these are to overall development; it should also represent a more challenging and stimulating means to approach and deepen drama for all children, offering them initiative and choice.

Problems when drama is intermittent

Examples of work drawn from many survey schools illustrate varying approaches and qualities but they do not reveal the problems caused by this variety. Sometimes children encounter challenging drama early in their school lives, but not in later years. At other times the pattern is reversed and drama is fostered more as they move upwards through the five to eleven age-range. Often one enthusastic teacher perseveres alone at some point in a school's class or organisational structure but even worse, there may be no-one at all in some schools who recognises the significance of drama. In these circumstances the extent and quality of children's experience is adversely affected and problems arise. Teachers emphasise the difficulties experienced when children have not built up social and dramatic strengths and come to drama with desultory attitudes. One teacher's words summarise what many other colleagues also maintain, "For many children when I say drama they look blank or expect to do plays. So it means that my job is to get them used to the idea of working in drama – not real development as I would like it but just that; starting to see what it's about. You can talk about it till the cows come home but they've got to start experiencing it before we get anywhere." There is a popular view among many teachers that discontinuity in children's dramatic experience necessitates returning to basic starting points, or perhaps beginning effective approaches for the first time with a particular group. Very possibly, lack of drama may be more significant at certain developmental stages but this is a question requiring more attention than a survey can provide. What can be stated with certainty, however, is that gaps exist in what many schools offer children as dramatic experience, potential educational advantages are lost, and teachers, even when interested, sometimes lack confidence in their own abilities to deal with the problems of building up dramatic and social strengths.

Of course, much depends on teachers' attitudes and how far they see drama as an educational process, so that two fundamental factors are commitment to dramatic activity and belief in its values for children's growth. This is where wavelengths in particular schools and between schools vary, a feature stressed by one headmaster who sees drama as important in his own school. He maintains that its values cannot be justified through words alone; teachers must observe children's development through drama and gain their own insights based on direct involvement. When old ideas springing from play production or story recapitulation are replaced by an emphasis on process and wider curricular links, then teachers will begin to discuss with more understanding what drama is about educationally. Meanwhile, many of those wanting to do something worthwhile are left with problems which can prove to be difficult and even intractible, unless sympathetic support, suitable material and strategies are forthcoming. With this in mind a brief examination of drama being introduced into three schools will illustrate approaches and some of the problems faced.

Coming new to drama

Example 1

A large modern junior school serving part of a small industrial town. Organisation is based on class groups each with its own teacher. The head master here was newly appointed but came with a strong drama commitment and considerable experience of drama approaches and organisation. He is keen on exploiting the integrative nature of drama within the curriculum and favours extended work which allows children to develop dramatically and draw on wider learning possibilities through classroom links. His own conception of development hinges on discovering a basic interest or idea that appeals to children, preferably their own, and then challenging them to determine how it should be implemented in practice. Discussion is therefore regarded as vitally important when plans are made and work subsequently appraised. The right kind of questions are important. Why did that turn out the way it did? What could we have done in particular circumstances? Why did a character react as he did?

He believes that teachers often find problems in the intangible aspects of drama and are unsure what to feed children and how to guide them, especially when drama has been lacking. His policy is therefore to strengthen teacher confidence and suggest ideas and structures from which they may choose, but setting these against some clear goals. In this he is guided by his County Adviser who emphasises the need for teachers to build up a range of experience which includes goals, strategies, criteria of assessment and appropriate material. The teacher needs to know how to evolve goals based upon possibilities as drama progresses and maintain a balance between structure on the one hand and spontaneity on the other. Therefore, they must nourish their own imaginative awareness along with the children's. Two lessons were observed, involving second and fourth year juniors respectively.

Lesson 1 : Second year junior class of approximately thirty children for thirty minutes. Children responded to movement "warm-up" activities chiefly exploring varying tree shapes, controlled by tambour beats. This activity was intended to stimulate both a move into drama and a structural consciousness that would stimulate ideas for a "story" based upon a forest. It did lead into a brief but useful discussion about trees, forests and picnics and the class evolved the idea of being lost during a storm and a subsequent adventure encountering witches. The majority of the children then assumed tree roles and used voice sounds to create a storm effect, moving, swaying and waving in response, so that lost children and witches had a believable environment. Group discussion followed as ideas for development were considered and group suggestions listened to. Commitment was obviously beginning to come, in tact the "storm" had induced a dramatic mood within which all children now seemed to be working with some enthusiasm. Patiently their teacher allowed discussion, comment and time for response. Had the spell been worked out? Yes, it had and was forthwith repeated. How did the lost children come into the witches' power? They had run with terror because of the storm and found themselves caught. What were the intentions of the witches? To keep and eat the children. At this stage time ran out and the class returned to their classroom.

These were children without experience in drama having to learn how group effort can build a satisfying outcome. They were beginning to listen and appraise, sort out ideas, and respond more positively as dramatic mood was created within the working structure. But the question of one boy as the lesson ended indicated something of the difficulties of the teacher's task, "Will we write a script and make it a play?"

Lesson 2 Fourth year junior class of approximately thirty children. This lesson, also thirty minutes, began with varied movement activities intended to increase awareness and focus concentration. How would you walk if you were an old man? Can you walk across a muddy field? There was a good response to these exercises and some degree of feeling was apparent. The children were then organised into groups and their teacher talked about mime and its qualities, drawing attention to detailed movement by demonstrating the threading of a needle. Each group then discussed its own choice of mime and was given time to exchange views, before beginning work in which comments from the teacher encouraged them to think more about quality of action and finer movements.

The main part of their lesson was concerned with a continuation of the Robin Hood theme begun a week or two previously and children recounted what had been decided and worked upon. It was significant that though these children were fourth year juniors their recapitulation stressed action only, and reference to role, motivation, feeling, ideas and the general kind of talk that comes when older children are busy constructing in drama were all lacking. Perhaps not surprisingly, action also dominated the drama itself in which a forest of trees was created, where Robin and a group disguised themselves and stole the horses of passing travellers. Language interchange was limited and unsure, though the possibilities for discussion and interaction in such an ambush and the range of concerns that might have been explored by this age group were wide and potentially challenging. Their teacher had an excellent relationship with the class who enjoyed his sense of humour. Yet obviously he was dealing with a group who were responsive enough, but lacked the dramatic experience and maturity to see possibilities and determine how these would be used. His structure and approach provided one means into drama for these children and gave them the opportunity to enjoy some measure of creative satisfaction; an achievement, when no active drama approaches had existed hitherto. Nevertheless, their dramatic journey is late in beginning, they have far to travel and a break in educational environment will come at the year's end. These children are fortunate, however, because there is now a commitment to drama within the school and an experienced staff to progressively build up and develop dramatic strengths.

Example 2

This is a middle school situated in an urban area with municipal housing. The headmaster is keen to see drama developed throughout the school which has a mixed ethnic intake, but recognises the difficulties teachers face when they are unsure about goals and strategies. He would like to see Colleges providing more insights into how effective work can be achieved, so that teachers come better equipped and willing to see that drama is not always movement or play production. His school is currently benefitting from a move by his education authority to focus attention on the wide range of educational opportunities fostered through drama, particularly those involving language activities. A teacher-adviser had visited the school and worked for several weeks with interested teachers. The lesson observed, however, was not his work but that of the class teacher concerned, and it illustrates how far a class may be moved on in certain circumstances. Approximately twenty eight children aged eleven years were involved for forty minutes.

Work began with warming up movements for a few minutes. Teacher and children then discussed space exploration and moon landings, using some of the factual data to support subsequent "moon walking". A drama game followed, with hoops spread on the floor for craters and several "dalek" volunteers standing with their backs to the advancing spacemen who had to dodge the obstacles but were killed if seen moving when the daleks turned to look. The main content of the lesson then began. First, discussion again centred on space exploration and the possible kinds of life on different planets. Three groups were then formed, one to represent a society of legless people, and the other two became astronaut crew members. Each group then went off to undertake certain tasks, the astronauts to use whatever was available in the hall, rostra steps, hoops etc., as construction material for spacecraft, and to determine layout, life-support systems and general crew duties; the legless people to create a society with work tasks and means of life. The class teacher then spent her time going round to each group guiding and supporting their efforts. She asked the legless group how they thought their life-style would be different and attention focused upon: means of protecting themselves; difficulties of working; kinds of jobs; how to move around; games and pastimes; construction of buildings.

Meanwhile, two imposing and quite different spacecraft had been constructed, with children showing considerable inventiveness and interest. At this stage the teacher suggested that spacecraft crew might consider landing and meeting the legless ones so that each could explore contrasting ways of life and inventions. An interesting exchange of questions and answers followed with the children showing commitment and involvement. The captain of one space craft asked his crew not to walk when they visited the legless people "so they won't be offended".

A final discussion brought the groups together to consider developments. What had been their problems? Finding what to say and what to do quickly enough; keeping a straight face at times;

working out some of the details. What had they achieved? They had made what they planned; helped "to find out about people and things"; worked hard but enjoyed it.

Afterwards the class teacher commented on her work. It was still very new to her and the children and she sometimes felt uneasy about control – that things could move away from her. Assessment was a problem because apart from control and children's involvement she was unsure what to look for. Nevertheless, she recognised that her class was beginning to work effectively together and could exploit imaginative possibilities, certainly within the present theme. Her problem would be where to take them next and how best to do this. Altogether this example does show how one class has begun to move forward in drama with a little skilled work beforehand building up disciplines and commitment and looks capable of making steady progress if appropriate challenge can be maintained. Perhaps the respect and trust which existed between teacher and children was significant.

Example 3

The third example offers a complete contrast in both types of school and the approach used to introduce drama. The headmaster wrote his own notes outlining goals, difficulties and achievements. Parts of this have been included as a valuable and interesting commentary on development over several weeks with children who had no previous experience of class drama and who worked with limited space. Two significant aspects deserve to be stressed. A dramatic consciousness begins to emerge through the active language emphasis and role differentiation. These children have become particular people with a real identity and problems. Though certain drama skills are missing, their role discussions begin to reveal a dramatic quality of feeling and thought which suggests they are moving forward effectively. Second, drama in this example is part of a broad educational approach and draws freely upon or feeds many curricular areas. It does not begin or cease with the drama interaction itself, but provides a continuing source of stimulation and reference for learning activities which take children into art, craft, discussion, research and many forms of writing. Thus from the beginning, these children have met drama not as a separate activity, but as an integral part of their learning.

Extracts from the headmaster's notes:
The School   A small village school with one full-time infant teacher, the headmaster and a part-time teacher who share responsibility for

the juniors. The school has three average size classrooms. Three fairly expensive housing estates have been built in the village during the past eight years, occupied mainly by white collar workers who travel to employment in neighbouring towns.

Why Drama? When I took up my appointment as Head I found that standards in basic skills were good, but creative language work was unimaginative. The children did not interact well in discussions. They would answer questions but were reluctant to propose their own ideas. They wrote what they thought the teacher wanted using factual language. They seldom used similes, analogies or metaphors and had no experience in attempting to write their own poetry. I was anxious to develop sensitivity in the use of language and to encourage the children to think for themselves, to pose problems and seek solutions in discussions with their peers. Drama seemed to be the vehicle which would achieve my aim. Although I was not drama trained, I built my classwork around the drama theme and used the enthusiasm it engendered. I knew what drama had to offer as a stimulus across the curriculum and that it could motivate children to write, discuss and use language as a sensitive tool.

I decided to link the drama to an environmental study of the village which is Saxon in origin. I favoured a theme which would allow the drama to be part of a wider study, and one which used the village as a focal point. I also wanted the children to be able to draw upon first hand experience rather than be completely tied to books. In this case it would be the experience provided by the drama itself and also that of the actual village environment to which they could refer. The Saxon church on our doorstep led us naturally into that period of history.

I began by describing the events leading up to the Battle of Hastings and the Battle itself. My story described how William collected his army by promising land to his knights. I ended the story by pointing out that a knight named Robert de Brus had been given our village as his Manor as a share of the spoils.

I then began a discussion with the children but found this very difficult. I had to continually ask questions to stimulate the thinking. Very slowly some of them began to make tentative suggestions, but I discovered that it takes some time to develop the art of discussion with children unused to oral give and take. One needs to treat each child's suggestion as a useful contribution and never voice all their thoughts. How far the children had progressed in seven weeks is illustrated by

this extract from a taped discussion – conducted with very little help
from the teacher.

Teacher	What about Robert de Brus. Do you think he's going to run away? If he goes, he loses our village, his manor and all his serfs.
Joanne D	If he wouldn't we could send the leper to talk to him. That would frighten him off.
Carol	If just one leper comes in when all the Normans have gone the wise old woman could try to cure the leper.
Joanne S	If your fingers dropped off, you couldn't get medicine to put them back on again, could you?
Carol	But it could stop the leprosy from spreading.
David	But you'd have to cut certain parts off. Wherever it was to stop it from spreading.
Phillipa	What if it started on your stomach. You couldn't really cut your stomach in half.
Teacher	Could they do surgery like that in those days?
All	No.

As a teacher, I learned a great deal from these discussions. I found it
difficult to keep discussions going without interjecting my own
thoughts and dominating the proceedings. Eventually, I tried the
technique of adopting a role myself as an ordinary Saxon villager and
this broke down the barrier. The children accepted me as one of the
group and began to speak more freely.

The children decided to start the drama with Robert arriving in the
village. Late evening was chosen because the villagers would be in bed
and they would have to get dressed. The children felt this would make
everyone bad tempered and aggressive and produce an interesting
confrontation. Robert would wake the blacksmith and tell him to
bring all the people out of their homes. There was a discussion as to
how he should do this. It was suggested that he could ring the church
bell but someone pointed out that the people might think they were
being attacked and cause a panic. It was decided that the blacksmith
should wake everyone up.

We attempted this first short scene. I was disappointed at the poor standard of speech and the children's reluctance to say anything. Clearly I had a lot to learn. It had all seemed so easy watching someone else. I had used the same technique – discussion followed by action. Very disheartened I tried to assess the situation objectively. I came to the conclusion that I was expecting too much and I had placed the children in an unfamiliar situation in which they felt insecure. There were a number of points to consider:

1   There was insufficient feeling and involvement.

2   They needed sufficient background information to support them in their role.

3   Children with no experience of drama seem to require time to develop the necessary disciplines.

4   Assessing children's oral capabilities is not the same as assessing writing skill.

My mistakes could have spoilt everything, I started immediately to rectify the lack of background information. We began working together to seek information on Saxon life – food, homes, weapons, farming and costume were all studied and so was the life of William and the Feudal system. The other three points would take time to correct. However, being aware of these factors helped considerably. I thought out my lessons much more carefully.

The next three lessons, one per week, were devoted to developing the confrontation between Robert and the villagers. Robert explained his position and stated his demands and new laws.

The villagers would be given a small amount of land for their own use. In return they must work for three days each week on his land. No one would be allowed to leave until the next harvest. They must build him a new Manor out of the stone. Until this was built two of his men at arms would be billeted with each family. Meat must be supplied to feed his retainers until his own land was producing. All game was the property of the lord for sport and poaching would be severely punished.

Many arguments ensued from this statement. The villagers faced starvation. He was turning them into slaves. Not enough time to work their own land. Why should they feed his soldiers? If they eat cattle none will remain for breeding. Warlike skills are not necessary. If the

Normans are so strong why do they need such an elaborate army?
What about the old people and widows – how will they pay their rent
if they can't work?

Each lesson began and ended with discussion. The children became
more confident and produced many interesting ideas. Progress in the
drama remained slow. Arguments were often not fully developed
because someone would interject a new idea before the current one
had been fully explored. There were still long pauses while the
children thought and they tended to collect around the Normans. This
poor use of space remains a problem, but I feel it is partly due to the
small area available. However, I could see development and the
children were enthusiastic. The introduction of simple props, shawls
and cloaks made from scraps of material helped the children
considerably. A sword was made for Robert de Brus and had quite a
remarkable effect. It seemed to lend dignity to the child and became a
kind of symbol of authority.

Conclusions

1   Actual drama activity ideally requires more than one lesson per
week, especially in the early stages. We did not have enough time.

2   The original aim was largely achieved. Language work improved
and enthusiasm was engendered for work right across the curriculum.

3   It has improved the children's ability to discuss and think
objectively.

4   It is a great spur to less able children who discover they can
succeed and consequently affects the rest of their work.

5   The children developed a tremendous interest in their own
surroundings because of the drama. They became very aware of the
generations between them and the Normans and the interesting
changes that had taken place in their village in that time.

6   It has social implications. The children are more aware of other
people's problems and are ready to consider them. They have learned
to listen.

8   Drama experience feeds on knowledge from all sources and leads
to greater involvement. At the end of seven weeks there were evident
signs of progress, but it would take much more time and effort before
these children could confidently enter and shape a dramatic situation.

References

The Child's World of Make-believe – J. L. Singer, Academic Press 1973.
The Effects of Socio-Dramatic Play on Disadvantaged Pre-School Children –
Sara Smilansky, Wiley 1968.
Beyond the Known – Brian Wilks.
(Drama in Education – No. 2 Ed. J. Hodgson & M. Banham, Pitman
1973.)

Drama and language

Drama as a language challenge

Many of the survey schools expressed the opinion that one of the values of drama in education was its potential for language development. A considerable number could go further and outline various language goals which they hoped drama would help to achieve, including:

1 Confidence in speaking.

2 Improvement of speech.

3 Development of fluency.

4 Development of vocabulary.

5 Development and expression of ideas.

6 Ability to communicate with people.

7 Spoken language as stimulation for writing.

8 Improvement of children's listening.

9 Awareness of language in different situations.

10 Ability to discuss, discriminate and evaluate.

11 Improvement of a skill basic to learning.

In addition, most of the schools visited also referred to other learning objectives which they considered an integral part of drama activities and which draw upon or enrich children's language resources. Part of one school's statement will be sufficient to indicate the breadth of these concerns – "To enable children to experience something beneficial to themselves. The understanding of other people, their situations and attitudes. A way of examining our cultural heritage through literature, poetry, and music. Another way of examining and learning about other subject areas, e.g. history, R.E. etc."

It is not suggested that these statements form a comprehensive list of drama objectives but they indicate that drama may promote language development. In practice, however, possibilities seem to be realised more through language activities associated with drama rather than through drama itself.

But on the face of things, it seems that even when schools do seek a broader and more challenging language programme, they often fail to recognise drama as a process into which language feeds and from which come many varied language possibilities.

Where schools fail to see the potential, both drama and language suffer. Missing in varying degrees is the discussion through which children actively shape and explore what they are making. Neglecting these aspects inevitably affects the ability of children to get the best out of drama. Furthermore, teachers and children are denied one important means of assessing development, whether this be in the shape and issues of the drama itself or how individuals and groups are responding. Language in this context may often serve as the hallmark for quality of experience, a fundamental concern which deserves closer attention.

The absence of a strong commitment here is sometimes paralleled in schools by emphasis on a more movement-based approach to drama which may not provide the range of experiences children need. This is not to undervalue movement approaches in drama; their considerable values are observed and recorded elsewhere in this survey and many teachers regard them as essential. Indeed in certain circumstances they offer the only effective way into drama for some children. Nevertheless, in many school environments, movement without spoken language or with associated peripheral language activities can become the accepted pattern of drama.

The crux of the problem here seems to lie in the fact that many teachers are not confident in their grasp of the theoretical and the practical implications contained within a framework of drama, language and learning. There is in schools some uncertainty about what should be attempted and what may be achieved.

Learning and achievement are two useful focal points for the consideration of language in a drama context. For though drama may present many situations which require different uses of language, they are means to an end in the search for fruitful experience and all the concomitant learning bound up in the drama process.

In practice the relationship between drama and language is often confused, with some stressing its potential as a "learning tool" and

59

others adopting a "drama first" attitude. There is, of course, a middle way followed by a minority that says there is nothing fundamentally unsound in regarding drama as a language tool to achieve specific objectives, provided that the integrity of the dramatic process is maintained.

Varying degrees of insight and commitment in this part of the drama field is revealed in how heads and teachers discuss the issues. The following statements illustrate and represent schools where some measure of concern is felt. Statements one and two are from headteachers and three and four from class teachers.

1 Children explore, consider others, go through new experiences and compare their own experiences in drama. I help them to organise and make decisions, value what they say and try to keep spontaneity. I see it as a way of learning, of feeding directly into reading and writing. But it's a long-term business."

2 "I like a movement approach. It develops sensitivity and can lead to good mime and dance. Drama is an emotional thing and improvisation is difficult to control. We've tried it. So I like vocabulary of movement rather than the spoken word and this can bring in music, poetry and language."

3 "The ability to use words is so important; many of our city children don't have this. Drama is an activity where you're saying to children, 'Don't give me back the information I've given you', but rather 'How does this strike you?' They need the ability to reflect and analyse which is so often hidden in class by limited language skills."

4 "I try to foster language in drama but they often get stuck and we have no language. I'm not sure what my aims are. I'm working in the dark really. If something good comes out I leap on it."

The justification underlying a particular drama approach is too often based upon negative reasons. It is often associated with uncertainty about the rationale but it is just as likely to involve a lack of knowing *how* to take children into certain kinds of drama situations and develop these. There are many teachers who would echo the view that, "There's so much theory about, but what we need is some concrete help".

Indeed, most teachers would seem to welcome knowing more about working effectively within a drama-language framework and certainly there is a pressing need for knowledge of strategies from which the teacher's own practice can grow. But both the *why* and the *how* need strengthening at the class teacher level if the actual practice in schools is to move forward.

These statements offer some explanation for the following Bullock Report observations:

"Drama has an obvious and substantial contribution to make to the development of children's language and its possibilities in this respect have yet to be fully explored. . . . We do emphasise that teachers should not retreat from language in their improvisation work for negative reasons; for example, because of the difficulties some pupils apparently experience with words."

At the same time statements about drama and language made by many schools reflect the growing concern with language policy which the Bullock Report seems to have highlighted. There was evidence of renewed thought and appraisal and some teachers referred to meetings in schools or in local Teachers' Centres where the implications of the Report were being considered, sometimes by the teachers themselves but often under the guidance of local authority advisers and Teachers' Centre Wardens. Teachers and schools are increasingly beginning to consider the interrelationship of all aspects of language and literacy, and the spoken word is enjoying more attention as part of a global language policy. In one infant school, for example, the head referred to how her staff were looking at drama in terms of a new school policy on language development, while a middle school produced a statement from which the following extract is taken.

"Human beings can only learn how to use language by using it. Therefore we must provide children with the experience of talking freely and openly to each other and to the teacher about themselves, their ideas and matters of concern to them. This leads on to an experience of working together in small groups with control, self-discipline and unselfishness. We must allow for the development of social awareness, 'The capacity to evaluate patterns of social action and judge for oneself the validity of current norms and conventions governing social behaviour' and the growth of the individual's fluency as a participant in social action.

I would suggest we should 'engineer' a wide range of social situations that may be foreign to the child at the time but that he is likely to meet e.g., people sitting in a delayed train. There may also be historical themes – of the locality or loosely connected with contemporary social environment – or heroic themes, incidents from myth, legend and fairy tale.

A complement to drama is an enjoyable experience of literature, and the reading and telling of stories. But probably the two most important of all experiences with which we can provide our pupils are:

(a)   the opportunity to talk with interested and concerned adults who will respect, listen to and respond to their ideas

(b)   a situation where drama is given prominence.

Drama of this kind relies on spontaneity, sensitive interaction and co-operation. It allows for the setting up of a dramatic situation where children have a problem to explore and discuss – it allows for the individual to play out evil in a legal framework, or to have to make decisions about moral values. Painting, talking, writing, movement and music making all contribute to it and are generated by it."

Play and language

To examine the practicalities of language in schools we need to examine first the scope offered by play since the roots of drama lie in most children's urge to play.

So much of what is achieved in education depends upon how effectively schools create a learning environment and this certainly applies to dramatic play. A school with S.P.A. status which serves an industrial suburb helps to illustrate this statement.

Here a large room served as the main play area. In one corner several Wendy House sections had been fastened together to enclose and create a "room" of real-life dimensions and within which was a complete range of furniture and household utensils. Against the opposite wall stood a typical Wendy House available as a "den" but which changed its function according to play themes. It had been a fire station, police station etc. but was marked out as territorially belonging to the boys. At one point, to emphasise this possessive right they had asked their teacher to write above the door NO GIRLS ADMITTED – KEEP OUT. Nearby was the girls' "domain", currently a hairdressers salon with a suitable range of props. In the centre of the room was a collection of large blocks and other objects useful for large construction work. A variety of clothes hung from a rack and nearby was a table holding helmets and hats – all offering a lead into dressing up and role choice. On the walls were pinned "adventure pictures" and photographs of people engaged in assorted activities. A smaller adjoining room and the corridor served as overflow areas and provided materials for smaller constructional play and art materials.

Typical play situations included: family roles played out in the "Wendy Room": hairdresser and clients in the salon: the construction of a "bus" using blocks, steps and a tyre steering wheel – the bus journey then took groups on imaginary journeys: children laying out hoops as moon craters and exploring these as astronauts: hospital and ambulance, policemen and firemen themes.

What are the hallmarks of productive dramatic play, particularly with regard to language? Could the following two examples be so classified? The first came from an urban school in the north and followed a visit outside to a building site, and the second from a small country school in the south.

Example 1

Five–six year old children. This group consisted of four boys who had earlier observed building workers nearby. They began their play by collecting the various wooden blocks kept in the classroom and then discussed the question of roles.

John	I'm the foreman.
Peter	I'm the builder.
Kevin	I'm a builder as well.
John	Put them down in a line right round.
	He starts to arrange the blocks in the form of a large square.
Peter	Zoosh, zoosh, plenty on.
John	It needs plaster.
Kevin	Cement you mean.
John	I know how ...

They meet up with some difficulty caused by the varying sizes.

Michael	Turn them round.
Peter	Yes, they'll have to go round.
John	They should go along, all along, long lines.
Kevin	And this way as well. Mine can go this way.
Michael	It'll fall. It can fall you know.
John	Not with the plaster on.
Peter	I'm finished my part. That's all the bricks.

They look at their work and move around it.

Kevin	It's got no roof.
Peter	Well, let's make it a camp.
John	Michael, you be on guard. It's the jungle.

They creep about.

Kevin	Keep a good look out for monsters and wild animals.
Peter	Kevin, you be captured by a monster and we'll get you away. A space monster.
Kevin	A dalek. With the death gun.

The play is enacted now in movement with the rescue effected by John as the six-million-dollar bionic man.

John	Send in a rocket.
Peter	Zoom, zoom – the end of the dalek.

This play extract clearly shows how any experience which has interested children may lead into a play sequence – in this case the stimulation was obviously that of the workmen observed earlier. But notice the integral place of talk in the play; without it there could have been little shaping or development of the theme. It serves to bind the group together and reinforces the common element by providing opportunities for individual needs and ends; they obviously want the play to continue and become more excited at the possibilities when the "camp" is established. Suggestion, even criticism, is accepted and the nearest the play comes to breaking down is when John reacts hotly to Kevin's correction of "cement" for "plaster". However, the collaborative urge overcomes temper on this occasion and the motivation to create and explore a satisfying theme is sufficient to ensure its development.

It is interesting to observe that aspects of the talking also seem to serve as feed-back to the individual children, in the sense that part of what they say appears to go out as an echo signal to confirm some conviction, uncertainty, decision, or to determine group reaction. For example, when Peter, convinced the wall will fall, states, "It can fall you know," or John's "long lines" to emphasise his views on the way bricks are laid.

Overall the language reflects the bringing together of knowledge, experience, concepts about the nature of brick structures and the television influence of daleks and bionic men. This move from reality into a more extended world provided many imaginative possibilities which depended essentially on language for their realisation. Dealing with imaginative possibilities in words is a strong challenge to children's developing linguistic resources at the infant stage and beyond. This has some significance for a school's approach to learning. There was a great deal of perceptive insight in one teachers' remark on dramatic play, "I think its value lies in the realisation of an experience". Without language, how far could children go in realising this imaginative play? Yet the language of this play sequence is, at first sight, unimpressive and reflects the "ordinary" conversations of everyday life. But when its functions are examined and we see what it achieves, then the significance of how it assists learning developments becomes more obvious.

A final observation concerns the closing stages of this play when the children were creeping round the space visitor and his prisoner in an effort to free him without being destroyed by "the death ray". There was much expression and communication in movement and movement-reinforced noises and words which coincided with the period of intense excitement. What explains it? Perhaps as one teacher said, "So often what they do at this age seems to run ahead of their words". A hint here possibly that the school has a wider language task than it sometimes sets itself?

Example 2

Village children five–eight year old, mixed age group. Witch theme.

M   Let's do a play about witches.

M	You're a witch and we're children.
H	I'm not doing it. Not that.
M	Oh, go on Henry.
L	I'll be the witch.
J	I'm the girl; we'll go through the woods to Grannie.
M	Yes, we think she's a witch. Do you think?
G	Yes, and she'll put spells on us, and we'll get away on her broomstick.
J	Where will her house be?
G	Let's make it here. (*They arrange several large blocks*)
M	Now she's asleep. Asleep in the other room when we come. What will we do then?
J	But she puts spells on us but we get away and take her broomstick.
M	Yes. You lie down there in the other room.
	(*The play starts*)
H	I wonder what's in this cupboard.
M	Oh a spell book.
J	Spell!
H	I don't know what I should do.
M	You're one of the children.
H	No. The cat, I'll be the cat. Shall I?
	(*Grannie comes out*)
L	Aah, Issy, Issy, Doo. Issy, Issy Doo. (*Waves her hands*)
M	Oh, she's turned me into a frog.
J	She's turned me into a monkey. Help me.
M	Quick (*children escape*).
J	We didn't get the broomstick.
M	Henry, you'll have to go back and get the spell book from the witch.

H	We'll all go. (*They creep back*)
H	I've got the book and the broomstick so she can't get after us.
H	Blast off. (*They go*)
M	Now we've got the book. What can we do?
H	Turn ourselves invisible.
M	Yes.
J	We could make gold.
J	Yes and turn bullies into frogs.
M	Or make a magic wand.
J	Yes and turn Grannie back.

Many of the comments made about the first example apply with equal relevance to this play. The making of something satisfying together is sufficient motivation to keep the children working at the possibilities and to support each other verbally. At the same time there are strong indications that very individual minds are co-operating here – notice the difficulty of keeping Henry within the agreed structure.

The stress on structure is interesting and indicates to some extent a growing capacity to create a conception of what they want their play to explore. Consequently, there is considerable emphasis on the planning aspects, not only in terms of structure, roles and the physical determination of space and location but also the consideration of a dramatic climax.

There is no hint of a language inadequacy or breakdown and interactive feedback is constant, sustained by fluency and commitment. The children are beginning to make conscious use of each other as sounding boards, an important feature especially evident in the non-role, discursive exchanges but also seen in their responses to each other in role.

One important characteristic of the two play sequences is the preoccupation of the children with choice of role. Many teachers agree that the attraction of the role is probably the most motivating aspect of dramatic play. It is also integrally bound up with language and wider learning possibilities. Consider the role situation and language from

67

one of the "hospitals" observed during the survey. A patient is brought in for treatment and received by the doctor and his two nurses – suitably attired.

Nurse	The ambulance is coming.
Dr.	Bring her in here, put her on the bed.
Nurse	Lie down we will cover you up.
Nurse	I think she's got German measles.
Nurse	Here's some medicine for you.
Dr.	Now I'm going to give you some tests. Hm. Hm. Don't be frightened, it's just my stethoscope. I can hear your heart with this.
Nurse	She's getting black spots.
Dr.	Give her some more medicine.
Nurse	This will make you better.
Dr.	Yes, you'll soon be better.

An observer would have noticed in the doctor a commitment to role and a quality of feeling in his actions, tone and choice of words. Some knowledge of doctors, hospitals and illness was being drawn on, and fed into a role which allowed him to experience himself as one in authority who could direct and organise, take decisions and proceed on a course of action. He had a choice of strategies which he could employ in this hospital situation, though these were bounded by his role understanding. Thus he was able to make decisions, express these to his co-players and in their response perhaps realise something of his effect on them.

This kind of active role-taking would also seem to be role-making. Just as experiencing the feel and challenge of role, and the response it evokes from others, adds to children's perception and insights, so the playing and understanding take on new meaning and teachers have commented on the effect of structuring thematic approaches like the "hospital" for weekly or fortnightly periods. Their own observations suggest an increasing quality of activity in these play environments in which being someone else is a core component. Clearly then, the opportunity for children to assume a range of role identities and enter varied situations in dramatic play is important. In essence they give

68

children an increasing number of ways to gain experience and assist in its interpretation. Language is necessarily and directly involved.

Unfortunately, not all the survey infant schools can report that language is well produced in dramatic play situations. Even though play generates a need for language, it is sometimes difficult to achieve that quality of play necessary. Play itself cannot really move far without language resources to help it along; there is an interdependent relationship so that good play is likely to foster extended language, while adequate language may lead to enriched play, given opportunity.

Where do the difficulties lie? The survey schools most affected (a minority), tend to be those from certain urban areas but this is not exclusively the case. Comments from teachers provide some explanation and understanding of the problem. They refer to "experience deprivation" in the pre-school years, a lack of discussion and involvement at home, an inability to readily enter imaginary situations or co-operate and compromise in order to realise a satisfying experience in play. In one urban school which had a very mixed ethnic intake, the class teacher for the youngest infants commented, "Their attitudes to play vary so much. Some just haven't enough English to go far anyway; some interfere with the play of the others and don't settle themselves for long in a play situation. A few of them are quite happy just to sit and hold a doll or walk about with a hat on. It's quite difficult to really get language going."

A policeman theme from children in two schools illustrates the problem. In the first, typical of the situation outlined above, a five year old boy wearing a policeman's hat was dealing with two malefactors. "You'll go to jail," he told them and they acquiesced willingly enough. It was not clear what they had done to be sent to jail but once in there, the play effectively ceased.

The second example also has another five year old boy acting as policeman. He announced that he was on watch at the moment. "He means on duty" volunteered another of the group. "He's keeping guard. We're all thieves." The policeman commented that they had been caught stealing cars and other people's presents so they would have to be caught. While the thieves were busy with their thieving the policeman "read" from his notebook. "Two men have stolen aeroplanes and gold, keep a look-out." An action sequence followed where the thieves were spotted and arrested. They wanted to know

would happen to them. A £100 fine was agreed on but before
g released they were warned not to park on yellow lines or it
uld be a fine of £180.

n schools where the first example is a typical situation there are
obvious longitudinal implications for drama and language. Peter
Slade comments that, "There's something wrong in the infant schools
if flowing improvised speech isn't fairly well in the saddle by seven
years of age." But clearly some schools are experiencing difficulties in
establishing this.

The difficulties of achieving effective play with some children is widely
recognised. Smilansky emphasises its fundamental importance for
creativity, intellectual growth and the acquisition of social skills.
Throughout the process, speech is the central tool used.

It is significant, perhaps, that throughout the infant age range there
are play themes which recur regularly in all kinds of school
environment, but there are wide variations in the extent to which
children gain from them. Most themes are capable of expansion,
replanning or being supplemented in various ways and it is this which
is so profitable to children. Indeed we need constantly to ensure that
there is scope for this to happen and help children towards an
awareness that these options are open and can be exploited. Children's
attitudes to play are bound up with these differences in ability to
exploit themes. Attitudes are not always positive and in some areas
indicate a desultory approach to the activity.

Schools seem to achieve active play more successfully where conscious
effort has gone into stimulating the potential abilities of children. In
this sense a "facilitating environment" means more than the provision
of materials, space and time; it involves a commitment on the part of
teacher and school to the energising of dramatic play with positive
attitudes and approaches. In short, it requires well thought out
strategies which use the teacher as guide, participant or catalyst, to
ensure that children really do encounter the challenges and
opportunities of dramatic play. Many teachers will smile wryly at such
statements even though they might agree with them. In discussions
about play activities they often express concern at how little time they
can give to guiding children or even listening to the language being
used. The demands of the curriculum in general swallow time and
play must often look after itself. This is increasingly so as children
move through the infant classes, and there is often a corresponding

decrease in the amount of dramatic play taking place in the older infant groups. To some extent (as seen in the Witch play theme earlier, page 65) an arrangement of vertically mixed age groups safeguards opportunities for play and may enrich it with the added experience of older children. Nevertheless, the problem of teachers' time remains. This is difficult to solve unless concern for play is supported by appreciation of its educational potential.

Overall, a wide variety of approaches to play provision were observed or discussed during the survey and most of these offered opportunities for language emphasis and enrichment.

1 Mixed age play groups. In one primary school children from five to eleven played together for an allocated time in a carpeted area known as the "studio". There was ample provision of play materials, blocks, clothes, etc. and also a set of cards compiled by the head which offered a wide range of play suggestions, though their choice of a play theme was entirely free.

2 A common play area. A similar idea to that described above but not involving any planned mixing of age groups. Children from all infant classes used the area for play and there was a natural interaction that brought together the language abilities of older and younger children.

3 Thematic outlines. Specific structural settings with appropriate props were introduced into classrooms, designed to lead to more active play situations, e.g. hospital, hairdressers salon, cowboy's bunk house, witches house, etc.

4 Active preparation for play. Infants prepared their own cakes, sweets etc. from clay or dough and sold these in their shop. Labels and price lists were prepared. Another group created a large-scale stable as preparation for playing out the Christmas Story in their own way.

5 Outside visits. These were found to provide a stimulus which significantly enriched play activity. The earlier reference to the building site is a useful example. One group which visited a "children's farm" maintained by an urban authority used the experience in play for several weeks afterwards.

6 Story and poetry. Many schools used stories, poems, rhymes, and discussion pictures to stimulate children's free play.

7 Audio-visual elements. Photographs of children in dramatic play situations were taken by the class teacher and used later for discussion purposes and the preparation of synchrofax "talking page" materials and accompanying illustrations. These gave opportunity for the interrelated development of spoken language, reading, writing and feed-back into further play.

8   Theatre in Education. Visits by T.I.E. bringing performances to the school sometimes led to play activities based upon the characters or story theme. Teachers commented that usually this play produced a blend of the children's everyday world and that of the performance.

9   Teacher-guided play. Adult linguistic resources and careful questioning greatly extends the possibilities of the total play situation. Strategies varied from overall teacher guidance and encouragement within a predetermined play structure, to taking on a role themselves or acting as questioner within children's own play situations. Role reversal techniques were sometimes encouraged so that children were challenged to deliberately adopt another person's role and viewpoint.

Infant drama and language

The distinction between "dramatic play" and "drama" in the infant years and beyond is a fine one based upon purpose and function. Situation, role, movement, gesture, mime and language are still the common framework for make-believe activity but now the broader educational objectives of the teacher are emphasised. What was intermittent and often a matter of choice, where roles could be slipped into and out of easily and the situation changed at will, becomes something more specific, time-determined, commonly shaped and explored by class or group under the purposeful eye of their educational guide.

So what is happening with children at five years old? The typical five year old moves slowly through a stage of building up relationships and discovering how to share, co-operate and shape in dramatic play. It is not surprising, therefore, that many teachers of this age group consider class drama lessons to be potentially overwhelming in the demands they make on children and regard play as more appropriate for language interaction. Nevertheless, teachers do structure and engage their classes in drama based activities variously related to language. Most commonly observed was the production of sounds, words or mime to accompany narrative, story and poetry read by the teacher and sometimes involving children in common or specific role taking. Though many teachers of infants seem to have an almost intuitive grasp of when and how to use dramatic techniques of this kind, there are some who exploit the potential to enhance children's learning and enjoyment more purposefully.

Drama "lessons" are another matter, however, and schools are aware of the possible insecurity and uncertainty of the five year old going into a wider and perhaps overwhelming drama environment (a feature not uncommon with any age-group coming new to this experience). Essentially, the pattern of class drama practised with first year infants is structured round their natural expression, with an emphasis on the stimulation and enrichment of sensory and imaginative qualities. The individual is at the centre of things, responding to voice, tambour or music, which also serve as a means of control.

Typically, the language challenge within the lesson is one of responding to words, suggestions or story; a snowflake drifting and melting; the plant growing up from the earth; being slithery like a snake; a giant going out for a walk and meeting. ... In one lesson, an actual string puppet was used to draw from the children a vocabulary of descriptive words and was followed by "puppet movement" activities as the children imagined themselves with strings attached. The impact of this lesson was seen later in some very vigorous paintings and accompanying captions composed by the children and written out by their teacher.

It is at the level of imaginitive response in discussion that some teachers find ways to lead their classes into more direct language participation during the early years in the infants' school. Again the stress is normally upon mime and movement within the activity though several schools in the survey encouraged conversation between children as they dramatised the action. Two examples from six year old children in post-reception classes illustrate approaches.

Example 1

A First School set in a Metropolitan area. In this school "monster noises" were created and recorded by the children prior to the actual lesson. Initially, children clapped "aggressive" rhythms and then extended these into voice patterns. At the beginning of the drama session the teacher suggested to the children that they would encounter something unpleasant. To tambour control, the children then met their imaginary monster and reacted to it. They discussed and examined the physical stances this situation might evoke. Subsequently, they assumed the role of the monster itself and made "horrific shapes" individually at first, then by combining in small groups. The children were invited to chat about how to do it, and they showed considerable confidence and fluency in doing so. A short period of movement exploration followed as the monsters moved around and the sounds created earlier were added to complete the imaginary effect.

At this point a problem was introduced by the teacher in terms of the school being confronted by such a creature. What could they do?

	We would just have to kill it.
Teacher	But it has fierce claws and fire.
	Get a step ladder and climb up on its back.
	Then kill it that way with knives.
	Just pull its tail and be friendly to it.
Teacher	How can we do that?
	Feed it with our best food. See if it will be friends, if we're kind it might go away.
	We could make a barricade round the door so he couldn't get at us.
	Hey no! Make a plastic model of him and give it to him as a present so he can see we don't want to harm him.
	That might not work.
	Well give him some food and put a lighted match in it and set him on fire.
	Throw a bucket of water in his mouth and put the fire out or sellotape his mouth all over his teeth.

The class teacher commented afterwards, "I try to get away from a purely movement approach and involve them in some sort of decision making, shaping and so on. It's not easy and you have to take them at their feeling and thinking level." In this lesson her intention was to encourage some tension and problem solving within the imaginative framework of the theme, yet within the children's emotional and conceptual capacities.

74

Another school visited had on its staff a teacher committed to exploring language in her drama work. The school was about seventy years old, of traditional design and served an area of terraced houses in a large industrial town. The visit took place on a cold day but the school had a warm and welcoming atmosphere.

A brief introduction was followed by time to look at examples of art work and written work on the classroom wall, then the six year old infants moved desks and chairs to the sides of the room and sat on the floor in front of their teacher. They talked of current matters but there was a quick focusing on the weather because there had been snow that week. What had they been doing? Building snowmen, a snowhouse, giant snowballs, having snowball fights.

Then they moved off in small groups to begin a recreation of snow constructions. Their work was a natural combination of mime and discussion, characterised by a fluency and attention to detail.

After several minutes the teacher called the children together again and they discussed their achievements and problems. Now she introduced a new challenge. Sometimes things happen in the snow. Could they think of anything connected with snow that would do for making a story in drama? Make a slide and slip on it. Make a sledge and go out on a search. Become snowed up. Be made so cold that the snow turned them into statues.

The last idea appealed greatly and was shaped in discussion to become the theme of a group trapped and frozen and having to be rescued. In the drama activity the language challenge was maintained, calling for discussions of rescue ideas and their implementation.

Kevin thought of a helicopter which could take the rescue team and a doctor with blankets and medicines etc. But other children objected that a helicopter couldn't land on snow. A rope would have to come down from it. But then you'd have to be very careful with the frozen people. No, you could put skis on the helicopter then it could come down. Another rescue group had thought of an automatic drill to get through the ice more quickly than the shovels some children were using. There was also concern that when the victims were brought out they should be given hot coffee and blankets.

In the final discussion the children touched on both reality and fantasy. The former centred on the concept of "disaster" and explored the notion that something terrible and largely unexpected had happened. Examples provided by the children included, the school being flooded: being knocked down on the way home: icebergs sinking ships like the Titanic: breaking your arm in P.E.: a volcano sending fire on people.

Three interrelated questions are raised by these drama approaches.

1   At which stage is it appropriate to move children into more language conscious and language demanding situations with role variety, opportunities for discussion, and decision-making procedures?

2   How early can we capitalise on the language abilities and imaginative ideas of the class group in addition to our own feeding in?

3   Do we need to consider more fully the nature and scope of the dramatic challenge we offer children in regard to language?

The work attempted in two more infant schools usefully extends the information required from these questions. In particular, the second school gives an illustration of work and problems with six–seven year old children at the beginning of the school year and again towards the end of the spring term.

Example 1

An Infants' School in an industrial borough. Here a modern building serves a residential area on the outskirts of a metropolitan borough. The class observed occupied an annexe classroom in which much of the drama took place. Their teacher was experienced in drama and enthusiastic about its values. Her commitment had strengthened in the past two years since moving from, "rather formal plays, almost productions", to a view of drama as a creative and learning medium. She listed among her goals the building up of confidence, initiative and decision-making ability as part of a language challenge inherent in drama and developing a feeling for structure and atmosphere. Quality of experience was seen as springing from depth of involvement and from the strong motivation which brought active enquiry. "If you have children wanting to know, wanting to find out, isn't this sound education? Drama can do this." She took an active role in the drama in order to supply "pegs of belief". At that time (beginning of the second term) she thought the class was ready for an extended challenge after their drama experiences of the first term when they had begun with an interest in faces and developed this into faces of people who make up a community.

The drama began with discussion between teacher and class (approximately 28) to find a theme which interested the children. Taking an idea from their recent Christmas activity, they opted for another play about King Herod, which the teacher resisted. However, the idea of drama with a king appealed to them so it was accepted along with "spinning wheels", an interest apparently drawn from a picture of the Sleeping Beauty on display elsewhere in the school.

Discussion centred on the king. What sort of a king was he? He was a bad king. Why did they say that? A variety of reasons and ideas were offered. (The teacher emphasised that at this point she placed stress on listening. "I like his idea, what was his idea again?")

Gradually a picture of the king was built up; one who took all the gold in the country, the young men and the guards and went off leaving only the old and ill to fend for themselves. This was the end of the lesson. The discussion had stimulated vocabulary exploration and children's contributions were written on the blackboard by the teacher and later transferred to a large card sheet for wall display.

a bully		stupid
wicked	THE	silly
mean	KING	naughty
selfish	IS	daft
idiotic	OLD	nasty
odd	AND	bad
sly	UGLY	horrid
sneaky		unkind
		cruel

Individual writing in children's own books followed, giving their own reasons for deciding the king was bad.

"The king left his country and went away to Ireland. And took his guards with him. And all the people wouldn't work. The farmers wouldn't work and the people did not have food. And all the streets were dirty."

For the next session the teacher prepared a "prop" for her own role; a scroll with ONE HUNDRED SPINNING WHEELS written in German. She intended to take the role of a critical outsider, a buyer of spinning wheels from a foreign country who had come to place an order. In that role she would introduce new words in context as a noble and educated foreigner, but primarily she would attempt to bring the children up against the reality of a situation which left them leaderless. By doing so she would also assess the extent of their commitment to the drama.

By word suggestion the teacher attempted to create the appropriate mood. "We'll be asleep. The King has gone. What little food was left has been eaten, the wood for fires all gone. We huddle in the cold and try to keep warm." She then entered in role, and the action began.

Teacher	I've come on my king's business but I suppose I'll have to talk to you seeing there's no one in the palace. And your country has given me a disease.
	(*She describes the symptoms of a cold*)
	It's called a cold, you'll get a cough.
Teacher	What we do at home is to go to the apothecary.
	It will make you sniff. And shiver.
	And you'll get headaches and earaches.
Teacher	What can I do?
	Keep yourself warm and go to bed.
Teacher	I can't. I have things to do.
	What have you to do?
Teacher	Wait a minute. I'll show you my orders.
	(*Unfolds scroll, children come to look. There is much comment among themselves.*)
Teacher	What's the matter, can't you read?
	(*Children accept drama situation and think before replying.*)
	There's only one here who can read.
Teacher	Who is that?
	(*One boy comes nearer*)

I'm the one who can read.

Teacher   Oh, so that's your scribe, the one who reads. Well read my order then.

(Boy takes the scroll and stares intently, turns it round puzzled. The others near him come and look at the scroll curiously. There is much murmuring and comment.)

Look at him, his eyes are just about popping out.

(Other children look at the scroll carefully and shake their heads.)

Teacher   Oh, I see you don't understand it. I shouldn't be dealing with you really. I should be at the palace. I'll read it.

(She reads it through. Children "translate" excitedly.)

One spinning wheel.

Teacher   No, not one, *hundert*.

A hundred spinning wheels.

Teacher   Yes, it means a hundred spinning wheels.

There are no spinning wheels left now.

Anyway what's your country?

Teacher   Leopold's country.

I've never heard of that country.

Teacher   I can't understand it here. Usually I'm given hospitality when I come.

What's hospitality?

Teacher   It means being looked after and being given food and a bed.

(Children respond by looking at each other and lowering their eyes.)

Teacher   Some of you look old enough to remember what spinning wheels were like. Who can remember seeing their fathers make them before they went away.

(Some children raise hands)

I can make a spinning wheel for you.

	So can I. So can I.
	We have a dungeon.
Teacher	That's no good to me.
	How many do you need? One hundred?
	There's some in the dungeon. I've seen them.
Teacher	No, I've been there. The rats have chewed them.
	There were some in the dungeon.
	Anyway we need food.
	The king's gone.
Teacher	Have you done something to your king?
	No we haven't done anything. He just went away and left us.
Teacher	How can you prove it?
	We'll take you there. You help us and we'll take you.

The teacher moved out of role and the children sat down. After a brief discussion the teacher said, "Write down a list of the materials you'll need and make a careful design for a spinning wheel. Then see if you can think of advice to give the village to help them improve their situation."

The class teacher felt that the lesson had not achieved as much as possible. She had hoped to steer the children towards a resolution of the leaderless situation, but time had run out. The weather had an undoubted influence in lessening the involvement, it was an extremely windy day with gale force gusts causing the annexe building to shake. Anyone teaching infants in these conditions will know how concentration wavers. Nevertheless, this approach exemplifies how it is possible to lead children into a situation based on their own interests and provide a challenge to thinking, feeling and language. The teacher working here in role structured a situation which seemed to meet the needs of the class. But by doing so, she did not impose her own ideas on the children. She established a supportive and secure environment in which children could explore the possibilities. This is not forced feeding or the confining of children's individuality and vision but rather, in the words of one teacher, "the establishment of trust and mutual respect encouraging growth in confidence, initiative

80

and a sense of responsibility, important if you want communication and interaction".

Example 2

An urban infants' school. This is a traditional building with classrooms grouped round a long narrow hall serving a local authority housing area. The drama work with older infants is taken by the headmistress who has a keen interest in its educational potential. She is willing to participate herself, especially with children "without the drama spark" but works much of the time as an observant and stimulating guide. A strongly held view is that for development and achievement in drama the school must give consistent opportunity to its children. "Drama brings a discipline-forming framework," which children absorb from a medium that cannot function without social rules and self control. She believes drama gives children the opportunities to extend their language. Her own language objectives are not always definite, "I'm prepared to take what comes". Nor does she find it easy to be sure exactly what specific improvement it will bring but she is convinced it has "spin-off" effects and shows children how much more is possible in so many ways. Any of the possibilities explored could be followed up in the classroom. Her drama work usually involved the older infants, approximately fifty in number.

For the first lesson of the new school year she took into the hall a large carved wooden head and used it as a "prop" to start discussion and evoke a dramatic location. This was a wooden head kept by native tribesmen in a foreign land to frighten outsiders away. Moreover, it was covered with gold and very valuable. The discussion moved on to the kind of life these natives would lead. What would they need? The headmistress admitted afterwards that at this point she had to use all her skill in asking the right sort of question to draw out a picture of life. They would cut trees for huts and hollow canoes, hunt animals and be farmers growing corn. "It took a while to get them really thinking but they enjoy this talking and planning. And it is semi-dramatic; getting them into a mental process of teasing out and creating."

Three tribes were formed occupying different areas of the hall and set to work hollowing out canoes and enacting other tribal activities. This concluded the first session in the hall, leaving the drama theme to be developed in art, writing or discussion in class time.

The next hall session aimed at introducing the extension of the tribal structure and possible tension between the tribes, perhaps leading to decision-making and interaction. With children sitting in tribal circles she posed the questions, "Who takes care of the golden head; where is it to be situated? Will the other tribes want to share in the possession?" She set the head on a stool near the central tribe as a starting point. Each tribal group at once became immersed in a babble of talking and splinter group movements. At length the children were asked to discuss the problem they now faced. What were they deciding. What was necessary?

	Our tribe is going for the head.
Teacher	Are you going to ask them first?
	Yes, we'll ask them.
Teacher	Are you all going to do that?
	(*Silence*)
Teacher	Would everyone go?
	We would send someone.
Teacher	Who?
	A general.
	No, a chief.
Teacher	Will each have a chief? If so, you'll have to elect one. Try to decide fairly. Wait, Shaun has something to say.
Shaun	The three chiefs should have a meeting about it and have a council in each village to sort it out.

The procedure of choosing a chief in each tribe followed; only in one was intervention necessary to secure a "vote" and resolve the deadlock created by the choice of three chiefs. The procedure followed in the other two tribes was based on consensus – much pointing and head-nodding. Each chief was then asked by the headmistress to choose his council members and discuss what they wanted to achieve and how it was to be done.

At last the central tribe were approached by the spokesman from the other two wanting the golden head. As if to demonstrate the independence of children in drama, the central tribe readily agreed that it was right to share; the others could take it. At this stage they were led on to consider more possibilities.

Teacher	Alright, what is going to happen now. Is the head safe?
	No some explorers come into the forest and see the statue. They see the gold.
Teacher	How much is the gold worth?
	Thirty-five dollars.
Teacher	Will the explorers think it strange to see this head? What will they think it is?
	An old thing from some old castle. They'd be frightened.
Teacher	Why?
	They'd get evil on them.
Teacher	You mean they'd be frightened that it would do them some harm. Does anyone know a word for when we're afraid of something and think it can harm us in a strange way? Well, we call it being superstitious.
	Oh, superstitious.
Teacher	Do you know now?
	Yes, like you could die or it could get you killed.
	It could be dangerous, dynamited even.
	The explorers could disintegrate if they touched it.
Teacher	What does disintegrate mean?
	Break into lots of pieces and disappear into nowhere.

After the session, the headmistress assessed her achievements and difficulties. She was pleased with the way the children were listening, especially in discussion and with the language outcome of the final discussion. Drama disciplines were coming too. However, the children's involvement in the village situation indicated that they had not yet established a group identity or the ability to work from that in terms of attitudes and language. She would have to wait for deeper involvement to come in time. Perhaps she had offered them a challenge which was a little too demanding at this stage.

However, there was clearly much of value in this work. Prominent again was the exploration of meaning provided by particular words in context e.g., "superstitious" and "disintegration". There seem to be two main points to emphasise here. The first is that enrichment of word meaning comes when the context offers something of the emotional essence in addition to the intellectual understanding, and this is especially true for young children. James Britton makes the second point that language occupies a key role in the business of representing the world and experience to ourselves – thus giving it shape and understanding. In this process "words become the filing pins upon which successive encounters with objects and events are filed". In the light of the drama examples considered, these two points would seem important when schools review their drama-language approaches.

The move from the canoe-building activities to discussion focuses attention on other crucial elements in building up children's ability to control their drama enterprises, e.g., an ability to listen, a requirement that clearly made heavy demands on the children when the varying tribes were making their decisions and it required direct teacher intervention to sort matters out. This raises the question of suitable strategies likely to help children cope with the increased demand for disciplined listening, without which any "meeting of minds" will be difficult to achieve. It was a problem fully realised by the class teacher who had to decide whether the drama should deal with procedures for chief-election, or move on and allow the dramatic climax potentially available when the tribes clashed over possession of the golden head. Again, an important question is raised for schools; how far is the opportunity for improving children's quality of listening fostered by the drama we provide?

A second, and perhaps more essential concern raised by the tribal difficulties over making decisions, relates to the demands made in drama for selection from past experience to meet the present situation. Clearly the infants here are entering a new phase where the interactive decision-making of their own dramatic play is going beyond their real life experience but they are learning to cope. Drama gives them the opportunity to try and in the attempt, perhaps bridge the experiential and informational gap. The survey examples show that this need not be a fearful encounter for either teacher or children; given the scope, they will work at their own level of understanding but can be led on by sympathetic and thoughtful support.

Revisiting the same school after six months confirmed the validity of these statements. The children had moved on significantly and a new drama was centred on two Indian encampments. Each had its own chief but with contrasting role characteristics; one was old, wise and peace-loving; the other young and aggressive, the product this time of selection and voting. They had been exploring the behaviour and relationships of the two tribes prior to the visit.

In the lesson, potential conflict between the two sets of Indians was averted by the news that white men (the visitor) had arrived. There was some discussion among the Indians about whether to meet them and this was followed by a confrontation, when their feelings were crystallised by the following comments:

> White men, we cannot spare you any food because we are short of hunters.
> If you fight us we shall all be killed.
> You will take over our country and we will be dead.
> If your leader is killed in the fight you will have no leader.
> We will cut some trees and make you boats and move them into the tide and you can sail back.
> We will give you some buffalo to take, rabbits and water.
> All the animals here are getting fewer and will all die.
> And if you go near them or touch them you will all die sooner or later.
> If you do not go away, we will fight for our country.

A very productive discussion followed without interference by the class teacher as the chiefs and their braves prepared for active clash.

	What can we do, these are clever white people. We will steal their guns.
	Yes, at night raid them. But there'll be a guard.
Teacher	So what will you do?
	Get him away.
Teacher	How?
	Well we could throw pebbles in the bushes and he'd go to look.
Teacher	Where would the guns be kept?
	In their tents.
	I have a good idea, we can camouflage ourselves with branches.

85

Teacher	Camouflage?
	Yes, like the grass. We need something to paint our faces so the white men won't recognise us. Like the Germans in the war. They had bushes all over them.
Teacher	I see, so you'll merge in with the background and look like trees and grass.
	David has a good idea.
David	I'll creep round the back and get in from behind. We could dig a tunnel to the tent.
Teacher	Wouldn't that take a long time?
	Yes and it could cave in. Give him something to drink that will make him go to sleep.
Teacher	How could you do that?
	Go up friendly and say "do you want a drink", like that.

The drama lesson finished here with the headmistress asking the children to think about what might happen if they succeeded in getting the guns.

Subsequently, a smaller group were involved in a continuation of the situation. But now one of the chiefs had been captured by the white men and held as hostage, threatened with death if his braves came to rescue him. After considerable argument and discussion within the group it became apparent that no one was prepared to stand down from a rescue attempt. The gist of their argument had been that the chief would not die because they were skilled in forest ways and the white men were not. Nevertheless, they realised that a whole tribe could not go on the mission and began to suggest ways of choosing a select group. "Draw the shape of a man on a tree and where his heart is we'll all fire an arrow. The best ones go. Find a stone, a canny big one, and see who can carry it to that tree. Have people throw stones at you and you have to stand and knock them away. Jump on the back of a moving buffalo. Run fifteen times round the forest and see who comes first. Blindfold him and put a beetle in his hand and see if he can tell if it's alive or dead. No, I know one better. Blindfold him and put things in his hand. See if he knows what they are."

Many more suggestions were made and approved or rejected by the group. Eventually they chose several as the basis for three braves to be selected for the life or death attempt.

It is interesting to note that when these "tests" are classified they deal with qualities of skill, strength, courage and cleverness, suggesting an ability in the top infant range to bring a critical and perceptive view to the problems and development of their drama themes. Together with their acceptance of group responsibility and decision making, this bears out the views of the school's headmistress that often we underestimate the abilities of infants.

Here the children readily found language for what concerned them because they were involved and the matters were relevant. The situation provided the experiential content for their feeling and thinking, something significant was happening and they reacted to it. This was an intellectual challenge, and also a social one in the sense of group co-operation and discipline, but the language fabric was basically woven by the subjective forces which generated the need to express and communicate feeling and thought.

Infants are still near the beginning of the long road to emotional, social and intellectual maturity and are supported on the way by the education provided by schools. Language is indispensable to the process, but perhaps schools could look with more profit on the integrated language and learning achievements evident in the kind of work examined here?

Of course, there are other productive ways into drama and language and indeed the majority of the survey schools serving the six–seven age groups tend to adopt their own approaches where they are interested in a drama-language emphasis. The next three examples will indicate something of the range:

Example 1

An inner city infants school. A street accident theme was used and related to a current road safety campaign. Discussion between teacher and children established the essential characteristics of road accidents, care for the victim, concern of the relatives, enquiries by police etc. The drama work itself was based on pairs or small groups of children. Parents visited the hospital to talk to their child who had been injured in the accident and to hear the details. Then policemen questioned drivers and onlookers to establish the facts. Further discussion dealt with how people were taken to court and what happened there. Finally the children did kerb drill and the lesson was concluded.

The class obviously enjoyed their drama and language was relatively fluent bearing in mind the mixed ethnic group involved. Apart from the road safety factors, some insight was gained into the concept of justice and the functions of a court.

Example 2

An urban first school. Group themes based upon an object formed the basis of the drama here. A camera, shell, gloves, pendant and purse were used as stimuli for short drama actions, each group being allocated one of them. Each group planned and discussed their play involving a good deal of language interchange. The plays themselves were mainly mimed by the children. Afterwards each group recounted their play episode in narrative form. A striking feature here was the children's obvious verbal fluency.

Example 3

A semi-rural infants school. Drama was stimulated by the story of *Hansel and Gretel* but very freely interpreted. From the idea of a sweet house the children moved to the creation of a village sweet shop. There was free interpretation of ideas in the building up of the play, with group assignments to discuss and work through various aspects of it. These included the use of movement, suggestions for characters and their relationships, and spells for the witch to use. The basis of the approach to spells was, "the idea that words could have a special quality, a potency". The play had considerable value from the viewpoint of spoken language but chiefly perhaps in terms of group discussion and co-operation rather than the opportunities it gave for active language give and take during the drama itself. However, the school was firmly committed to the use of drama as a focus for integrated work of which there was ample.

7–11 drama and language

When children have reached the age of seven or eight we should expect that increasing language competence and social awareness would lead into drama that builds effectively on these maturing skills and experience. Yet so often the practical realisation of possibilities is disappointing and drama fails to achieve a convincing and productive relationship with language. This is a basic problem which urgently needs solving because of its important implications for drama practice.

The problem of teacher commitment and insight is probably the key to the whole question. It has already been observed that many experienced and capable teachers remain unconvinced of children's capacity to develop language-based drama, or of their own ability in this area. The comment "I've read books on drama and language but I don't feel it's for me" did not come from someone new to teaching; it came from an enthusiastic teacher who had a sound relationship with her children. Sadly, too, many views expressed by both newly qualified and experienced teachers working in the seven to eleven age range concern the inadequacy of their College preparation for initiating and developing drama in which is an active agent. Clearly, there is a further need; in addition to the improvement of teacher insight into strategies, it is also necessary to prove that drama is a potent language medium.

In the context of these limitations and difficulties, what light does the survey throw on drama and language between the years of seven and eleven? A number of examples will help to show the range of activities and the kinds of qualities fostered.

Probably the most widely practised approach is that of exploring language through movement. Here language is used to encourage physical sensitivity and expression, spatial awareness, concentration and the stimulation and control of emotional response. It is often regarded as being particularly appropriate to lower juniors because it provides an effective framework for both individuals and groups during an age span teachers generally consider to be, "bubbling with energy". Several examples illustrate the kind of work undertaken.

Example 1

Seven year old children (approximately forty) in a First School serving an urban industrial area. The teacher is keenly interested in approaching drama through dance, but recognises children's need for a broad spectrum of experience. Nevertheless, she maintains that skill in movement is a prime requisite for further development of drama and refers to, "hard-working experience where concentration and involvement take effort". Her approach normally ensures that all the group take a generalised role and explore its possibilities and she sees her work as, "laying the foundations for more sensitive work in later years".

The children sat with eyes closed while a poem was read to them. It evoked a picture of jungle animals and stalking prey. An exploration of the poem in movement followed, with particular stress on the characteristics of the tiger; its stealthiness, velvet paws, and body like a coiled spring. At intervals the children's attention was drawn to the quality of movement using the poem for points of reference. Finally, "circus groups" were formed and created acts involving a trainer and tigers. Tambour and recorded music were used for control or mood.

Example 2

Nine year old children (approximately thirty-two) in a junior school serving an overspill urban area. The emphasis in the school centres on the "natural motivation through drama to build up and act out the emotions". A strong expressive element is regarded as integral to drama along with developing qualities of co-operative endeavour and tolerance.

The lesson itself was chiefly concerned with the exploration of the sea and children worked individually and in small groups. They made varied shapes; "rounded" and "spiky" rock shapes, knotted sea-weed, and gnarled drift wood, followed by the creation of an underwater scene. Imagination was stimulated by the vocabulary used and accompanying percussion sounds. From this point the children moved on to explore the world of boats and ships with miming of rowing, sail hoisting etc., before landing on an island and exploring. There was a commitment in the children's work and a positive response to the vocabulary and word pictures used during the lesson.

Essentially, both examples are concerned with children's responses when they enter an imaginary world partly created for them by evocative language where the vocabulary, nuances and rhythmic quality are important. As a result those images made or recalled in the drama provide raw material for its shaping and exploring power through which expression and meaning may be enhanced. We noted earlier that this kind of work offers the possibility of a synthesis between language, feeling and thought which enriches a child's subjective world and may also increase his awareness and understanding of the outer world.

Perhaps it is necessary, however, for teachers to consider the total nature of the challenge of drama in education. Can we really exclude from children the opportunity to create and explore drama experiences in language; to plan, shape, and discuss, to interact linguistically to the significance of role and situation, review developments and finally reflect upon and consolidate a whole spectrum of learning? There were schools in the survey sample which recognised this challenge within the lower junior age range, but though they provided a range of approaches not all were equally demanding. Two examples illustrate this:

Example 3

Eight year old children (approximately thirty) in a junior school serving an urban residential area. The teacher was experienced in drama work and took many of the classes throughout the school. She was thus able to compare developments as children moved upwards through the classes. The class in question was regarded as a group, "with good drama sense and commitment to work". They were ready to be challenged in terms of imaginative creation and language fluency.

The lesson began with the children working individually "cleaning their car" to the accompaniment of lively music. This was followed by pair work in which the car was being sold to a reluctant buyer. Discussion was fluent and lively.

Buyer	I'll see what it's like inside. H'm good comfy seats.
Seller	Yes, and strong.
Buyer	I hope they're not too springy though.
Seller	Not really.
Buyer	What are these things for?
Seller	They're the latest seat belt fastenings.
Buyer	And this is the hood catch?
Seller	Hood?
Buyer	That's what they call it in America.
Seller	Bonnet we call it here.
Buyer	What about the engine?

Seller	Oh, it's down there, very powerful.
Buyer	Can I test it?
Seller	I'll open the sliding doors to let you out.

There was a period of discussion in which the teacher and children examined the kind of approach and language likely to be used by a prospective buyer and the seller.

More buying and selling followed. The children had a free choice of the article bought, which turned out to be faulty and a complaint was necessary. Then the children organised themselves into groups of six to plan and build any sort of machine. Among the "constructions" were a chocolate-making machine, a bus, a Formula 5000 racing car and a saloon. Finally the groups were asked to use the car and plan an outing on which, "something would happen". Several situations were created, most of them involving some kind of accident, with much telephoning for police and ambulances, subsequent despatch to hospital and arrival of relatives to enquire about the casualties.

There was considerable emphasis throughout the lesson on the conscious use of language in varying situations but it never became an exercise; "being and doing" were evident throughout. Planning, interaction and discussion were well balanced within the overall structure provided by the teacher who encouraged individual and group contributions.

Example 4

Nine year old children (approximately thirty-two) in an urban school with mixed intake. The school from which this example is drawn has a commitment to the language possibilities inherent in drama. It seeks approaches relevant to children's needs and interests which often allow the development of drama themes over a period of weeks. Essentially, situations are sought which involve the whole class in language interaction and encourage active role taking. However, within the overall structure there are many opportunities for group language activity feeding from and into the central concerns of the drama.

For this second year junior group the theme derived from the story of Beowulf the Warrior, which engaged the children's interest and suggested a framework for dramatic exploration. The work began with a discussion on the kind of community to be created, people, families and occupations. Subsequently, a meeting called to discuss complaints was interrupted by the arrival of Grendel the monster who carried off a sleeping guard. The language interaction included these exchanges:

You're the best, you're supposed to be the best man. Why don't you do something?

You saw he had a go at the monster. The sword just bounced off him – it's impossible to fall it.

We'll have to try. It will be very bad if he takes everyone.

Many ideas were put forward in the course of a prolonged language give and take, exemplified by the following extract:

I wonder if he would eat animals?

He wouldn't have took Karl if he was after animals.

He wouldn't have come here, would he?

What about poisoned meat? Say there was an old man dying and so if we fed him some poisoned meat and tempt it outside, we could drop a boulder on him or something like that.

What if he could smell the poison?

Murmurs. No that's no good.

I thought we had great men who could fight anything.

Yes, but the swords just bounced off. You saw, bounced off.

Our blacksmith could try to invent something. He's good at inventing things.

The chief's council was given the task of considering the suggestions and arriving at a decision. Part of their discussion dealt with the moral aspects involved in using a human life.

Teacher   What do you think about that idea of the old man?

             If he's going to die, it's better than us all dying.

             Yes, because it's going to be suffering. We could ...
             Well if we could get all the old men together and toss
             up. Or ask which one really wanted to die in the
             village.

Say we have two very old men who want to die. They might say, use me and then we could feed them with poison.

A lot of them do want to die with the monster around.

Just feed them a bowl of poison and give them to the monster.

Teacher But I don't think the family will agree with that.

All the families don't like people to die, 'cos they're all upset.

Well we'll pick out of the hat.

Yes, but that's going to be awful to the person.

Yes, but the ones who want to die. We don't want to die.

Teacher If I were you I wouldn't tell him.

And let him die if he doesn't want to?

Well I think it's really good but there's only one thing wrong. What my guards said about drawing out of hats because it's a man who's dying and wants to die is the best. That's not really fair on any person. Say, if we had everyone's name in the hat, and we stick to the person who's. . . .

Teacher He could be a child or anyone.

No but only the old people's names go in, a younger person's got more life in him.

Teacher But it's up to the man whether he wants to die or not. Just say we picked and we got a man and he didn't want to be killed and we did give him poison. Well that would be against his will, he wouldn't like that. What if that happened to us. What would we feel like?

We wouldn't feel very nice about it but anyway we'd be dead.

We keep picking other people not us.

We've got more life than other people.

Yes, but we don't want him to get everybody so just one for the monster will be alright, isn't it?

	It wouldn't be fair to the old man – he's got to have his fair share.
Teacher	What does the Thegn think about that?
	Well, it's alright if he's in pain and going to die but if he's not, it's not too well for him.

What we have here is a group of young juniors involved in deep discussion motivated by the need to find a solution to their problem. Ostensibly, the difficulty is finding a way to destroy Grendel but the underlying issue centres on two real moral dilemmas; the value of one human life, and the right to choose, freely. It illustrates the potential exchange of thought and language when children enter a drama world. A rigorous "thinking through" is taking place with children free to contribute and develop their ideas while slowly moving towards a consensus.

Notice how they have moved on from the action of the story itself to their own ideas. This story is now their drama and able to hold a variety of concerns and possibilities within its developing form. Not that the issues and language engendered are context bound; the drama permits and encourages both imaginary ventures into possibilities and reference back to children's own knowledge. There is too, the challenge of how far analogy drawn from their own past experience suits the needs and purposes of their present dramatic problem. This is seen in the doubts expressed over the "drawing of lots" and the fact that here it concerns a man's life. When children examine life in this way they often find meaning through drama.

It might be said that the kind of exchanges taking place in this example of drama represent a slowing down of the action without losing the essential motivation to take it further. But "further" need not necessarily mean sequence of action; it can, as in this case, lead to deeper exploration of issues in which the role-taking qualities help. Allowing children time and opportunity to get under the skin of someone else as a dramatic character can have advantages in many drama situations, and there seems to be no basic difference between role-taking in this context and the role-playing examined in young children's play.

Throughout the drama interaction, language controls and influences, regulating the social situation which holds a group of children together and encouraging expressive, persuasive and interpretive powers. What a commentary on the significance of language and the power of words for an eight year old boy to say, "Make up a word and make something to go with it that might kill him".

The last example points towards the potential for language and learning inherent in drama where children are allowed to enter as active participants and begin to explore and understand something of the "humanness of human beings", a process in which language is fundamental.

Of course, it is possible that children remain at a peripheral level in terms of linguistic challenge in drama. An example illustrating this possibility was seen during a visit to an inner city school where a class of eight and nine year old children of mixed ethnic origin were developing their version of the Wooden Horse of Troy. They had previously established the Trojan community, prepared name-plates and undertaken other written requirements for the shops and stalls in the market place. Now their teacher wanted them to consider the new presence of the wooden horse so they discussed who would see it and what might happen. In the event children remained preoccupied with their shop situations and the total language interchange was sparse and relatively unchallenging. An outsider observing the activity might have been forgiven for concluding that the children had rather poor linguistic resources and were unable to shape and develop the situation.

The class teacher knew better; and though her children had language problems, she was fully aware of what they could do in drama, an ability evidenced by the earlier planning discussion. On the day, however, it had been necessary to allow their exploration of a phase which obviously interested them.

The message from recent linguistic research is relevant here: language is effectively used, and learned to be used, by exercising it in a variety of situations. What children learn to do with the language they possess depends upon a developed awareness of the self as an active participant in situations in which, as Peter Doughty puts it, "the activity of language involves a process of selecting continuously from a wide or narrow range of possibilities, wide or narrow according to the circumstances in question". Doughty further maintains that language competence depends essentially upon an individual capacity to read or interpret the situation which one finds oneself called upon to deal with in language terms. He stresses the need for children to experience situations where certain ways of speaking are appropriate depending upon the issues and roles involved.

We can add to that Andrew Wilkinson's views on children's language capabilities and their awareness of its possibilities. He emphasises three aspects; that children know what language is and will often make their choice of what to say on the basis of the whole situation in which communication takes place; that they are aware of what language does in expressing will, mind and heart and accomplishing tasks like finding out and communicating views.

With such views as a backcloth, can teachers afford not to look more closely at the possibilities offered by drama for the creation of varied situations where use of language requires recognition of, and adjustment to, role, context and listeners? What we seek are dramatic activities where children's language resources are enhanced and extended through the collective nature of the activity and where the necessity to deliberate, choose, implement decisions and assess consequences is an essential part of a dramatic and educational learning process. The statement made earlier is worth emphasis here; drama and language are mutually enriching given opportunity, suitable material and appropriate strategies. With this in mind, we can now look at the older age groups.

Example 5

Eleven year old children (thirty-three) in a Primary School serving a socially mixed urban area. The teacher in this example has a firm belief in the challenges and opportunities for learning presented by drama, and that the great majority of children from all environments can work constructively within a drama-language framework. He believes it is essential to build up attitudes to drama which encourage commitment and application to the task in hand. His approach is summed up as follows:

1   Material with an intrinsic appeal to the children concerned and drawn from any source, but potentially able to lead into many areas of learning.

2   Matching children's needs and interests with the provision of opportunities to take them on from where they are. In this sense "taking them on" includes seeking involvement at appropriate feeling and thinking levels through interaction and discussion which builds upon their growing confidence and abilities.

3 Providing opportunity for varied role-taking, with an emphasis on allowing children to discover the challenge of role and responding to the interaction of roles within the dramatic situation.

4 Giving the drama and children time to develop. This means that often drama will not be primarily a sequence of events. Instead, there will be occasions when children explore the complexity of the situation itself, the underlying concerns and the interplay of different roles.

5 Encouraging appraisal and constructive criticism; giving time for review or reflection and the chance to discuss during the drama or later. Discussion may be organised on a group or class basis, perhaps involving children only, though sometimes the teacher acts as chairman or assumes a participant role.

This next example of drama arose from a study of the old fishing area of the town and the disappearance of a thriving fishing community because of Victorian industrial development. The challenge was to recreate the community and explore the issues raised. Prior discussion established the roles and situation. At a special meeting they were informed that their landlord was selling out to the dock company and their way of life would be affected. After community discussion they chose a deputation to explain their point of view but were unsuccessful.

Land Agent	You've been given enough time.
	The doors will all be locked and we're not opening them.
Agent	Look the land's been bought so you're just wasting time. If you don't agree, my orders say I unfasten that water pump.
Leader	Your orders say, we say no. We can't drink sea water. What a thing to say.
Agent	Well, you've been asked to move. You could have land near the mill.
	What miles from the sea. We're fishermen, can't you understand?
Leader	You don't understand, we're fishermen. It's like teaching a worm to fly to say there's a piece of land, go there, we're not farmers.
	No we don't know what to do.

Agent	It's not my concern. I've got my orders. (*Moves towards pump*)
Leader	You'll not touch that pump.
Agent	Look, you're speaking to these people, right? Well look out for trouble now. (*Agent leaves scene*) (*People talk among themselves*)
Leader	Listen, he'll be back soon.
	What can we do?
	He's going to fix the pump.
	Pull one of the boats up and block the road.
	Oh, he'd just
	Or worse, smash it for spite.
Leader	We need to see Mr. Jackson.
	We've tried, haven't we?
	He won't, won't.
	What about a letter to him. (*Murmurs of approval*)
	You can write. You write it.
Leader	What shall I write. Tell me what to put. (*Crowd call out comments to be included*)

The letter was composed and meanwhile a fishing boat was filled with water as a safeguard. But bribery and betrayal by one of their own community eventually ended the affair.

Some of the significant points of this drama were summarised by the teacher.

1   Although the situation concerned the problem of a small community giving way to development, there was exploration of a number of basic underlying themes: community obligations and attitudes: moral obligations of companies: rights of individuals: treachery and revenge: fear of insecurity.

2   A blending of feeling and thought related to an extension of the

children's emotional world but feeding an intelligent awareness which was sometimes reflected in the language used.

3   The development of a "dramatic environment" as children became absorbed and showed an increasing linguistic ability to direct and shape the experience. Related to this were the moments when the drama exerted a "grip" and the basic experience of being there changed to experiencing the significance of what was happening.

4   The interplay between role personalities which at this age seem to take on more importance. With younger children, conflict, tension, agreement etc., are more often concerned with the situational elements but by ten or eleven many children seem to focus on individual or group identity and its impact as well.

5   The letter became an important symbol invested with community significance. It represented a crystallisation of their hopes, fears and attitudes.

6   The importance of discussion within the drama was increasingly "recognised" by children as a reflective phase allowing for absorption of the dramatic developments and insights, and as a sounding board for group views.

7   In drama, the language was supported by the natural factors of nuance, pitch, rhythm, gesture and movement which aided a more complete response and added their own contribution to the meaning expressed or received.

8   Children responded to role challenge. The "leader" in this drama was elected by the community at a time of crisis. He matured in his responsible role as did the other children in theirs.

9   The presence of the crowd was significant in its effect on the language exchanges between the chief protagonists. Each seemed more conscious of what he said with an audience present.

Example 7

Ten year old children in a junior school serving an industrial urban area. The school in which this work was observed does not have a drama tradition built up through the age range, but has one teacher who is enthusiastic about its possibilities. She works exclusively with her own class and succeeds in establishing positive attitudes towards drama among her top juniors. In discussion she refers to a "balanced diet" of drama experience blending movement and language. Her approach is global and drama feeds freely into and from classroom activity.

The drama began in class with discussion and a choice of historical period and subject. After some consideration of possibilities, the children opted for the past, "time of the galleons, Miss", and a sea voyage round the world. There followed a "fact-finding" discussion led by the teacher to establish a basic shape and content for beginning work. What did they know about ships of that time? What were the physical challenges to sailors? What were the functions of the crew? What was the nature and discipline on board?

After allocation of roles (with children having choice) the class moved to the hall, used the rostra, tables etc. to establish their ship and began work in movement on their various tasks. However, within this movement-oriented activity, there was some language interchange, mainly involving comments as the ship's work proceeded. The lesson ended with discussion, partly centred on aspects of movement and spatial quality, but also focusing on one incident, that of a lazy crew member reprimanded by the duty officer, and the implications in terms of authority and punishment.

Two weeks later the classroom showed evidence of research into the period. Children had prepared a vocabulary list of nautical terms and occupations on sailing ships of the Tudor period; details of ship construction, life on board, and a proclamation inviting men to serve in the navy with the certainty of prize money from rich Spanish galleons.

The subsequent drama activity illustrated how a movement-based approach may lead into language challenging situations. From the physical exploration of work tasks and the knowledge of seafaring life gained in their research, a dramatic situation developed over a quarrel between crew members about the heavy workload, their trial and the mutiny that followed.

Officer   Stop this arguing.

Crewman   He said I wasn't doing my share of work.

Crewman   Get a witness, he'll prove it.

Officer   Did anyone see all this?
             (*Silence*)

Officer	Stand up you. Who started this fight? (*Points to one crewman*)
Officer	You'll get 50 lashes.
Crewman	He doesn't deserve that. (*The accused men are taken before the Captain, the crew listen*)
Captain	Stand up the witnesses. How do you know this man didn't do enough work. Weren't you working yourselves?
Witness	I saw him.
Captain	Saw him doing what? Was he sitting about?
Witness	No.
Captain	So he was doing some work? What about the man he was fighting?
Crewman	But he sleeps in the next hammock, Captain. He's protecting his friend.
Captain	Stand up the other witness. Did you see this fight?
Witness	Nods.
Captain	Why didn't you come forward then as a witness. What did you see?
Witness	I saw Andrew start the fight.
Captain	Anyone else anything to say. (*Silence*)
Captain	Right, you'll get 25 lashes.
Crewman	25. Too many. Yes too many.
Captain	Well, I'll give you three minutes to decide to tell me what you know. (*To officer*) "Watch out for any trouble." (*The crew move together and complain among themselves about conditions*)

The action finished with the crew taking control of the ship and locking the officers away. Discussion followed and was basically a review of the drama events.

The teacher then assessed the lesson. She was satisfied that the drama had taken on an "organic shape" and was beginning to develop. However, both the movement and language lacked the qualities sought and she considered spending more time on deepening the "movement mood" of work and deprivation on the ship, or to focus more thoroughly on the roles, attitudes and substance involved in the trial and mutiny. There was already the exploration of fairness, justice and authority beginning in this situation and more would undoubtedly come. It could be fed by questions and discussion or from further research in class. However, she felt that the movement emphasis contributed to the crew's underlying feeling and could lead to richer expression in language. Whichever course was adopted would involve the class in discussion and their views would help to move the drama forward, while their readiness to contribute was evidence of a classroom tradition their teacher had fostered.

Discussion

The willingness and capacity of most children between the infant and older junior years to discuss constructively within a drama context is characteristic of their work and can be an effective language tool. Older children, in particular, seem to appreciate and exploit this aspect of drama work, perhaps because of their developing ability to perceive and reflect upon dramatic possibilities.

We are referring now to when children quietly consider, take stock and absorb the significance of the drama events, either as a class or in smaller groups. It is an activity that can be undertaken at any point in the drama process from the initial choice of theme and preliminary shaping, to mid-lesson review and concluding end of lesson reflections. The survey indicates that wide variations exist between schools in the forms and extent of drama discussion but wherever it is encouraged teachers agree on its importance to the total drama process.

In one sense this kind of discussion represents the reflective edge of a spectrum of feeling and thinking contained within drama and its associated outcomes. When the younger juniors in example four (page 94) moved from the impact of Grendel's marauding visit, they entered a phase of reflective consolidation which returned with them to their classroom after the lesson itself was concluded and influenced the subsequent talking and writing. Here events and thoughts were clarified and shaped so that David could eventually compose this piece.

Searching for my only son
Behind the bush I look but no sign of him
Six of us look for my missing son
But six of us have not found him yet.
I look upon their gloomy faces
And each time they nod their faces to the sign of no
I look upon his best friends' faces but all I see is sad eyes
But just a minute I see a hand
And behind a bush there lay my one and only son
We carried him in the Hall,
Now all the people with sad faces look,
I cover him with his cloak.

The same process was observed in this next example.

Example 8

Eleven year old children (approximately twenty-five) in an urban
Middle School. After preliminary discussion, rostra blocks and chairs
were used to create a tortuous pot-hole cave. Roles were decided upon
and the drama began. Somehow things went wrong and what had
been intended as a cave rescue turned in to a cave disaster. The
following day a "Court of Enquiry" was set up in the classroom,
chaired by the teacher. Its primary function was to focus thought on
the structure of the lesson and draw conclusions helpful to future work,
but in the process the class found themselves reflecting on other issues
as well.

Teacher	Why were so many allowed down the shaft at once?
Manager	Well it wasn't my fault. I thought they had permission from the Safety Officer and they said they had. They were lying to me, you know.
Teacher	How could they have stopped people going down?
	With a barricade. They could have put a barricade up.
Teacher	It's all very well but the people who went down are here today. They should tell us why they went down.
	Well it was silly bringing people up before the doctor got there. If someone's badly injured by the time you get them up they're probably dead. You need doctors down there to give treatment.

Teacher	Did you go down the shaft?
	Yes.
	Why do you murder people?
Teacher	Do you know what he means?
	No.
Teacher	Clarify what you've said.
	Well there was people like you stopping other people getting out and just murdering them. Yes just murdering them. There was only 30 seconds left while people were still going down there. People were dying.
Teacher	This is true. Didn't you feel you were in the way? Why did you go down?
	To see if I could help. And I was just trying and other people came down.
Teacher	Anyone willing to admit it was their fault people were killed?
	Well, I suppose when someone shouted "thirty seconds" I just said "free for all" and started to fight to get out. Well it was the reporters and photographers' fault.
Teacher	We're fond of blaming other people aren't we?

This example illustrates three points; first that a teacher can use himself to stimulate discussion either by participating or simply as class teacher, and in this way can regulate the area of exploration and deepen thinking on the issues raised. It also enables him to maintain children's commitment and encourage a balanced expression of views within the group. Second, these children reveal how effectively drama roles and the impact of dramatic experience linger after the lesson has ended. They are still strongly immersed in their "role self" so that attitudes of the role, its relationship with other role occupants and the shared experience promotes productive discussion. Some teachers insist that much of this kind of discussion is dramatic, whether the children speak explicitly or implicitly in role, basing their argument on the "internal representation" within a child created by involvement in a drama situation. Third, there is the significance of the satisfaction children gain from reflective discussion, manifested here in a readiness to contribute and in the insistent way they focused upon the human concerns of the drama.

When the dramatic action is over, children often wish to reflect and consider it. If teachers apply these two perspectives when they view the language of drama, it is possible to distinguish the kinds of demands made on children's feeling, thinking and language in different situations and phases. In the discussion about the malfunctioning of a cave rescue it is still possible to detect role identities and attitudes. To that extent then, the children have not moved outside active involvement, nevertheless it is also possible to recognise in their comments a savouring of what happened down there. Within a wider frame of reference, the cave panic of yesterday now becomes irresponsibility and even "murder" in the light of reflection. The art of leading children into reflection and discriminating judgment, the apprehension of the shades of grey in life and people, is one particularly well served by drama when the opportunities are recognised and seized.

The next example illustrates how children can engage in productive discussion among themselves, accepting responsibility and working sensibly to achieve consensus.

Example 9

Ten year old children (approximately thirty) from an urban junior school. This school has a sound drama tradition built up continuously from the first year. The work is normally part of a year group project and feeds into and from integrated work areas. Drama is seen as a challenge to "doing" which accepts thinking as an integral aspect of it. One teacher remarked "Further up the school thinking about drama is as important for children as the doing. Otherwise it doesn't satisfy them." The fourth year was engaged on an Egyptian project and the work was striking evidence of an informed and lively approach. A large and realistic burial room for a dead Pharaoh was being constructed and offered a lead into the discussion theme. "Consider that a new Pharaoh must be chosen; whom will you choose?" Groups of six or eight children worked on the problem in their roles as Egyptians. The extract is from the discussion of one group.

> Well, I understand the peasants and I think they need more money and things. If I were Pharaoh I er wouldn't cut off their hands. I'd give them more money and a life.

You can't give them more money for stealing.

With money they wouldn't steal.

But then they'll want more, won't they?

Yes, they'll all want more money.

Yes, and then we'll come to the same econol, economically position as Britain. You know all strikes.

They're greedy, those peasants.

Well what's that got to do with it? They're willing to work, aren't they, and if we don't give them money, they're going to starve.

Maybe we can get prisoners.

If I was Pharaoh I would change the rules and not have so many harsh laws. I'd change the religion. It costs the country a lot of money with all these gods.

We could just have one god. You know to rule over us all. It's not good for the country having these hundreds of gods

I know but if you change the gods and have only one the peasants and craftsmen are bound to start arguments.

There are more peasants than the army. If they started an uprising they would soon wipe out the army.

Get the peasants into the army and conquer more lands then we'd have enough people to do our work for us.

Slaves for us?

Why? We've got enough other lands already.

This is getting us nowhere.

Yes, if I was Pharaoh I would do about the same as David but I wouldn't give the peasants quite as much justice. We might get overrun. They might take the country over. But I believe in justice and really getting slaves from other countries is a bit off.

No it isn't.

It is, it is. Look. How would you like it if you were in another country and someone came along and put you in chains and started making you work?

I'd bop them.

If they tried to take us over there'd be a massive war.

We're getting nowhere. I think give the peasants more money and change the laws about stealing. If you cut off their hands they can't work.

The discussion eventually ended with a form of voting devised and approved by the group. Each candidate would be given points shown by a number of fingers raised. In the event of a tie, a second vote would decide the issue.

Once again children demonstrated their capacity to find language for dealing with ideas and feelings. Role played an obvious part in the discussion – bearing out the earlier contention that it provides an attitude for children to adopt, and use in a process of discovery – learning about themselves as well as the imagined Egyptians.

In making a choice, the individuals contribute from their own experience and bring their particular language resources to the task; each adds something which collectively makes up the group viewpoint, and from which they take whatever modifies their own internal world of attitudes, feeling and knowledge. Each statement represents a language venture into the discussion arena and challenges children's capacity both to find the necessary words and structures for communication and their own ability to understand and reflect on the contributions of others in the group. This process is seen in the exchanges concerning the slaves, and reveals an increasing recognition of independence and interdependence in daily life and a separation of fact from opinion. "They're greedy those peasants." "Well, what's that go to do with it. They're willing to work aren't they?" Here is drama involving a group of children in role and exercising their ability to solve problems considerately. The value of the group is that in comparison with the individual, it can provide more plausible solutions and effective criticism; the value of the drama is that it can create problems which cover the whole range of human endeavour, provide the motivation, and foster the language necessary to achieve a satisfying outcome.

Other ways of stimulating and using language in drama are illustrated by the following examples. Role play may be used in a wide range of situations from the "incidental drama" occurring during a subject lesson to drama sessions based upon it. Most teachers use this term to mean identification with a character within the constraints of a fairly

108

rigid situation. Some teachers favour its use when there is no tradition of language-conscious drama in the school or when other difficulties make a simulated situation approach a possible way in. Subject matter varies, but is often related to domestic, neighbourhood or work themes. There seems to be general agreement among teachers that role play may be a useful way of leading children into language, but that it cannot match the challenge to create and develop in a full drama sense.

Word music

Relevant here are those approaches in drama which stress the power of words in an explicit dramatic context. Not many examples were recorded but one useful illustration came from third year juniors working on a charm. Grouped in a circle the children experimented with a 'word round'.

> Poison cannot kill you
> Water cannot drown you
> Arrows cannot harm you

Here, words were arranged into an effective mystical blend which seemed to heighten and extend their symbolic nature and meaning.

Words from movement

Sometimes after a movement lesson in which a dramatic element has been encouraged, associated vocabulary is drawn from the children. A straightforward example is that of a class of children working on the theme of "Struggle" afterwards used "weariness, tiredness, fierceness" etc. to crystallise their mood and imagery. This approach represents one way of seeking a language form to express and interpret children's subjective experience.

Language from music

In one school, upper junior children listened to recorded music which "changed mood" several times. They then discussed in groups what sequence of events the music suggested to them. Their drama themes were subsequently enacted, mainly in movement and mime but also generating some language interchange. All themes had the same underlying shape; normal activity being overtaken by something fearful or dreadful, obviously the outcome of that particular music. Afterwards the children recounted their plays and discussed them with teacher and classmates. The work gave considerable scope to children's fantasy, but perhaps its chief language characteristic centres upon how music evoked a mood and imagery which was reflected in their drama and language. However, this was not extensive nor especially challenging whereas the language of their planning and reflective discussion clearly revealed a school approach which exercised these aspects within a drama framework.

Language and mime

Language is sometimes found as the instrument of thought within a mimetic framework, perhaps assisting in the planning, giving subsequent interpretation of the experience, or dealing with problems. One illustration comes from a class of first year juniors who were "shrunk" by their teacher during drama and had to plan where to live, what to do etc. and then proceed in mime (page 77). Afterwards, they discussed their solutions for living, avoiding dangers, and the problems they experienced. In these approaches language is very much a supportive element enabling the mime to be shaped and appraised.

Drama and writing

The relationship between drama and writing

Dramatic activity in the five to eleven age range has been seen to initiate situations in which a wide range of language functions are exercised and developed.

How readily, though, do children move from the face to face situation of drama into the production of written language and is there any reason why they should? Are the language challenges and qualities of oral interaction and discussion likely to influence the quality of writing? How far does movement-centred drama feed written work? These are some of the questions posed when a survey focuses on drama and language and they are important issues for drama, children and their teachers.

Teachers themselves hold different views on the relationship between dramatic activity and associated writing. A minority are convinced that purposeful involvement strengthens later written expression and they would agree with the comment made by one experienced colleague "Work in drama generally helps the written work of children – for once they have fully identified with an experience they find it easier to write about their reactions to it. The thoughts and emotions aroused in the drama makes their recapture in words easier and the writing produced is vital and interesting." Another teacher expressed her view more succinctly "I don't always get poets on their feet in my drama lessons but there is no difficulty in finding them with pens in their hands afterwards". Schools were visited in which the whole language activity of drama was regarded as interrelated; spoken and written forms, including reading, nourished the total drama process and were extended by it. The infants' theme concerned with the bad king (page 77) is a useful example of this approach.

On the other hand, many schools held somewhat reserved views on whether drama should be used to stimulate writing and doubted if doing so fostered any special qualities. A significant number of teachers were uncommitted on the issue; they felt that drama encouraged spoken language but had not themselves explored written possibilities to any real extent. Among this group were some who worked in difficult areas where the achievement of written language was often "a painstaking process".

It is difficult to assess effectively the relationship between spoken and written language. Nancy Martin has emphasised the variations between the purposes of the two language forms and the attainments achieved in them by children (and adults). Some people are fluent speakers in familiar situations, but have a low level of literacy generally and the opposite is also true. Most children cope with writing close to talk but often have difficulty with reflective or argumentative writing. Thus the problem facing teachers is "essentially that of first distinguishing clearly between the spoken and written forms of the language and of applying standards appropriate to these different uses, and then of applying standards appropriate to the different levels of attainment of children. The difficulty is that there are no norms other than those built up by experience in teachers' minds." We have seen how true this is when looking at earlier examples of spoken language in drama and how teachers must tailor their approaches and challenges to suit individual children. Nevertheless, Nancy Martin's observation implies a challenge for teachers in a further sense; to venture into areas of language concern and build up their own experience in terms of what is possible for children and themselves.

On the face of things drama might be thought to offer certain advantages as a link between spoken and written language. To begin with there is the nature of drama itself, an absorbing activity where children enter and explore experience collectively and afterwards discuss and reflect, first as a group, but later shaping their own thoughts in written form. In this way children organise their reality and communicate it to others.

Second, attention must be given to the strong motivation drama offers, which can send children off to writing assignments with enthusiasm and commitment. Young children find a satisfaction in writing which deals with themselves, the sorts of interests they have and the things they do; even when they have moved from the egocentricism of the five year old this remains true and is exploited in the imaginative story writing of the junior and his personal involvement in accounts of first-hand experience. Where drama scores so heavily is that it legitimises many activities normally excluded from the school environment;

children can become other people, live another life, take enterprising decisions and do so within a context of commitment and talk. In these circumstances it is not surprising that writing associated with drama carries much of the same motivational flavour. The other side of the same coin reflects a different need; that of being liberated from the dynamic situation to respond individually to the experience and seek a written shape that fits the task. This is increasingly obvious as children move up the age group and gain both an extended consciousness of the language challenge and their own satisfaction in meeting it.

Finally, drama makes available a number of different language models for children according to their age and experience. Some teachers refer to these as the "voices" of drama and are aware of the varied contributions they can make to the total language fabric, as planner, persuader, narrator, commentator, critic, recorder or role participant. James Moffet claims that if we want to improve our methods of bringing children to language awareness and competence it will not be through "asking children to read about writing and write about reading, but by asking them to practise the skills themselves with actual raw materials and audiences". In the situations for language provided by drama, the writing often has a clear purpose and encourages a growing sense of function and achievement.

Considerable research has already been undertaken in this area of the functions of writing by Nancy Martin's team and the Schools Council 'Writing Across the Curriculum Project' and it will be useful to quote from their pamphlet *Why Write?* "Younger children's writing is seen as essentially expressive, in which it is taken for granted that the writer himself is of interest to the reader and he feels free to jump from facts to speculations to personal anecdote to emotional outburst . . . thoughts may be half-uttered, attitudes half-expressed. . . . This kind of writing may move in two different ways – either towards the transactional or towards the poetic. Transactional writing is that in which it is taken for granted that the writer means what he says and which can be challenged for its truthfulness to public knowledge and its logicality . . . it is the typical language of science and intellectual enquiry, of planning, reporting, instructing, informing, advising, persuading, arguing and theorising. Poetic writing is that in which it is taken for granted that "true or false?" is not a relevant question at the literal level; what is presented may or may not be a representation of actual reality . . . but the language is not being used instrumentally as a means of achieving something but as an end in itself. The three forms may shade into each other."

Through the writing associated with drama it is possible to see these three functions exercised, especially as children move up through the age range towards eleven. In addition, however, drama writing from the survey schools falls into three broad categories according to its function in the drama process;

1 that associated with planning and preparation,

2 that which acts to take the drama action further or deepen its significance,

3 and writing which is a culminating act, assessing, appraising or reflecting upon experience undergone and formally ended. Each category can be conveniently examined separately, though their relation to the three basic functions of all writing noted earlier should be borne in mind.

The functions of writing

How early does writing for planning purposes start? If we accept the play situation where the class of five to six year old children prepared labels and price lists for their "shop" in preparation for the play activity, then possibly it can be discerned in the first infant years. However, by the six to seven year level, there are more substantial indications of its place in some drama activities and one example has already been examined (page 77); that of the class beginning their work on the "bad king" when they were led by the class teacher to compose a novel picture of the king and write in their own books what they considered he had done wrong. In this way the use of a written language approach assisted the children to construct a meaningful basis for a challenging theme.

A similar process was observed with children of the same age elsewhere. Here the class teacher used a map drawn by herself to begin discussion and lead into drama. They would be pirates going for treasure to the island shown on the map and all agreed that a plan was necessary before setting off on such a long and dangerous journey. So they returned to different parts of the classroom and in groups discussed two aspects; what practical help could they give the expedition and what things would they need to collect for the journey? After discussion they were to write down their ideas so that these could be used for further class discussion and selection. The subsequent writing illustrated a wide range of suggestions, some of which are given here:

Someone good at fishing. On a ship if you ran out of food you will need someone to fish.

And you'll have to have someone to tell you which way the ship has to go.

I would be a guard. I like being a guard. If any horrible creatures come, I can shoot them.

A digger to dig for the treasure. I'll need a pick and shovel.

A nurse to make them better. If they fall in the water the sharks would get them, they'd be cut.

A map drawer to show where the treasure is.

Among the list of objects required for the journey were: weapons, compass, landrover, bombs, knife, spade, food, and matches "to light a fire, keep warm and frighten off anyone who wants to rob".

Not all the planning activities of this age group are so explicit. In one class the children began to explore a space theme in which they would leave earth as astronauts and visit a distant planet. In the initial lesson they discussed and tried out the kinds of movements astronauts and space creatures would make before beginning a journey homeward. Afterwards their teacher asked them to think more carefully about the world they were to visit, and outline the features as a planning function. This was one plan that emerged.

"When I landed on the strange planet I felt pleased and proud. My space ship was no good because it had run out of gas and my six-legged dog called Pockled Dust was lost. I saw funny creatures with television aerials on their head and one of them knocked me out and took me to their village and put me in a cage and when I awoke I saw Pockled Dust getting the keys off the strange creature with his six legs. He found the keys in the top pocket and let me free and I went back in my rocket as fast as I could go. When we got back I gave Pockled Dust a crater of dust for saving my life because it was his favourite dinner."

The opportunity to "plan" for this infant (and many more in the class) was also the opportunity to create a fantasy in very expressive language. It is difficult to tell how many personal functions this piece of writing fulfilled, but that is a feature of so much infant writing anyway. Whether an uninformed reader would have recognised a planning function is doubtful; what should be clear, however, is the essential individuality of the writer and her closeness to what she writes. She plans within the context of her own narrative which gives shape to her ideas of what may be found on the strange planet and the kinds of adventures possible there. The teacher here remarked of her drama aims, "I want it to breed responsibility and get them to use their imaginations constructively, to be able to look at problems and implement ideas and develop language, not only in the drama but also in the classroom generally.

Planning in the junior and middle school varies widely. One of the interesting language tasks noted earlier (page 96) was that associated with a mixed ethnic group of nine year olds from an inner city school, working on the story of the Trojan Horse and painstakingly preparing captions or lists for their stalls (and enjoying the activity). Obviously different language demands are made when planning for drama in different circumstances and it is necessary to consider the total situation, including the important lead-in before deciding what language planning is appropriate or desirable. By contrast, a group working in a very different environment formulated a proclamation inviting applications from venturers interested in joining an expedition to the New World and received letters written in reply at the "Sign of the Bull's Head". One example is given.

"I would like to join your expedition to the New World. I am 25 years old and strong. Besides I am a blacksmith so I will be good at making weapons for you or tools if you need them. You say £25 is needed and has to be paid before we go to buy supplies and things. I can deliver the money by Friday. I am not afraid of wild beasts or Indians and I am not married so I can easily go."

A first year junior boy could also write about his role self at the initial stage of drama and in language which indicates how close he is to the infant astronaut. Yet the language task is different because the junior has to grapple with personality characteristics even though he is helped by imaginative details in his narrative.

"I am an Indian brave. I am called Fleetfoot. I have long black hair and I am big and handsome. Once I had a competition. I had to throw a tomahawk and I won and I had to walk over red hot cinders and I walked that too, and I like hunting in the forest and I can run as fast as a deer. I have a long face and a crooked mouth and my nose was broken in a fight and my ears stick out and when I go out to war I wear warpaint."

Language activities of this sort are motivated by the children's urge to get drama going but also serve another purpose; they help the process of character building and create a sense of commitment to the drama process. Here are the first intuitive feelings of initial characterisation, drawn probably from many sources, being shaped into a concept of the role character. Later, after experience in the drama, it will be possible for writing of this kind to reflect deeper awareness and more personality facets.

A contrasting approach was seen with older children in the planning stage of their drama on "relationships" who used a local community as their material. First they had grouped themselves into families and then intended exploring the possible kinds of situation when people are confronted by a crisis or the unexpected. To encourage deeper observation and perception of character, they wrote about other people.

> "On Tuesdays he goes for his dole. He collects it and steps across the cobbled stone in his boots held up by strings. He opens the club door and descends down the steps to the bar. 'Pint please' he says. One of his famous words."

A further example is taken from another group of eleven year old children working on a new "city state" which kept their own town and institutions as a frame of reference. Different groups were allocated "areas of interest or significance" as part of preliminary planning, before the whole concept was considered by all the children. One member of the group which was formulating proposals for education in the new city state gave her ideas on a school.

> No headmasters – because they are too strict – only headmistresses.
>
> Don't need maths.
>
> History and geography, art, music are important. Piano lessons would be liked.
>
> P.E. and Games would be included.
>
> There would be men teachers as well as women.
>
> Children would go to school every day except Saturday and Sunday.
>
> There will be homework. Children can choose which lessons to go to and there would be different teachers for each lesson.

No assembly or prayers.

Teachers should go for tests to see that they are not too strict.

There should be school trips.

Children should all go to school until they are sixteen.

They can choose to do exams or not.

A teacher should be kind and helpful. And cross with the bad ones only.

This is a drama planning task obliging children to work within a structured framework, sort out their ideas and express in writing those they consider important in an approach. It is also a language task obliging the children to concentrate firmly on the intention behind the writing and in effect exerts its own shaping power. Just as important from the drama viewpoint is the experience of "thinking through" which together with a greater awareness of their own attitudes will support the dramatic involvement. Significantly, the teacher responsible for this group recollected that when the suggestion was later made to exclude schools from the new city state, it led to moving drama as children argued eloquently for the ideas they had worked on.

The close links drama may forge with reading are also evident in some of the planning assignments, especially where teachers encourage children to research and build up a significant background of knowledge which underpins their drama roles and activities. One example comes from the fourth year junior group whose discussion on the choice of a new Pharaoh was noted earlier (page 106).

When the Pharaoh died his court went into mourning and the priests stopped shaving their heads.

The body is then taken to the house of Vitality. The mummification was done by doctors who were priests.

This is why the Egyptians know a lot about bodies and are good doctors.

This is how they did the mummification:

1 Remove internal organs.

2 Remove the intestines through an opening in the left side of body.

3 Hook the brain down the nose.

4 Then wash out body with wine and pack it with linen soaked with perfume.

5 Plug the eye sockets out with wads of linen.

6 Then the whole body is buried in bed of natron (which is a chemical) to absorb all moisture and body fat.

7 The body is then treated with preserving ointments.

8 Then each finger and toe is bandaged separately.

9 In between bandages they put jewellery, pendants, rings, etc.

10 At each stage the priests would say prayers, magical spells and they would pour ointment over the body.

11 Last of all they put the death mask on, then the body is put in the gold coffin and then the shroud (which is a red blanket) is wrapped around the whole thing.

Writing of this kind is very factual and complements the more poetic language possible in drama activities. Very often it is an accompanying feature of a developing theme and informs and extends the drama action and issues. Of course, it represents a form of writing often achieved in other ways, but the point stressed by teachers is the motivational power of drama to bring children willingly and productively to research and thus effectively link reading and writing with the spoken language of discussion and active interaction. Those teachers who look for a fruitful interrelationship of oracy and literacy might well find it here.

Writing stimulated by dramatic interaction

Several schools used drama to stimulate writing; sometimes moving the action forward or deepening the significance of an issue already being explored. The formulation of a "charm" to defeat the fear and effects of plague or a "treaty of peace" drawn up between Indians and settlers provide ready examples of this approach. Because writing normally represents a specific task within the drama, the writers bring a strong sense of purpose to a relevant language challenge. They can see why the writing is necessary and how it relates to the ongoing drama so they usually make a constructive attempt. Very probably the issue will have been discussed during the drama and later in the classroom, the points of reference clarified and the framework for the writing established. A framework of this sort is supportive but it also obliges children to select from their language resources the appropriate material. Since the work is often basically significant to their drama, a class or group will usually take a keen interest in the content and quality of the language product and show a readiness to contribute suggestions if these are required and encouraged. When the "threatened fishermen" (page 98) were preparing a letter to their unresponsive landowner they discussed for some time whether their statements should reflect defiance or helplessness. Children often recognise a special significance in writing produced for particular drama situations and they can reach a stage of drama and language maturity where the influence of written forms is assessed from a dramatic perspective.

One of the youngest groups to illustrate the language approach discussed here was the class of five year old children whose play-drama world of Bogglybogs (page 18) had helped to formulate several words and phrases of special significance for entering and leaving the magic world or transforming themselves into Bogglybog creatures. Their activity was considered in an earlier section of the survey report and included reference to the ordering of the Bogglybog world through "rules" which emerged in discussion and were written down with the help of the class teacher.

A class of slightly older infant children worked on a drama theme concerned with a magic carpet. Their carpet had been "lost" so attention and effort were focused upon the production of "spells" to find it. Here is one spell:

  Izzy, pizzy let's get dizzy
  Cart, carpet, I need to go to market
  Carpet come and take me
  Carpet take me to the market
  Izzy pizzy, my carpet's gone dizzy.

Spells for drama are relatively popular assignments in the early junior years, probably through the influence of witch, wizard and monster themes. They develop into rather more complex mixtures as children grow older, no doubt gaining something of their substance and form from reading. When used in drama they rarely fail to yield an awareness of the potency of words and an insight into children's acceptance of the magic and mystical. This second example comes from a second year junior class:

Stir in some frogs' legs
And slugs and worms
A thousand caterpillars
A hundred flies
The jelly from two bees
Five spiders
And four apple pips.

Language to invoke a magical response is one task; language to evoke
human response is another. Situations are sometimes reached in
drama where intercession or representation is required, and though
this will be achieved in most cases through the spoken word, there are
times when written forms are effective.

Lord Pharaoh, Our life is a misery working down in this quarry.
Our throats are dry and parched because of lack of water. Some of
the children are fainting and most of them are so dizzy that they
can't keep their balance on the rock and just fall off like dead flies.
There is not enough water for the wedges neither is there enough
food for the men who work on the rock. Their bones weaken, they
are that weak they can hardly lift a hammer.

The tools the men use are no good. When they touch the rock they
break. We need more tools for these men to work with. Maybe you
could give some with stronger handles. Then if you did, we will be
able to do twice as much work.

In our conditions, there are many dangers. Down here we live in the
huts with many people. Some of them have diseases that we could
catch. Our conditions are not fit to live in. You have a palace with
proper beds. What do we have? A mudhouse with a mat to sleep on.
We are asking you Pharaoh to help us. Signed, The Elders.

This group was primarily concerned with the persuasion of language –
how to convince, but in doing so they were also expressing and
communicating much of the feeling, involvement and concerns of the
drama. In searching for a vocabulary and style to suit their purpose
they received active support from a drama situation which gave
strength and urgency to the business of composition and to its content
and tone. They were learning how to shape an argument through
thought alone. The task demanded a marshalling of relevant facts and
feelings, selection of those considered important for the purpose, and
discrimination in using words which will be effective. It is possible to
regard writing of this kind as a blend of active and reflective roles; on

the one hand, activated by the drama situation, something purposeful is being pursued; on the other, an obvious reflective process is influencing the composition. Once important issues are crystallised to any significant extent drama is no longer the same. The situation may remain unchanged or it may move on, but role-taking, awareness and insight may be different and often deeper.

This process is seen at its most effective where children have established a drama tradition and developed a dramatic sensibility, yet it also influences the early stages of drama with children who have little dramatic experience. The headteacher beginning drama work in his small village school chose the village itself and its historical associations as a source of raw material and his older juniors settled on the confrontation between Saxon and Norman as the main theme. His notes (page 52) outline the children's interest in a new activity, but also indicate his own difficulties in deepening the experience, particularly the awareness and significance of losing freedom or land. This is how the idea of writing a "Will" evolved, as a strategy for giving the Saxon villagers their basis of argument in defending traditional rights. The careful production of the wills and their suitable "ancient appearance" testifies to the children's interest and commitment.

Last Will and Testament of Oswy, Thegn of Heorot

I, Oswy, Thegn of Heorot, would like to give this land to my only son, Leofric. If he is dead I would like to give it to my brother, Henry. I want you to take good care of this land like I did. I want you to share the cattle with the villagers. I want you to give every villager a fair share of land. Give every villager two pieces of gold and six pieces of silver and also a bag of corn each. I would like you to give my sword to the blacksmith and give the wise old woman my waist chain. When I die give a big feast, kill two cows and an ox. Give the church one acre of land to build another part of the church on. I also give the church four bags of gold to pay for skilled men. I hope this Will will be carried out.

The children discovered in the Thegn's Will a symbolic representation of the meaning in holding a possession as one's own and the freedom to make community and individual decisions without coercion. It crystallised the feeling and bonds of community, bringing villagers together as people with a history, rights and privileges, now facing the threatened break in historical and social continuity. These are quite fundamental and important issues; they reach the roots of human concern and to gain insight into their nature is to learn something far more significant than the facts of Norman Conquest. So the Will became both symbol and catalyst, encapsulating a range of concerns while providing for the drama a means to deepen role, commitment and situation. Nevertheless, it was not a magic wand; role-playing, sensitivity and argument were deepened, but children also need experience to exploit drama opportunities fully and this means building up confidence, tolerance, trust and all the disciplines relating to dramatic interaction.

Two further examples indicate the spectrum of writing possibilities available. One group of ten to eleven year old children developed a theme centred on 19th century factory conditions and kept a "drama diary" in which they recorded the significant events and thoughts of workmen struggling for better conditions. A typical entry reads.

> Friday 13th May 1872. We have been on strike and have just got out of prison. We stole some money – twenty shillings to be exact from our master, the factory owner, and he had us thrown into that filthy place. It all started when one of the workers had an accident and we asked for better machines and more money. He promised us two pennies more a day and better conditions but he didn't pay up, so we stole the money.

Where the drama situation suits this approach, it offers the advantage of a language model in which regular recording of events helps children to reflect and comment on them so that it becomes the individual's account of a group experience. There is a mutual feedback between the action and the record with a probable strengthening of each.

Another group of children of the same age but from a different school considered how they should set about electing and installing a new leader. In discussion they agreed that an improvised approach was inappropriate for their purposes and a formal arrangement was required. Different groups undertook the task and finally produced a set of "laws" governing the election and a ritual ceremonial for the leader's installation. It was interesting that before the latter task had been accomplished the group explored the obligations and rights of leadership and incorporated the most important of these into their text.

Writing as individual reflection on experience

The greatest proportion of writing associated with drama falls into the third category; it does not primarily represent planning, persuasive or "instrumental" compositions with drama development in mind, rather it offers an opportunity for children to reflect upon experience and crystallise feeling and thought. As writers they are detached from active involvement but use drama as the basic experience to begin a process of clarification and interpretation. They are able to go back over events in an individual capacity, savour mood, or explore possibilities and implications.

It seems important to recognise, however, that while all experience provides raw material which children may work and shape in writing, the experiences of drama present them with an organic material whose qualities may promote insights and awareness within the active drama context and can continue to influence the strength and sensitivity of children's later written reflections. Writing that follows drama, not as an imposed exercise but where mood, role and situation appropriately lead into written models, frequently supplies evidence of maturing minds and can continue to influence children's later writing. Examples from children's written work will help to outline progress in this respect between five and eleven.

Among the drama activities referred to earlier was a class of five year old children who created in movement their own interpretations of string puppets and afterwards painted pictures of themselves in action. Beneath these paintings they added written sentences such as "My string is pulling my head up to the ceiling", and "I am stretching up tall".

Not surprisingly the paintings express more of the experience than written language can achieve for this age group and provide some insight into the impact and significance of young children's "being and doing". Similar examples have been noted throughout the survey. The play-drama world of Bogglybogs noted earlier led to a class book in which paintings and accompanying statements recorded some of the experiences. One picture of a distinctive blue creature resting on the top of a red house bore the observation, "I have painted an invisible Bogglybog". Often the class teacher assisted in discussion so that words and sentences currently beyond the children's ability to write could be used. In this way it was possible for the following story to be written.

There is a Bogglybog on a roof and when we catch it we will kill it because it is a naughty Bogglybog. It drops litter. The other Bogglybogs don't drop litter because they are happy and kind.

We are the Bogglybogs
The boggly woggly Bogglybogs
Be nice to us or we will gobble you up.

There is a parallel between these examples and the comment made by a teacher of younger infants, that so often their experience runs ahead of language ability. Yet it is only by meeting opportunities to deal with experience in language that children can begin matching some of the vitality and significance so often seen in their paintings, and begin to organise and shape it in written form. Spoken language begins this process in which drama can play a major role, by providing enterprising situations calling for all forms of language awareness, and where the sharing of experience provides an essential basis for individual development. Dramatic activity can help provide a strong linguistic foundation, supporting the developing written structures in which children discover how words can work for them. Most infant children soon progress from single sentence comments and begin to write the "story" of their drama. One six year old, Andrew, followed his hall lesson with this written account:

On Tuesday we went into the hall and I built a snowman. He had a black hat and a carrot for his nose and I put a red and white scarf on him. First to make the body I rolled a ball round and round and then I put it down. And then I rolled another ball round and round and then I put it on top of the other one and put on some buttons.

Again the writing echoes Andrew's talk, matching almost exactly his words used in the hall when the children were asked by their teacher to tell her about the snowmen they had made. His story indicates, however, a developing grasp of how words can be used to shape a detailed and logical account of a make-believe situation.

By the time many infants reach seven, writing derived from drama may show a developing awareness of language forms and the technical facility for getting words down on paper. Consequently, their reflection on the drama experience is enhanced by an ability to select from the most interesting aspects. Very often the result takes them beyond the actual experience to an imaginary extension of the drama world, allowing scope for exploring fantasy and imaginative possibilities through written language. Two examples from this age group illustrate the point: the first comes from an Eskimo theme and could be classified as "poetic"; the second "expressive" story, "The Pirates", not only records part of the adventures originating in a pirate play but comments in its choice of imagery on the power of imaginative involvement to evoke feeling and extend language even with young children.

Crack, crack, goes the snow
Heave, heave I make an igloo
Swosh, swish goes the oars
Whee-ee whee-ee goes the harpoon
Into a walrus.

Once upon a time there lived on an island three pirates. One day the pirates were bored so they went for a walk on the island. One of them saw strange creatures. He even saw a water dragon and when he saw it he was scared out of his wits. And he ran to his cave quickly as he could with his arms sticking out and his legs running like a lion. And he was shouting so loudly that he thought his mouth would fall out.

The stories children read and hear, and the drama situations they create have a strong sense of sequence, so it is a natural development to find "reflective" writing following drama taking the shape of a story and using it for many language functions. Sometimes this entails moving away from the literal representation of the drama so that the writing becomes like the pirate story, a blend of dramatic activity and imagination. Even so, children will often maintain that such expression is an account of "our drama" or a "story of our drama" and thus indicate how the activity is serving as an intellectual and emotional stepping stone, enabling them to achieve a variety of purposes through their subsequent writing. Teachers who use an active language approach in drama with infants and foster associated writing, have commented on the close relationship between the make-believe world of dramatic activity and more general imaginative writing. One experienced teacher stated, "Before I used drama I had some difficulty in encouraging children to write their own stories, but now they seem to be able to do this with ease. I believe drama experiences help to feed interest in words and imaginative writing". Drama viewed as a sponsoring agent with potential of this kind should not be overlooked by schools seeking children's fuller development and their ability to use spoken and written language more effectively.

These aims are basic: so is the interrelationship between them and attention needs to be focused upon them. Yet writing originating in drama is more commonly practised during the infant years than between eight and eleven. At first sight this appears strange, given the greatly extended language resources of most junior children. Why should it happen? A number of reasons seem likely. First, there seems to be wider acceptance of the values of the play-drama world during the five to seven stage, and the lively imaginative mode of representing and exploring self and world which language reflects. Second, there may be greater acceptance of the seamlessness of learning; all experience is grist for the young child's mill to be talked over and written about, with play and drama providing many of the fundamental experiential steps towards maturity; Third, more specific language teaching in the junior and middle school years lessens the emphasis given to drama involvement and associated writing. The links between drama, learning and language forms are sometimes difficult for many teachers to determine, and hence the potential contribution of written outcomes is often undervalued even where drama itself has an accepted place in the curriculum.

Between eight and eleven expressive-poetic narrative is the most widely practised approach to reflective writing following drama and it continues to perform the same functions for juniors as for infants. Nevertheless, depending upon the strength of drama tradition in a school and the kind of work undertaken, important characteristics appear in writing as children move towards the upper age groups. Children begin to show a capacity to move from face to face interaction towards constructive criticism, description, and generalisation in writing chiefly contained within a narrative form. This degree of achievement, however, depends heavily upon the opportunities offered to children by the drama work undertaken. Where drama provides scope for getting under the skin of character, researching into relevant background and developing related situations, the possibilities for writing and extended exploration of issues are obviously enhanced along with the motivation to undertake written tasks.

Schools using these approaches are a minority of the survey sample and most schools visited tend to adopt a programme of single lesson activities or relatively short-term themes, which do not, in general, foster much associated writing. If there is an exception, it is probably to be found in a movement approach to drama. At first sight this appears somewhat paradoxical since the active linguistic background underlying so much reflective writing has already been stressed. In a few schools, however, movement is used to create strong mood as dramatic situations or themes are explored and later contributes to the shaping and content of written expression. Dramatic ideas, consciousness and sequence are developed, as are sensitivity and awareness in a movement framework which complements and nourishes a language output. In general, however, achievement of written language from a drama-movement base does not seem to be extensively practised. This example from a top junior working on a space theme illustrates the quality of language that can result from appropriate movement activity:

The Enchanted Forest

We landed with a thud
My head throbbed like a drum,
The air was dark and damp,
I dragged myself through the eerie forest,
"Oh! what's that?" something had tapped me on the back,
Some mystical power was urging me on and on,
I could hear groans and squeaking branches of trees.
I was terrified and afraid,
Again I felt some magical mysterious presence,
Then I heard somebody screeching with laughter.
It went right through me,
I looked around but there was nothing to be seen,
Then came a strong wind,
Which blew me off my feet,
Before I knew it I had been blown across the forest floor
I landed on a mound of grass,
Before the feet of two horrible witches,
And a rather stupid-looking wizard,
What was to become of me?

The writing is rich in imagery which lends strength and sensitivity to a well-shaped "poetic" narrative in which Steven has been given imaginative freedom to create his forest in words and comment on the happenings there. It offers a considerable contrast to ten year old Clare's story, (page 52) an outcome of drama in the small village school referred to earlier, where the problem was to keep their freedom and rid themselves of the occupying soldiers. Part of her work is quoted.

We suggested lots of things to get rid of the soldiers but nothing seemed to turn out. Then Godwin suggested leprosy and someone said "I wouldn't want to get leprosy and let my fingers drop off and my skin crinkle up". But the Thegn said "It's either that or you'll be beaten and put in chains", so then he agreed to get the leprosy. Our fingers might drop off and we wouldn't be able to feed the babies or get food for ourselves and do things for each other. Most people said it was a good idea but some people thought it was mad. Some didn't know what to do because if they had a lovely daughter they didn't want her fingers to drop off and all her skin to crinkle. So the Thegn suggested we had a vote and leprosy won. But then someone said "Where are we going to get a leper from now?"

Her story is long and detailed and goes on to outline the reactions of the villagers when it comes to implementing their decision to bring in a leper with all its attendant risks. The writing has shape and purpose but differs from a typical ten year old girl's story because it deals closely with people their relationships, concerns, actions and consequences. It is not a mere chain of events; instead it offers a quite moving commentary on the village dilemma and the difficulties of decision-making. There is a sense of commitment and purpose throughout and the observations on the horror of infection mark a move from the surface situation to an examination of the underlying issues. At times the story becomes critical as it shapes Clare's reflections on the arguments and decisions. These are important considerations for teachers interested in language stimulation and quality, especially in the light of the headmaster's comment quoted earlier that the school had little tradition of imaginative writing and none of drama.

An example follows from a school where a tradition of drama does exist and illustrates how two upper junior children have reached a stage in drama and language control which enables them to move from a narrative model and work convincingly within a framework of reflective introspection; a challenging task for any junior. They had been working on their drama theme for several weeks, building and changing as discussion, interaction and research fed an awareness of possibilities. This example helps to show the individuality of children within their drama role and situation.

After what I've done for those people in the village, they promised to me and to the Thegn that they would never go back to those non existent gods. Now I have heard that they have gone back. The Thegn off all people has turned against me and I thought that I could trust him. Never again. As for the old priest he has been evil ever since the day he set foot on the earth. One person said that he had been brought on earth by the devil.

I stopped them from making sacrifices and told them that the proper god does not take lives and he only wants to bring happiness. The Thegn ordered the woodcutter to chop down the sacred tree and stopped them going to the place where evil brews. Myself and the monks made a bible for them in such detail. Now! they have turned against me. They are actually going to sacrifice a man. I have taught them not to fight or quarrel or steal. The man they are going to actually sacrifice is very important to them. They are saying without proof that he stole 7 bags of flour. But he is a very honest man. Of the 6 months I've been here he has never told a lie to me not just that he is a pleasant man to. This is the most outrageous thing I have ever heard going back on their word. I must try to get them back to me or 6 months work will be wasted. I must get them back to me. I must.

This example represents internal discussion and reveals the impact of role and dramatic situation being worked over in language of strong feeling and insight. The shape and function of the work makes greater demands than narrative and though story elements are woven into the fabric, they serve chiefly to reinforce expression which conveys attitudes, recrimination, description, speculation and comment. Argument in written language is rare in the junior years. Here is one of the specific "voices" of drama helping the writers to explore their drama personalities (and their own selves) not by writing the whole story but through a particular focus and selection. The boy has not lost sight of his purpose which was to argue and comment from within his role.

The approach is one particularly enriched and made possible through drama. The child comments from within the drama situation on people and relationships bound up in a "willing suspension of disbelief" and in the process of discovering some of the characteristics of the human condition. Two forms of knowledge crystallise in the writing; the traditional knowledge of historical background researched from the reference books; and "experiential knowing" evolving largely from the drama itself.

How then has the writing moved him on? First, by allowing scope to reflect upon and savour more deeply the world of "imaginative reality" provided by drama, in which problems and achievements were sufficiently convincing and relevant to engage children's full commitment and allow a quality of experience that fostered shape, purpose and insight. Second, he has successfully coped with an individual language task by exercising and extending his own language resources, not only in terms of words and constructions but within a framework of particular purpose and discipline. Third, because he knows he has looked himself in the face and given form and expression to part of his feeling, thoughts and attitudes, gained further insight into himself as a person and realised the creative satisfaction of the writer. Fourth, he has gone over the events of drama experience in his own language and made it more his own.

In most of the schools which approached drama in the ways outlined, a continuing use of reference material to support research was seen. We have referred to this previously when research was used to assist in planning; by far the greater proportion, however, is produced during the life of the drama or later and often represents a considerable language output.

It is part of the "organic" nature of drama that it helps to fuse research and role-taking in this way and bring to the facts extracted from books a vitality of life and significance.

The importance of self expression in writing is generally recognised by teachers and has been effectively stressed by the Schools Council Writing Across the Curriculum Research Project Team. "To allow children to engage meaningfully and represent their world depends on how much experience they are given to write expressively." Yet it remains true that many children choose to write within a framework or use a language model which does not always challenge their developing language resources and this presents a constant problem for their teachers. If we accept the mutual relationship between language and learning exemplified in some drama work, this may open one way to achieve disciplined and expressive writing which carries the unique qualities of personal and group dramatic experience, generating its own strong motivation and language voices.

Drama and literature

Why use literature for drama?

Dramatic activities reviewed earlier focus attention upon three major interrelated problems facing teachers: the encouragement and choice of appropriate subject matter for children's drama ventures, a suitably supportive framework within which they can profitably work, and means to enrich the quality of experience. Teachers differ in their awareness of these situations and how they respond to them, but a number of schools provided evidence that one resource for dealing with the problems involved was literature, especially story.

Nevertheless, the rationale supporting the use of literature for dramatic purposes varied considerably between schools and provided a spectrum of comment when discussed. The most common view expressed appreciation for the support given by story to both children and teachers and is typified in the remark, "I use story for the magic web it spins". Here the motivation and interest of story was stressed in addition to the framework of support provided by its shape and characters. Within this view, however, several differences of emphasis were evident; story could be liberating and experimental giving children the chance to compare their own feelings against those of the characters; it allowed for a basic shape and approach but might be altered in some details; there was nothing to hinder children freely improvising and using the story structure as they wished.

Other teachers reflected these views but regarded story as only one part of their approach to dramatic work, but there was common agreement that motivation was normally strong when children used story as a drama basis.

One headteacher of younger children welcomed the supportive framework and motivational interest brought by story to drama but saw its primary purpose in terms of appropriate emotional involvement. She was anxious to create a drama environment which drew upon the kinds of material, issues and emotional tone found in the stories, poems and songs typically enjoyed by her children. A headmaster colleague, on the other hand, considered that story offered drama two major strengths – a structure which allowed children to encounter moral attitudes by actively experiencing situations where these were raised, and an artistic awareness imparted by the shape of the story and its language.

The use of more general literature for dramatic activity was less strongly supported by explicit comment except in several schools where it formed part of an all-inclusive approach to drama. Here story was enriched by background reading and research which drew upon any relevant material and contributed, sometimes substantially, to the events, issues and roles explored. One school summarised its policy in these words, "We see all literature as a vital element for much of our drama, not only to provide a theme or framework when this is appropriate but also because it adds valuable background material to any work we undertake".

How far did views vary between teachers working with different age groups? There was fairly general agreement on the potential value of literature for drama, but far less on how and when it should be used. Choice of story was another matter and was obviously an individual decision. With younger children the characters and actions of typical infant stories were sometimes thought to be appropriate for play and class drama situations, with the magical world of witches and wizards following on towards the top infant years and early in the junior school. For the middle junior years and onwards some teachers seemed to be looking for stories which contained the kinds of characters and situations which would lend themselves to evolving drama disciplines; stories of strong action, definition of character and recognisable people with actual ways of life. Cave dwellers, Egyptians, Greeks and Trojans, Norsemen, and the sagas of the Bible were some of the examples used in the survey schools along with the people created in the works of modern writers who seem able to capture those qualities essential to drama.

It is the shared concern for people, their values and beliefs and the experiences they undergo which makes story useful to drama. In this sense story is not only fictional narrative but includes all accounts of human endeavour, myth and legend which serve children as starting points or basic material for their own dramatic re-creation. It provides opportunities for taking on the roles of those read about or making new and related roles, and allows children to share many experiences and emotions. One paragraph of the *Plowden Report* indicates the closeness of story and drama. "It is through story as well as through drama and other forms of creative work that children grope for the meaning of experiences that have already overtaken them, savour again their own pleasures and reconcile themselves to their own inconsistencies and those of others. As they 'try on' first one story character then another, imagination and sympathy, the power to enter into another personality and situation, which is a characteristic of childhood and a fundamental condition for good social relationships, is preserved and matured. It is also through literature that children can feel towards the experience, the hopes and fears that await them in adult life."

Literature and drama in practice

Three basic approaches to the use of literature for drama were evident in the practical work seen in schools and in the comments of teachers.

1 A more or less faithful re-shaping of the story. The interest here centres on special qualities produced as a result of dramatisation and how it differs from the narrative.

2 The use of story or more general literature not so much as a rigid experience, but with stress on its use as a flexible framework to permit re-shaping, re-patterning, an increasing understanding and possible synthesis of the narrative with personal experience. Here the story is retained as a tentative structure providing something of a blueprint, but obliging children to face the practicalities and challenges of construction through drama.

3 The evolution of story as the outcome of dramatic challenge which begins perhaps with a single situation but builds up and develops over a period of time. Very often the stimulus provided by the drama sends children (and teachers) to a variety of related literature and background material. Both factual text and fiction may serve as sources of information and a background of experience from which analogy and understanding can be drawn.

Strict narrative drama was observed in several schools, both infant and junior. It seems to have particular significance for the youngest children who frequently "mouth" the words of favourite stories when these are read to them and faithfully echo both action and language in subsequent dramatisation. They act almost as if they seek a confirmation of experience rather than an extension of it; certainly they reflect Margaret Spencer's observation in seeming to, "believe that a story has a certain kind of accepted pattern and do their best to be faithful to it". But drama is a transforming agent, allowing children to identify with story characters and achieve a more active experience through the freedom to initiate and not simply imitate. In this sense the imitative drama of young children seems to parallel the same stage of play and the verbal interaction, events and roles are imaginatively sustained. Even in their own play following story, children of this age group will often go through the story sequence and closely match its detail and language, though sometimes they take elements and recombine them in other forms.

There are several explanations for this; the relative immaturity and egocentric nature of young children and their inability to respond fully to the demands of creative drama making; pleasure derived from reproducing story in dramatic form and the security offered by story roles and situations. Nevertheless, role-taking and dramatic action of this kind obviously excites and interests most children and presumably gives enhanced awareness and meaning through the process of "becoming" someone else. When children are old enough to discuss their role-taking they invariably stress the accompanying pleasure but they also hint at how strongly the experience is felt. It is this motivational pleasure and involvement that can heighten the normal level of awareness and response, which explains why older children are usually willing to dramatise story and keep strictly to the shaped pattern of events and language. But how many opportunities are lost in schools because of this when children capable of creative and enterprising drama from story, able to exploit its possibilities for life and language, remain bound within its predetermined pattern.

Most children find the use of story exciting and satisfying when it permits the discovery of challenging possibilities and gives scope to respond constructively. In this way they re-shape the story to suit their own interests and purposes and gain added motivation from the active involvement. Story may take on added life and meaning when it becomes more than something read or listened to but yields its content, characters and issues for children to work upon and extend. Where the opportunities exist, teachers often become excited themselves at the possibilities inherent in a re-creative process. One headmistress spoke of a story read by her juniors which dealt with the era of cave-men and the birth of civilisation. Subsequent discussion revealed that much of the content allowed a wide range of choice when children planned how to use it for drama; the struggle for survival, necessary laws if people were to live together, fears and superstitions and possibly the importance and significance of the artist in society. This drama, unfortunately, was not observed but it illustrates how a perceptive teacher and her class of juniors could see story in terms of dramatic challenge as well as enjoying the reading. Other examples of a "story approach" included:

1   A visit to an infants' school on the outskirts of a small mining town showed how the ability to find dramatic scope in story may begin relatively early. The visit coincided with work being undertaken by children of six and seven on their own adaptation of *Hansel and Gretel*. Two features in the story had outstanding appeal for them; the fascination of witches and the idea of a house made from sweet things, and these were used as the basis for their own drama in which, "discussion and free interpretation of ideas built up to form their own conception". The shaping took several weeks to achieve, but during that time a village was established with its sweet shop, distinctive roles were created in addition to the witch, and the improvisation involved both language interaction and movement. Children experienced different ways of reacting in movement to the fear and threat provided by the witch and her attendants, adding this aspect of drama to the language fabric built up by the central concern; how the witch occupied the village shop and the efforts required to get rid of her. Among the writing related to the drama was the composition of potent spells, one of which is given as an example.

> Witches put in their pots
> Legs of earwigs, frog's skin, bats eyes
> A witches spell is twirly whirly
> Slide and slither.
> Witches fly and dance
> Witches giggle then skeletons dance
> Owls hoot and ghosts float
> And the witch flies on her broomstick
> I was one of them
> I can turn you into anything I like.

2   In the same school six year old children heard their teacher read an eastern fairy story *Kahakura – The Worst Fisherman* and used it as the basis for drama. Kahakura is in trouble because he catches no fish but this was because sprites were catching them at night. He discovers this by hiding one night and seeing them, but becomes entangled in one of their special nets. This, however, he manages to keep. Again, significant parts of the tale were used and adapted to children's own creative wishes and it was the imagery which seemed to appeal most here. From discussions between teacher and children the idea of

making a "sea world" was developed, with a sea king, mermaids and weird creatures. The various roles were tried by all children, largely in movement, who also created a physical and sensory environment with wind, waves, rolling pebbles and sea plants. Within this "story world" they enacted their own sequence of events stimulated by the original tale.

3   In another school, with a tradition of using story for drama, an unusual choice for lower juniors was *Hamlet* – but treated loosely as a "murder play". The children's enjoyment and creative satisfaction showed most clearly in the scope they were given to build their own ideas into the drama. A procession with drums and solemn music in which all took part gave a feeling of courtly dignity. Later, movement and interaction combined naturally as the class created a swirling mist through which a ghost appeared and brought alarm to the castle guards. The exchanges between guards outside on a cold night were stimulated and reinforced by a feast being held inside with entertainment and revelry. The question of story choice is often challenging for a teacher and *Hamlet* is perhaps surprising material, but its use in this school has to be considered against a wide experience of drama activity enjoyed by children throughout the five to eleven age range. As a result they have a well developed dramatic maturity.

4   Some second year juniors built drama round the story of *Pocahontas* and created a tribal culture to explore. They established a hierarchy of chief, medicine man and braves ranked by one, two or three feathers. Ceremonies were devised in discussion for occurrences like a brave's initiation and totem offerings with rules and procedures to be followed. The conflict element came largely from the arrival of white settlers and the ensuing confrontation. Lengthy arguments developed over rights, attitudes and strategies to be adopted, culminating in the decision of the settlers to dam the Indians' water supply. The example illustrates how similar dramatic material – in this case Indians and settlers, often recurs throughout the age range but is handled with increasing dramatic competence. Pocahontas as a story served simply to introduce a basic theme, stimulate interest and provide something of a background for children's own drama making.

5   Third year juniors in an S.P.A. school used the story of *The Burghers of Calais* as a flexible framework for improvisation and it became an experience of community life in hazardous circumstances. Early discussions established "siege rules" under which the city was to be governed, and allocated meaningful roles. Tension, events, issues and interaction grew from this community experience and provided

their own fabric of sequence. Research during the drama fed in essential knowledge and a number of outcomes found expression in art, craft and varied writing.

The total work provides a useful illustration of how traditional stories became children's own dramatic themes within which a variety of events were possible. Drama, unlike the story, is not finished and polished but may develop beyond the actions of the written page. It is then more than a narrative and need never be envisaged as merely retelling story because it goes further and deals at first hand with actions, commitments and consequences, constantly moving and throwing up fresh issues for consideration.

One of the few stories told and read throughout the five to eleven age range is that of the Nativity, a narrative account often assuming a ritual significance with content closely shaped and actors assuming prescribed stances. Nevertheless, because several schools encouraged children to enter the story situation dramatically at their own level of understanding and allowed flexibility in how they shaped and explored a group recreation, some illustration of how different age groups responded to drama through story is possible. The significance of a "received pattern" within which we work referred to earlier was again evident in the involvement and activities of younger infants. They had heard the story from their teacher and in the corridor arranged a spacious "stable". The language was flexible because the story had been told rather than read on this occasion. Consequently, they faithfully kept to the shape of events and used their own language.

Angel	Don't put the baby's face in the straw.
Mary	He's all right there.
Angel to King	Who said you could come in?
1st King	Well, we knew where he was. We followed a star.
2nd King	I want to see the baby. Ah, gutzee, gutzee, gutzee.
1st King	Moo, moo. I'm making the cow say hello.
3rd King	I can't see.
1st King	I hope you have a nice time.
1st Shepherd	I know how to do it.

2nd Shepherd   We can't stay. We've got to go to our work.

Mary   You haven't stayed very long. Don't lift him up.

Perhaps we need to ask if the language that creates and extends
experience in story for the youngest infants is always conducive to the
dramatic process when it is read, or whether drama is better served by
a teacher's spoken account. In several schools the view was expressed
that storybook language can imprison even young junior children
when they dramatise verbally but earlier examples in the report make
it evident that where a drama tradition is established, discussion
encouraged and children allowed initiative, the language of an author
can enrich the process. Even so, there are many occasions when
teachers prefer to narrate their own version.

The ability to work flexibly within the Nativity framework was
demonstrated by a class of seven year olds in a school where they have
many opportunities for drama ventures. In their recreation of the story
Mary was questioned by the village women about the angel's visit and
the practicalities of moving to another town, the menfolk worked in
discussion and mime on recognisable occupations, shepherds debated
what the risks to their sheep would be if they were left unattended and
Herod's attendants danced for the wise men. The class teacher had
given an overall structure to the drama, notably through a class ballad
which involved children in much incidental work on rhyming words
and a discipline of composing lines to match the chosen rhythm.
Verses and chorus were sung to connect story sequences and added to
the shape and enjoyment of the drama which was developed over a
period of weeks. Part of the ballad is given here:

They travelled on the dusty road
Joseph walked and Mary rode.

They went down to Bethlehem town
When they got there, no where to spare

The only room was in a stable
Jesus was born, laid in a cradle.

King Herod sent a regiment
To find and bring the Baby King

Mary Joseph and the Babe
Ran to Egypt and were safe.

Given opportunity, the ability to improvise within a story structure develops progressively as children move through the junior years and by their tenth year they may show convincing evidence of maturing dramatic originality.

One such age group again using the Nativity framework was challenged by their teacher to assume appropriate roles and decide how the story might have developed had they been involved themselves. The passive role of Herod in the narrative was criticised and he consequently became a more active menace during enactment, obliging the wise men to devise a subterfuge by which he could be detained until Mary and Joseph escaped. Afterwards the teacher explained that he challenged his children to look at issues through the eyes of particular characters.

How far children are aware of character in drama helps the teacher assess their dramatic maturation. The interest in characters and their relationships is one of the major reasons why story appeals so greatly, allowing children to combine an outward looking interest in people and their situations with an inner exploration of themselves as developing personalities seeking their own control of events. Younger children are usually more interested in the actions of people; it is what they do to each other that is important. As they move upwards through the age range, however, concern in what people are like grows, how they behave in varying situations and the motives behind their actions. By providing a wealth of characters for role-taking, opportunity to actively explore the situations and issues which confront them, and constructive freedom to develop or re-shape when the dramatic process requires it, story represents a basic resource for both content and maturation in drama.

References

A Language for Life (Bullock Report), H.M.S.O. 1975.
Schools Council Project, Communication Skills in Early Childhood, Joan Tough.
The Effects of Socio-Dramatic Play on Disadvantaged Pre-School Children, Sara Smilanksy, Wiley 1968.
Child Drama and Its Value in Education, Peter Slade, E.D.A. 1966.
Language, English & The Curriculum (Schools Council Programme in Linguistics), Peter Doughty, Edward Arnold 1974.
The Foundations of Language, Andrew Wilkinson, O.U.P. 1971.
The Speaker (Talking & Writing), James Britton, Methuen 1973.

Stages of Progression in English (Talking & Writing), Nancy Martin, Ed. Britton, Methuen 1973.

Why Write? (Schools Council Writing Across the Curriculum Project), N. Martin, P. Medway, H. Smith and P. Darcy, Schools Council/London University Institute of Education.

Drama. What is Happening, J. Moffett, N.C.T.E. 1967.

The Linguistic Sciences & Language Teaching, M.A.K. Halliday, A. McIntosh, P. Stevens, Longmans 1970.

Stories in the Classroom, Margaret Spencer (Children Using Language), Ed. A. Jones and J. Mulford, O.U.P. 1971.

Integration

What is meant by integration?

When the class teacher whose infants improvised and developed drama based upon *Hansel and Gretel* (page 136) later discussed the work she referred to a flow diagram drawn up by herself which outlined a broad integration of normal class activities feeding into and from drama. In addition to language stimulated by children's dramatic involvement these included music making, chiefly through percussion, a wide range of ideas expressed in art and craft, stories, poems, songs, movement, vocabulary and rhythmic chants. It was quite clear that drama did not exist here as an isolated activity but formed an integral part of the schools' total learning approach, in which its power to draw together different areas of the curriculum was especially valued.

Many of the other survey schools also maintained that drama has an integrative force with distinctive educational advantages, though often their views indicated differing conceptions of what was meant by "integration" and the kinds of objectives achieved through it. A few examples will illustrate the point. Some stated that drama is an activity in its own right which can draw from any source, but may be used more specifically to promote insights within a given area of the curriculum, e.g. history.

In one teacher's words, "It lets children make more sense of history and geography by allowing them to experience in drama the integration of facts and their own present circumstances". There is a difference though between these views and the earlier stress on curriculum integration outlined by an infants school staff and echoed by a primary school headmaster who thought the day of the drama lesson with its activity regarded as separate and complete in itself was passing quickly away, to be replaced by recognition that drama tied the curriculum together, motivated learning in many different areas and broke down unnecessary subject boundaries.

Essentially the basic distinction between the integration referred to in these examples lies in the fact that two kinds of integration are being referred to and sought as goals. One is concerned with the fusing of knowledge and experience within the actual drama process; the other reflects a desire to offer children motivational and learning scope through a broad and relatively undifferentiated school curriculum. The two aspects are important to education and are often closely related in a school's approach to drama – but they represent integration at different levels.

There is a third distinction necessary when schools refer to group integration through drama, which also has two levels. Firstly, the integration that occurs when a group develops its own sense of awareness, identity and attitudes as a result of dramatic events, and secondly, the social integration of children as ordinary school pupils when they work together in a disciplined and responsible manner to build up a dramatic enterprise or develop subsequent outcomes. Again both aspects are important though the latter goal is stressed more strongly by teachers.

In examining these views an important feature stands out; the extent to which teachers agree in acknowledging that drama has an integrative capacity. How effectively and in what manner this functions and is encouraged in particular circumstances varies with their view of how children learn; whether the school's approach is enquiry based; and the organisation of drama activities. Where these allow drama to exercise its integrative potential, the outcomes often provide significant indicators for assessing the quality of children's experience and learning.

Not all teachers agree that the integrative functions of drama need to be stressed and maintain that its integrity as an art form is sufficient justification for its educational acceptance. But this is to deny its full place in the learning process and some part of its own nature. Certainly it is a creative art in its own right but it is also an activity that engenders critical and constructive thought, comparisons, judgments and discriminations. Within a drama framework many problems may be posed and solutions sought but neither problem nor solutions exist in an experiential vacuum; they are the result of what is brought to the drama and what happens there. As such, drama exists as a frame of reference as well as a framework for activity.

There is, of course, a close connection between the integration fostered by drama and the relationships it helps to forge within both curriculum and school. Several headteachers referred to how it "draws the school together", and others to "the way drama links school and parents". These are distinctive functions and need to be considered separately from the integrative processes outlined.

Some basic questions

In this section, the survey examines how schools make use of the integrative power of drama to advance their own educational purposes and some useful focal points are provided by several basic questions.

1 How effectively does drama, in practice, draw on the potential contribution offered by many areas of the curriculum and by stimulating a wide range of outcomes act as a curricular integrating force?

2 Children's involvement in drama offers them a unique means of "being and doing" in which material from many sources may be integrated within the drama process. Does this add anything important to children's learning?

3 How far may this same integrative experience with its learning aspects serve a particular sector of the curriculum and offer a means to explore responses to situations, ideas, acts and consequences in areas like history?

4 How is drama used as a focal point itself for project and thematic work?

5 Are there changing needs in this area as children grow and mature?

6 How does it serve to foster interrelationships in schools?

Reference was made earlier to the considerable variation in drama practice and approaches observed during the survey. These differences were reflected in the language challenge offered to children and not surprisingly they also influenced the integrative aspects of drama and their potential power to help children experience and learn. It is essential to be sure of what we are seeking at both the real level of co-operative endeavour and the imaginative level of dramatic involvement. If social integration seems important, and no drama will go far without it, development can only come through group challenges and situations where children are obliged to sort themselves out and observe certain conventions. They need the scope for initiative, sensible discussion, tolerance, and practice in a whole range of decision making activities. When the six year old infants creating their own witch drama worked as group or class to suggest and develop ideas they had this scope; they also had basic material which was appropriate and satisfying.

To seek a level of integration within drama that encourages quality of experience, we must know how much is offered to children through the basic material, in addition to what they bring as personal experience. We shall want them to use all their knowledge and experience to support their imagination, consolidate their understanding, to ask questions, relate to others through drama, implement decisions and ideas, shape, build and appraise. Within this kind of framework, drama will integrate not only other areas of the curriculum but also personal and group learning. But the same reservation applies and is borne out by the survey observations; where teachers are conscious of the drama they offer children and how far it satisfies abilities and appetites in their own school circumstances, they are more able to realise the potential development inherent in the drama process.

Perhaps because in infants schools the curriculum is often based upon an integrative approach anyway, few problems result from subject boundaries, though some schools stress more than others how effectively drama unites the curriculam. The most significant differences lie in the actual drama work and the possibilities available. Both *Hansel and Gretel* and the Indian theme examined in the language section, were built up by six or seven year old infants. In each there was the beginning of a dramatic group identity and response to the drama concerns which enhanced development. Furthermore, the activities revealed how varied elements feeding into the drama may fuse and enhance children's awareness and understanding. In this sense both fantasy themes and reality contribute to learning. Third year juniors in a small village school still remembered their work of the previous term when they had created a world of "Gedunks", peculiar creatures with strange characteristics. Essentially, however, their challenge was that of building a community. They needed to establish rules, patterns of behaviour and work tasks, using analogy from their own world of experience and examining alternatives before deciding which should be adopted. The possibilities for integration of learning and experience are apparent and in favourable conditions many curricular areas could be brought together to support the process. In general, however, this seems to require a more conscious effort on the part of junior teachers and schools except where the possibilities of drama and belief in an integrated curriculum exist together.

Some middle schools face problems here resulting from curricular specialism which can inhibit the full use of resources and broad approaches to drama work. This was a point emphasised by one or two specialist teachers of drama who experienced such limitations and consequently were obliged to plan a more independent drama programme. On the other hand, not all middle schools in the survey sample were similarly affected and several encouraged thematic approaches that fostered integration. One example has already been referred to; the "cave disaster" forming part of a drama theme centred on "Underground Exploration". The same school also used "Routes" for drawing together material on explorers, adventurers and all who travel, recreating chosen experiences in drama and drawing freely from all sources. More specific examples from schools will illustrate fuller appreciation of dramatic integration in practice.

Example 1

This First School is situated in an industrial urban environment and occupies buildings originally intended for older children. However, careful adaptation has provided pleasant conditions in which the younger age groups can work effectively. The school has a strong tradition of integrated thematic work in which drama and literature are recognised as vital agents and they are both seen as part of the same spectrum. Literature is not regarded solely as a story or theme for working upon but essentially as enrichment, feeding drama through its capacity to relate the world of children to that explored in the theme. The headmaster stressed the "point of contact" often provided by analogy from story or poem that establishes a relationship between reality and thematic exploration. Within the framework offered by the theme certain areas of subject matter are explored more fully to achieve "heightened awareness and meaningful experience". The framework is always kept flexible so that both teacher and children can choose, though the headmaster stressed his belief that part of a teacher's role is to lead children towards significant areas of experience while recognising their specific level of interests. Within the age range of his own school (five to nine years) great value is placed upon encouraging imagination but intensity of concentration is also regarded as a key factor together with an effective movement vocabulary. The belief is that in the earlier years a movement-centred approach will eventually bring a greater quality to drama.

Work done earlier in the term illustrated the school's approach when children had been looking at early fairs and the use of animals as entertainment. Subsequent discussion led to exploration of bull dances and dancers in movement based upon the rituals of Knossos and drawing upon several stories to feed in awareness and establish "points of contact". From their drama the children returned to the classroom where they continued with associated painting, or writing, and consolidated experience of the past with understanding of the present.

The school was currently developing a medieval theme and groups of eight year old children came into the hall for drama activities. Approximately seventy children were involved but three teachers shared the work. First the groups "warmed up" through a variety of movement exercises to increase concentration and sensitivity. A monastery situation was then introduced as part of the children's exploration of medieval life and they assumed appropriate roles. Hall columns became "cloisters" and silence, solemnity and the religious atmosphere of monastic life were reflected in the movements and activities of the "monks". A contrasting approach followed, centred upon the experience of being punished in the stocks with its physical restriction and torments from onlookers.

In another group the preparation of a giant pie for consumption during a medieval banquet formed the basis for movement and language activity. There was much discussion about kitchen roles and the tasks to be performed before ideas were put into practice. Sub groups undertook specialised tasks accompanied by further discussion, mime and movement, until the pie was eventually baked. Children in all groups showed a commitment to what was asked of them and it was obvious that they were familiar with movement challenges and discussions.

In the classrooms they continued with research and related activities feeding from and into the central theme. A large, carefully composed proclamation inviting the school to a medieval feast had been carried round to each class by children dressed in hats and tabards of the period. At each stopping point they played a piece of medieval music on their recorders and read out the proclamation and invited letters of acceptance. On one classroom wall written reactions from children sniffing and tasting varied spices formed part of a display which included illuminated art work, spinning and weaving artefacts, maps and plans of monasteries, knights banners, helmets and weapons. At a central point the school had set up a resource collection of books, pictures and useful objects from which children could borrow what they required. The whole approach reflected a vitality of learning and a global curricular involvement.

Some of the children's writing reflected imagery and awareness evoked in drama and discussion.

Silence in the Monastery

The monastery was so quiet I could have heard a ghost creeping beside me.

So quiet I could hear the sound of a lord in the Middle Ages.

Laughing heartily.

It was so quiet there I could hear the sounds of the whole world whirling round the sun.

Poaching in the Forest

Creeping in the Forest
Tip toeing stealthily
Hiding behind the trees
Where nobody will see you.

You are going fast as the wind
Somebody is here,
Stop dead.
The dull bushes hide you
In the dark night.

Moving swiftly from tree to tree
The leaves are crisp
And go crunch, crunch
The shadows are creepy
And the poaching is done.

A human body
A human man
Poaching in the Forest
A rustle and a crack
Why do you make a sound?

Clearly the school has a well defined rationale which underpins the approaches illustrated here and explains the vigour and quality of much that is attempted and achieved. The approaches to drama match the emphasis on movement and the goals sought from it; and one can discern how it serves the process of integration within the school's thematic structures. Obviously, however, the kinds of structures within which we ask children to work on drama differ in the demands and possibilities they offer for learning and each has implications that need to be recognised in any formulation of goals and programme planning.

Example 2

In contrast to the first example, this open plan junior school is relatively new and serves a large village on the outskirts of an extensive conurbation. The intake is drawn from varied social backgrounds. Work observed here provided an outstanding example of drama based upon an integrated curricular approach. A strong tradition of drama has been established and children work productively on group and class improvisations or a range of outcomes involving research, writing, music, art and craft, indeed on anything that is grist to their dramatic mill. The existence of a drama tradition has ensured that those disciplines and capacities essential to co-operative enterprise are strong. These include application to the task in hand, initiative and confidence to participate fully in discussion or verbal interaction, the consideration and appraisal of suggestions, ability in decision making and consciousness of dramatic shape and possibilities. In short, a creative and critical competence fostered through drama and exercised in a school which supports the development of these qualities in children.

Two year-groups, third and fourth year juniors, worked upon a drama theme concerned with the conquest of the Aztec people by Cortez and his Spaniards, though second year juniors were also involved. At times, group work was appropriate while on other occasions up to thirty children would work together. From the beginning a resource area was set up within the school where relevant books, pictures and information sheets could be located; these included books borrowed from libraries and contained a wealth of challenging reading for junior children. At the same time work began on two strands of the drama; preparations for the Spanish voyage were explored through discussion and movement, chiefly the loading and rigging of a contemporary vessel; and group improvisations based upon aspects of Aztec life. Both activities reflected knowledge drawn from research, the ship loading group having prepared a list of weapons and supplies for shipment to Mexico, while improvisations drew heavily upon facts gleaned from a variety of reading. This was part of the dramatic process considered important by the school. The mutual feed-back between the on-going drama and its supportive research meant that "finding out" activities were increasingly motivated and directed by children's involvement in direct experience which created a need for specific background information.

One small group explored the justice meted out by the Aztec market courts and set up their own situation in which a thief was caught.

Seller	Buy my fruit, fresh fruit, good fruit.
Seller	You want something?
Thief	No not really.
Seller	Hey, you took something from there.
Thief	I did not.
Byestander	You did. I saw you with my own eyes.
Seller	You'll go before the priest then. (*Gong*)
Priest	What is this man on a charge for?
Seller	Stealing from my stall.
Byestander	Fruit.
Priest	Did you?
Thief	No.
Seller	He did, he was seen.
Priest	Did you steal?
Thief	Yes I did. I need to keep my family.
Priest	Does he have any family?
Guard	No.
Thief	I need to keep my relatives, my aunt.
Guard	He has no aunt.
Thief	Well, alright, she's dead but I have to keep myself somehow. Don't I?
Priest	Stealing is wrong. You know that so why did you do it then?
Thief	Well I have to keep myself from starving.
Priest	Well I know a place where you won't starve. Behind the line. Ten days.

Head	Well what did you think of that?
Guard	The fruit seller didn't seem real. She should have been more excited when the fruit was stolen. Shouting more about it.
Seller	And he should have been resisting when they wanted to take him to the high priest. He wouldn't want to stand behind the line (Aztec punishment).
Head	What's special about the market courts? Something about them?
Priest	They have guards who go round to investigate?
Head	What about you? What is your job?
Priest	Well, I'm the High Priest. I have to be different. I decide like a modern judge – I can put them behind the line

A further example illustrating how the process brought children and their literature together, followed development of initial improvisation to a point where Cortez and his men first encountered the American coastal Indians. The drama quickly revealed that certain basic cultural facts were needed to establish a believable tribal community and after discussion the following list was drawn up and displayed.

What were their occupations?
What sort of names they had?
Which gods were worshipped?
What sort of punishments were given?
How were the reed boats made?
How was water carried?
What metals and dyes were used?
How they slept?
How were pots made and baked?

One teacher remarked at this stage "Once they realise they don't know something, they go readily to the books. It's not until you're discussing later with them that you realise what a depth of knowledge some of them have gained."

Research took children into historical and geographical background but it also related to science and invention. The cannon and firearms of the period were carefully studied and reproduced in drawing, so was

the armour used by the Spaniards. Discussion of these drama-based
outcomes was encouraged and here a group of children consider brain
surgery and effect of altitude.

> The Aztecs were good at brain surgery but didn't know how to
> travel.
>
> Yes, they used to fit gold or silver plates when there was a bad
> accident.
>
> But they didn't have the things they had to have to travel.
>
> Anyway brain surgery is more important than travel.
>
> Yes, but they had the equipment to do brain surgery. They should
> have had equipment to do a simple thing like travel.

Music was also explored using knowledge of probable rhythms and
sounds gained from various sources to compose original pieces. Words
were added to some of these and they became evocative songs.

Art and craft activities accompanied the evolution of the drama,
notably some striking screen prints on fabric prepared by children
working from Aztec designs, a wide range of artefacts made from a
variety of materials and collages illustrating scenes of Aztec life.
Second year juniors worked on two craft assignments which led
directly into other drama-related forms. Initially, they constructed
from paper and chicken wire a group of large hobby horse heads to
represent the animals taken to Mexico by Cortez, and subsequently,
word music was composed based upon a selection of verbs describing
horse movements. Later they became involved in giving form and
substance to the dream of Montezuma (Aztec Emperor) in which a
number of symbolic monsters appear. From their conception of these
creatures created in craft activities, the group then built up a distinctive
and evocative vocabulary for each monster, and used this as a basis to
begin movement enactment of the dreams. The word lists included:
flounder, lumpish, massive, ponderous, block, blunder, weighty, clod,
cumbersome, grope, glide, drift, hover, poised, grand, swoop, skim,
graceful, majestic. These words were explored in movement, initially
by groups working independently to build up their own conceptions.
Guidance at this stage was crystallised in their teacher's advice,
"Think of a word in the list, say it, and let it go right down to your
fingertips".

With most forms of school learning children follow a programme of
study in a given subject through a building up process and systematic

progression, using the facts or experience previously undergone to provide new meaning and insight. So does drama, of course, in many important respects, but it may also provide a non-linear experience when children encounter several layers of information, attitudes and feeling on a more integrated and immediate level. During the development of the Cortez-Montezuma theme this was apparent at several points; the challenge to improvise on reactions to Montezuma's capitulation provided one group with an awareness of the layers they had absorbed and were having to accommodate. Part of their discussion serves as an example:

Teacher   What sort of things will you say about him?

               That's the trouble, we can't be sure.

               We don't ever say bad things about him.

               And if we did someone would tell him.

               If we are invaded we wouldn't have much freedom and we'd have to pay taxes.

               Or be slaves to work for them.

               We might have to worship their god.

Teacher   Would that be important to the Aztecs?

               Oh, yes, because we believed that if enemies destroyed our idols and things, the gods would be angry and punish us.

               We wouldn't be allowed to sacrifice to the gods and would get very worried about it.

Teacher   Is Montezuma concerned about his gods and the effect this will have?

               Well, he thought Cortez was a god anyway.

               He was slightly afraid of him.

               He didn't want to harm him for fear of revenge.

Teacher   So that was the undoing of the whole thing – he was a god too?

               Yes, we could have had him when he first landed.

               If we went to war with them they're maybe more powerful than us so we'd make friends and not be beaten.

	We wouldn't normally give in.
Head	Would you be able to criticise Montezuma?
	No.
	He's not to be even looked at. Lower our eyes.
Teacher	So what has happened to make you feel critical?
	Well, the ball game was probably the start. He lost the ball game and there's been other omens.

These children are bringing to their drama a developing awareness of events, language, ritual, belief and power. Many cultural areas had been explored and discussed, including the superstitions of the Aztecs and how we are influenced by similar fears today, the way they made decisions, and how their ideas of authority and justice contrasted with present day conceptions. They knew in this discussion what they would like to do as fighting warriors or modern soldiers, but they were immersed in a culture whose peculiarities had to be explored in relation to their own present and Aztec selves within the global and synthesising process of drama. Their discussion indicates one point of entry, but they have gone further because they discuss in role terms. The emphasis is not upon the Aztecs only, it is "we" who are facing the problem and accommodating to several layers of awareness and meaning simultaneously.

A purposive role in drama often seems to foster significant integrative learning that may be apparent during interaction and discussion or show up later in children's writing. This need not be a "major" role: the essence lies in giving every child a base from which to operate and tangible relationships which bind all roles together in the common endeavours of the drama. So when some of Andrew's observations on his role as Cortez are examined from the viewpoint of integrative learning, it is useful to remember that he has developed as one member in a group enterprise.

Myself as Cortez – Andrew

Teacher	What else has helped you to know Cortez?
	In the acting we did, where the other men came up and said the ships were sinking and I looked surprised but I knew all the time. I was a bit sly then, a sly man.
Teacher	Have you built up a picture of him as you've gone along?

Yes, it's a big jumble in my mind.

Teacher   You mean you haven't got him sorted out yet?

Well, I know a lot about him but when I'm acting I sort out when he's sly. When I act him, I know.

Teacher   Cortez was a leader. You'd need to know a lot about people for that?

Yes, he had to be clever or people would outwit you. I outwitted them – when the deserters wanted to go back.

Teacher   How far has drama helped you to understand him?

A lot. Say a person came in who hadn't been doing much, just writing and had lessons and came in here and wanted a competition with me about how Cortez was; or tell more about the information, not what he did but what he was like inside, I don't think they could do as much as I could.

Significantly perhaps, at one point in this discussion, Andrew comments:

"You can't do it sitting down. You can't get the feeling of what you're going to say."

Clearly reflected in this discussion is the role awareness and maturation developed during the drama process. Andrew has come to know Cortez so well that he can speculate on his reaction to hypothetical events. But there is something much more fundamental and important here, implicit in the whole content of his observations and explicit in at least several of his statements. He acknowledges two forms of knowing; one derived from his reading and general research, the other springing from being Cortez in the drama itself, of having experienced the significance of his role within a dramatic context which drew upon researched facts as part of the basic raw material and breathed life into their dry bones.

His drama has been a discovery process and remains an instrument of enquiry while still providing an art form that allows human actions and situations to be recreated, experienced and appraised. A dramatic journey through the sixteenth century world of Spanish conquests has encouraged a deeper level of intellectual life and ability, integrated as it is here with feeling and values. Very often written outcomes reflect the same "drawing together" and indicate how children have grown through their drama towards informed attitudes and values. The poem on Gold reflects one child's development.

Gold

Gold, gold beautiful gold
How I love your shine
Gold, gold men crave your brightness
How I love your gold.

Gold, gold, people desire
People wanting more
Riches, riches, eager to find
Some selfish and unkind.

Gold, gold, men love you gold,
They love your sparkling light.
Gold, gold, you make men greedy
When you're in their sight.

Men, men, you greedy men
Digging for your gold
Men, men, you greedy men
Praying to your gold.

An important reference used by the children was a translation of the journal kept by Bernal Diaz who accompanied Cortez on the expedition. Though only one of many books feeding the drama, its detail and style seemed to influence them a good deal and it was absorbed into their own creative activity. Sometimes echoes could be heard in spoken language, for example, when messengers brought the first news that Spaniards had landed.

Terrible things are going to happen.
Strangers have come to our coast.
Yes, men seem to rise from monsters' backs
What will happen to us? What shall we do?
Have the gods returned?

All the work outlined here represents a sampling of the total activity which was always fluid as ideas were framed, implemented or discarded and the levels of children's awareness and understanding steadily increased. Discussions with staff provided some useful indicators to their approaches and assessment of developments. The children worked at first on more general aspects like the ship loading, etc. but created more specific situations as the drama built up. This allowed experience to be deepened, character to be more sharply defined and response to each other and the group strengthened. Thus the two forms of group integration were fostered; situations like the creation of an Indian settlement, or a planned mutiny united children at the real level of co-operative endeavour and encouraged tolerance, discipline and critical appraisal, while they also established a dramatic group identity based upon who they were and what was happening in the drama.

Emphasis was firmly placed on the experience being "first hand", with children sharing in the development as a result of their involvement. Nevertheless, when children are placed in historical situations, far removed from present day circumstances, they must have information about time and place even though many of the concerns are fundamental to all people. How far can children go without this necessary feeding? Certainly it must be seen as one of the school's tasks to provide the raw material from which understanding and development can grow. When children become recognisable people in drama, their research feeds in the specific information they know is needed; their role develops and so does the drama itself.

Language is a prime facilitating agent throughout the process and as a result develops in varied ways through discussion at different levels and in the verbal give and take of dramatic interaction. In all this, teacher expectation and trust is important, summarised perhaps in the words of one teacher, "I don't think I'm good at drama. But such good comes from it and I enjoy the working relationship with the children that it gives and the things we can look at. You let children go on with their ideas and you know it's moving away from you. But you wait for it to 'gel' and it goes."

Example 3

In the previous school, curricular, dramatic and social integration involved the total resources available but this example looks at one teacher working relatively independently in an older junior school serving a mining area. She regards drama as a means of learning and integration, believing in its capacity to provide deeper understanding by "living through" experiences she looks for situations which lead to the stimulation of ideas, sympathetic understanding, expression of feeling and fruitful discussion. Much of this she believes is synthesised within the language of drama and for that reason language and learning mutually benefit. Drama has potential here because it provides a variety of situations and circumstances for children within which they often show unsuspected abilities and become capable of deep involvement. Yet it always remains an enjoyable activity with strong motivation. Though the example of her work here is historical, she offers children a wide range of dramatic activities throughout the year and is just as likely to use story, poetry or current events as a basis for improvisation.

The drama example involved approximately twenty eight children for weekly lessons and developed from a study of Victorian history being undertaken in the classroom. During preliminary discussion of long working hours and poor conditions one girl said, "I would have gone on strike, I wouldn't have worked under those conditions", to which the teacher replied, "I wonder what would have happened if people had decided to strike in those days?" From this question came the decision to create a Victorian cotton factory and explore conditions there.

At this stage the class teacher formulated her goals for the drama activity.

1   To involve all the children (very mixed ability) in the drama.

2   To develop, clarify and extend their knowledge of life and factory conditions in this period of time.

3   To attempt to help children realise that when people do attempt to strike, many situations arise that will not have been thought through before and that only when they are actually in the situations will they realise and understand more fully and see the consequences of actions.

4   To attempt to introduce some idea of tolerance, compromise and responsibility towards others.

5   To encourage all children to communicate with each other and by allowing them to experience different situations and use language more effectively.

All the children were quickly involved in the drama, establishing a factory and work patterns. They discussed arrangements and implemented decisions with their teacher acting as guide. Very soon a dramatic atmosphere was created with cruel, autocratic owners provoking resentment in tired and underpaid workers which led directly to a clash of interests.

Strike Leader	I say we go on strike. Are you all with me?
Worker	What about our families? I have six children.
Strike Leader	Never mind your family – we all have families, but if we don't stand together we'll never get anything better. So come on follow me. (*They pick up their placards and march – chanting*)
All	Better conditions and more pay.
Owner	Stop! What do you want – come on tell me.
A Leader	We want better conditions in this factory. Look at it – it's filthy and the machines are dangerous. People are hurt every day. Why Mary lost a finger only yesterday. Not that that would worry you.
Owner	New machines cost money.
Worker	Yes, we know that – but you've got plenty and if you don't do something about it you're losing us.
Owner	Right – I can get better people than you and plenty of them. Go.
Leader	Well, we might stay if you give us 3 pennies more a day.
Owner	Three pennies more – I can't afford that.
Other Owner	Now if you want better conditions you draw them out and show them to us and then we'll see what we can do about them.
Strike Leader	We haven't got brains to do that – we can't write it out for you, but we'll tell you – won't we lads?
Workers	Yes, yes, we'll tell him.
Owner	Well go home and think about it and we might be able to sort something out tomorrow.
Strike Leader	Never mind you might – you will do something or we're out. Come on lads.

Support was given throughout by the class teacher when she felt the children needed it. Essentially she wanted to ensure that everyone was

159

involved in some way and that the drama challenged the abilities of children. Within fairly short-term drama situations (the theme lasted only a few weeks), this teacher found it helpful to focus attention on key aspects and was ready to support children if their role demands became heavy. She was willing to participate in role herself but not to carry the drama, just doing enough to encourage the flow of language and ideas. When discussion was necessary she took a key role and attempted to stimulate reflection on the drama events and issues.

Teacher	Now it looks like a deadlock. I wonder how this can ever be resolved?
Worker	They just have to give us better machines and more money.
Owner	But we haven't got any more money.
Teacher	We are really making very little progress in this dispute. What do you think is wrong with these negotiations?
Strike Leader	They (the owners) are just plain stubborn.
Owner	So are you.
Teacher	Well I think that you are going to be out of a job and you are going to be without workers unless you find a solution, quickly. Anyone else got any ideas about this deadlock?
Girl	Why we'll all have to give a bit – that's all.
Teacher	Yes, I'm sure you are right. We often have to give a little bit and it's hard, but let's see if it would work. Go and discuss the situation in your two groups (owners and workers) and then we'll have a meeting in the factory at 7 o'clock tomorrow morning.

Research aided the drama and reference books were used to build up a factual basis, so that the story of the Tolpuddle Martyrs who were transported to Australia proved both relevant and stimulating. The teacher regarded this aspect of the work as important who actively researched with her class and encouraged them to seek out appropriate material. She hoped that within the integrative framework offered by dramatisation a deeper understanding would evolve, taking children beyond the insights gleaned from a normal history lesson or when they looked at pictures of Victorian workers.

Writing was an integral part of her approach and though the opportunities for extensive writing are more limited when the theme is short-term and restricted by organisational constraints, a dramatic content and flavour was already beginning to characterise written expression and illuminate aspects of learning derived from the drama experience.

A Victorian Factory Worker. The country is in a terrible state and it is our fault say the people who have tea with Queen Victoria. What do they know about it? It's all very well for them to say these things, but how about us working for what? Why for four pennies a day! I have six mouths to feed in my house and I work thirteen hours for those four pennies – without any rest. The overseers watch us and bad language is often thrown at us and sometimes we are whipped. But do we mind? Oh no, we don't have to mind because we have no brains or we would be somewhere else. For us it is all toil, so what can we do? We'll go on strike and ask for more pay and better conditions. There must be better conditions in the factory. Why only yesterday there was an accident – I work a weaving machine and two children, who only get two pennies for picking up the fluff that comes off the thread, got caught in the machinery and were badly hurt. One of them will probably die and the other will be a cripple for life. Oh, who knows, perhaps one day in the future, life in the factories will be as we want it to be – perhaps when everybody considers everybody else – perhaps when the bosses care.

Eventually desperation led to theft from the owners, imprisonment for some workers who would not compromise and the destruction of their factory. Discussion at this stage revealed the teacher attempting to lead her class towards an appreciation of consequence but perhaps they required more time in their drama before issues could be fully explored.

Teacher	Well, now you have lost the factory, you have lost your jobs and even worse, some people have suffered severe injuries in the fire. What do you think about the situation now?
Worker	I think we were stupid, we shouldn't have listened to them.
Worker	Oh, I don't know – they were doing their best.
Teacher	Do you think the situation could have been handled in a better way?

Worker	I think we should have had a vote on it.
Teacher	Yes, what does a vote allow you to do?
Girl	It lets you say what you think.
Teacher	Yes – it lets you speak for yourself – providing that you do think for yourself and are not influenced by the people near you. Do you think workers would burn down a factory today?
Class	No, they would know they would be out of a job. They would have more sense.
Teacher	What do you think they would do in this situation now?
Class	They would talk about it. They would talk to their Union and the Unions would talk with the bosses.
Teacher	And hope to reach an agreement or a compromise?
Class	Yes, maybe.

This example illustrates the tantalising choices often facing teachers and children in drama; how much time can be given for developing particular areas or approaches and which threads should be teased out. Here a good deal of the time was spent on evoking a factory atmosphere, where owners and workers could develop their own group identity and interests. The fluency of the verbal exchanges and the strength of views expressed, especially by the workers, illustrate how cohesive the two groups had become at the level of dramatic belief and identity. Underlying this achievement, and largely making it possible, was the social co-operation and integration which encouraged children to work together and take their drama forward. Afterwards the teacher referred to the many strands running through dramatic work and how some issues could have been developed. Time is always the enemy, particularly where drama opens up the factual background and allows exploration on a more human level. In these circumstances choice becomes important for both teacher and children, especially where curriculum boundaries impose constraints. Nevertheless, this example illustrates the capacity of drama to bring what is present and familiar into a meaningful relationship with the nineteenth century individual and social world.

The scope for curricular integration

Though many of the survey schools confirmed that drama has close links with the greater part of the curriculum it was a minority of the sample who seemed to consistently pursue curricular integration through drama. In practice, however, there is a good deal of variable or intermittent dramatic activity which fosters integration at the curriculum level in proportion to the stimulation and challenge offered by drama approaches and how far a school's learning organisation is kept flexible.

Where challenging drama coincides with real possibilities to exploit the outcome fully then its integrative strength is clearly seen. The examples illustrate how some schools approached the task of using drama for wider learning purposes and attempted to extend the benefits through a variety of related activities. All have in common a strong measure of motivation and an interest base that can take children from dramatic involvement to pursue research, writing, art, craft or music. In this sense the total drama process requires even more than Douglas Barnes' essential notebook and pencil; it needs the library, pictures and information sheets, paint, card, cloth and scissors, in fact a large part of the school's resources. The various examples clearly show that a view of drama restricted to hall activity is limiting and generally unnecessary. It is also important to stress the effectiveness of a two-way process where drama feeding other curricular activities strengthens children's commitment, belief and willingness to work constructively and sensibly in discussion or dramatic interaction. In other words, the links between drama and its wider curriculum outcomes can be dynamic and not merely a passive means to convenient follow-up activities.

Where schools are interested in the quality of activity and learning, any approach needs to be assessed in terms of how effectively drama functions in this respect. Are we looking simply for drama to assist in curricular integration or do we recognise that with the establishment of dynamic links the scope and quality offered by drama may be reflected in activities subsequently undertaken in class? When children are asked to enquire, then the purpose and focus – or perhaps just as important, the necessity involved, will crucially influence how they set about it, as well as the breadth and depth of their enquiries. If we wish children to write in any of the "dramatic" voices previously examined, they may find this difficult without an adequate drama base. Indeed whatever the activity, in whatever part of the curriculum, we cannot divorce the quality and range of outcome from how wisely a particular drama approach was chosen. Infants explored music possibilities to create an appropriate atmosphere and sound for their witch and her movements; juniors faced with communicating with Aztec Indians discovered how Aztec words were constructed and used this as the basis for their own interpretative "language", while children elsewhere delved into how nineteenth century law dealt with issues developing in their factory drama; a dying sailor on an ice-bound ship reflected in his "log" something of the tragedy that ended a promising venture. All these children had in common a supportive framework for curricular activity provided by approaches which recognised the nature of effective links between drama and its possible outcomes.

The last-mentioned example taken from a theme concerned with "Adventurers" (page 116), illustrates how some schools use drama as a focal point or process to relate activity and enquiry within a chosen framework structured by broader thematic interests. Not many schools in the survey used this broader thematic approach and those examples seen or discussed tended to serve the nine and eleven age groups. It is an approach that offers similar possibilities and challenges in terms of curricular integration to those created by more specific drama concerns like the exploration of a Victorian factory or Cortez and his Aztec conquest, but some teachers maintain that the potential range of material for children to work upon is often greater in practice. Others emphasise a need with their own children to shift the dramatic situation fairly frequently or stress how resources for research in one particular area may be inadequate to sustain detailed and prolonged activity. Certainly, broader themes do draw from and combine many concerns and may feed many interests. In one school the social, historical and geographical development of the neighbourhood had been recreated and explored through such a theme and had led to extensive activity right across the curriculum; in another "Routes" provided a focal point for drawing together contemporary and historical material which stimulated varied individual and group topic work within the theme. Productive work in schools indicates that alongside teaching ability in drama we need an awareness of its force as a global process with wider educational implications and opportunities.

Where does the "single situation" drama lesson stand here? Many teachers organise their drama in this way and the majority are interested in "follow up" possibilities; in fact the report has already noted several examples of language work with associated art which were outcomes from single dramatic situations. Drama created and explored within one lesson only can be and often is a satisfying experience and there is no reason why a range of related activities should not follow in the classroom, taking children into reading, writing and making. There are schools where this happens, but it has to be observed as a survey generalisation that the wealth and quality of outcomes resulting from extended work are not usually matched by "follow up" activities based upon single lesson approaches. Of course, children's age and maturation play a large part in determining what approaches a school will use and whereas many infants' teachers claim that single lessons are most appropriate for their classes, it becomes obvious as children grow up that most of them increasingly require, and can cope effectively with, the challenges and opportunities offered by extended themes. Getting the feel of dramatic shape, wanting to get under the skin of character, deeper interest in what motivates people and influences events, all contribute to a need for drama material in which these factors can be exercised and developed, leading as we noted earlier to more productive links with the curriculum generally. These are certainly considerations to influence junior and middle schools, but the extended work observed in some infants' classes suggests that here also children could profitably create and explore through longer-term drama themes, when conditions are appropriate.

Drama, history and geography

The examples show how drama is often linked with historical or geographical areas of knowledge and raises the question of how it serves children and the subject area itself. Probably the most important point to emphasise is that drama functions no differently in specialised concerns than it does throughout the whole curricular range. Whether we take an event in time, people in particular circumstances, the examination of a moral problem or interpretation of factual data, drama will illuminate and provide meaning within the context of human experience and response.

When teachers are asked why so much historical material is used for drama purposes, they often reply that it provides a means to "stretch" their children both intellectually and emotionally by creating certain situations in which new characters, events and issues must be encountered. On the one hand it widens the frame of reference for children when they meet new material and people, but it also means they must be historically discriminating to some extent in their drama venture. They face a challenge to organise an alternative and convincing world to their own but in doing so maintain significant points of comparison and thus relate the two. Not only does this allow children creative and exciting drama situations; it also is one means to enliven dry facts and through active experience make problems and issues easier to understand.

Things are alive in drama when the emphasis is on the discoveries made rather than mere implementation of factual knowledge to create a "received" world. Children working within such a dramatic framework require a knowledge and information to develop ideas and issues. This is usually confirmed by references to background knowledge and the degree of research undertaken when children become actively involved and need to know more.

One teacher discussed a dramatic project in history undertaken with lower juniors where the main aim was, "to explore the possibilities of using drama as an educational tool to teach historical concepts". Associated with this were various subsidiary aims which he outlined as:

1   To get children to really think deeply about decisions they had to make.

2   To learn to listen to other people's points of view and accept majority decisions.

3   To introduce the idea of drama as a way of exploring living so that children had to be real people in real situations. People with whom they could identify.

4   To give children a sense of satisfaction and achievement.

The theme was chiefly concerned with one of the early industrial lords and his influence on a major city and its surrounding countryside. Within this framework the children were asked to explore many factual areas; the contrast between life styles of rich and poor; what life was like in the nineteenth century countryside; how one man's inventions could create a factory system and change a city.

It was not a case, however, of teaching facts then consolidating them through drama. Instead it was hoped that children would build the "story" and discover a need for information, allowing them to create situations where people had contemporary problems and desires. So

166

when work began on building up a village community and life
tentative and exploratory, gradually adding detail and feeding
and into research, writing, making and discussion. Similarly, w
move to the city when country jobs were lost, time was taken to
an urban and factory atmosphere which grew as detail fed shap
interaction.

This maturing historical and dramatic sense was also seen in the work
of those ten year old children whose Aztec theme was outlined earlier.
The warriors musing upon the idea of criticising their Emperor,
accepted the cultural constraints and hypothesised within an
appropriate perspective in role, but they also posed the problem as
twentieth century boys with a contemporary viewpoint, apparently
recognising the distance between their world and the sixteenth century
and having some consciousness as observers. Thus the poem on Gold
with its condemnatory overtones reflects the disapproval, more
explicitly expressed in discussion, that a civilisation should have been
destroyed so ruthlessly. At the same time, the young Cortez could
defend himself and his actions by agreeing that he was a stern leader
but arguing, "He was on an expedition in a foreign country. I think he
was everything a man should have been. A good leader for them." To
achieve the recognition and operation of these two perspectives within
one young child's mind or within a group, and have related judgments
and hypotheses actively discussed and tested in drama, is an important
step towards historical, social and moral insight.

Not many of the survey teachers who use historical or geographical
material in their drama actually quote "subject-based" claims as
justification for their choice, but hold to the view expressed earlier that
it provides children with an extended challenge and new concerns.
They do think about the problem, however, as one teacher did when
she said, "I sometimes worry when I use history; I worry about the
factual accuracy". In general though, both teachers and children seem
to maintain a fair degree of historical sense in their drama even if they
do not always manage a totally factual basis. They will experiment
with situations and test people's reactions but this is the essence of a
dramatic approach anyway; not to teach facts, but rather to
illuminate people caught up in particular circumstances. Children are
aware that their drama world is an imaginative product and they have
the power to make things happen but normally they are happy to
search out and apply factual knowledge to sustain dramatic
credibility. This characteristic increases with age and the survey
examples show that by ten or eleven years (and sometimes earlier) the

factual basis is normally of some consequence to the group concerned. When the ten year old Tudor (page 116) venturers agreed to pay their £25 and outfit a ship for exploration they wondered what sort of money it would be and where it would be kept; their letter writing within the drama showed a preoccupation with wax, seals and choice of address; and log book entries contained research data making the voyage credible. All were indicators that point to historical awareness within drama.

It is obvious then that some schools recognise how drama activities in subject areas such as history or geography can add important insights to children's knowledge and awareness. As with Andrew as Cortez or Hilary as a factory worker, this can be an individual realisation but it comes through a shared experience in which group insights and attitudes also develop. A significant characteristic of all this work, however, is the degree to which general concerns underlie subject matters and relate the past and present. Issues involving families, relationships, law, authority, religion and belief are never far from the surface in many drama situations and can often be recognised as fundamental elements shaping dramatic intentions and outcomes.

Drama and moral education

Subject based drama also serves moral and religious education in its broadest sense. When the Victorian factory workers (page 161) decided to burn down their place of work because the owners refused to improve wages a whole range of moral concerns was available for discussion, just as the varied motives that moved Spaniards to conquer Montezuma's (page 156) empire could be explored by children.

Teacher   What do you think about what the Spaniards did?

They destroyed the civilisation.

Yes, but they did things like sacrificing people.

The Spaniards wanted to make them Christians.

Yes, but the Spaniards killed people as well so they deserved to die.

For gold. But they went to make them Christians as well.

Teacher   What went wrong?

Well they (Aztecs) had a kind of dictator.

We shouldn't have interfered.

And we couldn't understand each other's ways.

Greedy.

Of course, these general concerns stimulated by drama are not confined to historical themes, they are part of everyday life. Poetry, story, fantasy or present day experiences explored through drama lead just as effectively into moral and social issues for children. Should a witch be punished once her power has been removed? How far should we obey a bad King? Is a community's well-being worth the sacrifice of one human life? What rules are necessary to create a viable community? These are all questions highlighted in the infant or junior dramatic work considered earlier and implicit within them are concepts of obligation, loyalty, justice, co-operation, commitment and interdependence. Drama provides opportunities for experience and reflection in fundamental areas like these through many different situations, thus leading children to discover, try-out and consolidate attitudes and values.

Several examples were seen however, where drama was used more directly in teaching Religious Education. These chiefly involved straightforward classroom re-enactment of story with little further development, though teachers stressed how this "incidental drama" seemed to illuminate the story, particularly with younger children. Two approaches show how teachers can deepen understanding in these circumstances.

One group of lower juniors looked at the story, "The Boy who cried Wolf" and considered it from the viewpoint of responsibility. How should this boy be treated by a community when he acted in an irresponsible manner? How many chances should he be given? What sort of things would be said when villagers met to consider his case? Older juniors looking at the story of the Good Samaritan discussed the implications and were then challenged by their teacher to devise their own modern versions in groups. Subsequently these were enacted before a classroom audience and involved the following themes: assistance for a man robbed of his wages, helping an elderly pensioner with work in his garden, going to the assistance of a milkman whose delivery lorry had broken down.

These approaches took children beyond simple reenactment to thinking and feeling through situations more directly, bringing their own experiences into contact with the source material and testing their responses to particular ideas and circumstances. Nevertheless, work observed during the survey suggests that for teachers to hold a narrow "teaching tool" conception of drama may lose them the advantages of its creative potential. We need to know more about the learning qualities that develop as a result of children experiencing through drama and the ways in which these can be deepened or extended. Perhaps more emphasis on drama as a process rather than an activity would improve insight into how it functions and our efficiency in using it as an effective method of teaching.

Drama and music

The strong and often integral relationship drama shares with music is apparent in many examples of work observed and requires some discussion. Because drama involves both feeling and thinking, the capacity of music to stimulate and heighten emotional and sensory experience is used by many teachers in a variety of ways. Important here is the extent to which it stimulates imagination in a dramatic context and forms the basis for many movement approaches. Mood and purpose often crystallise in rich imagery or promote imaginative insights, expressed and communicated through the movement sequence but sometimes being used later as reflective material for writing and art.

The effect of music begins immediately, quickly creating mood and atmosphere. In these circumstances children seem to respond expectantly with a sense of anticipation that deepens commitment and involvement. It is doubtful whether the first year juniors going to bury their dead king would have moved so solemnly and convincingly, reflecting in their faces the significance of the occasion if music had been entirely absent. Nor can the human sacrifice made to the Aztec gods have been so dramatically heightened without the pulsating rhythms and sounds that caught children up in moments of vivid experience. Watching children at work and using music in this way, it is possible to recognise how the mood and atmosphere engenderd encourages both confidence and dramatic consciousness.

Sometimes music prompts children into various dramatic activities. Examples already examined included a junior class who used recorded sound to stimulate their entire drama and based both movement and speech content on imagination and interpretation. Several infants' schools found that songs led children directly into dramatic situations which were then developed independently.

Of course, the definition of music must be interpreted widely and includes far more than recorded sound. It may be the simplest of created rhythmic noises like the fingers of children tapping on a floor in slow crescendo to signify the plague of locusts steadily approaching, metal tapping together as accompaniment for historical nail makers, the slow beat of a tambour keeping Viking oarsmen in co-ordinated motion or voice music simulating machines in a Victorian mill. When we consider either these simple accompaniments to dramatic actions or the more complex represented by infants' percussion for their witch and her attendants, a work song required by Pharaoh's slaves toiling in their quarry and the eerie cacophony of sound needed to provide atmosphere for a night time Saxon pagan ritual, it is creative music making a challenge in its own right as well as providing essential dramatic material. Once again, the two forms of integration are apparent; that implicit in the drama itself where music, mood, rhythms and dramatic involvement fuse into a single experience; and the work stimulated across the curriculum drawing music, drama, language and art together.

One example comes from juniors whose school serves a well established residential area in a market town. They were using a poem as the basis for moving into drama and sat on the floor of the school hall while it was read by their teacher. The theme was frost, and how it transformed the world into a brittle whiteness. The poem had been practised as choral speech and this accompanied interpretive movement, together with some original music composed by children and played by a small ensemble. Three groups worked as separate units but combined finally in the total victory of frost over a resistant landscape. Movement was strong, sensitive and extremely expressive, building up a deep mood and combining with voice and music to produce what was obviously an artistic and aesthetic experience. Language came through discussion when teacher and children looked at qualities of response and planned movement sequences together.

Afterwards the headmaster and class teacher discussed how this work reflected school approaches and their view of drama. "We use a movement approach; mime and dance which builds up a vocabulary of movement that can take the children into dramatic situations. Control and quality come that way and we can combine music, poetry and the language of literature naturally. We give some structure to help, but children contribute too. This brings discussion and involvement, while they grow in confidence and ability. Drama is an emotional thing and we try to make them more aware of emotional tone; how they feel and how others feel. They develop ideas of order, sequence and shape in what they do. We see drama as helping children's development but from a junior educational viewpoint. The question has to be asked, is drama being done for performance or for children's benefit? It's a creative challenge and the emphasis here is on what children are getting out of it and their experiences, though we do sometimes share our work in school assemblies."

Another interesting example which usefully illustrates this whole process came from work in a junior school where the children explored nineteenth century poverty and used choral speech, songs and poetry created by themselves, together with movement and mime to build up effective pictures of the period which was both emotionally strong and morally significant. Movement sequences explored several aspects of life, children searching in river mud for food, working as child labourers or existing in poverty on the streets. The song writing was an intrinsic part of the work and clearly reflects how feeling and reflective thought spring from dramatic involvement. The example illustrates the point.

In the Dirty City   *Sarah*

In the dirty city in the dirty town
In the dirty old mill
The bobbin goes up and then comes down,
In the dirty city and town.

A skinny little child stands ragged in the street
With legs like bones and filthy feet
Body like a skeleton
And wan little face
In the dirty city and town.

He wanders, O he wanders
Along the dirty streets,
He is so thin and he never eats
His home is in the gutters
With litter all around,
In the dirty city and town.

In the dirty city in the dirty town
In the dirty old mill
The bobbin goes up and then comes down,
In the dirty city and town.

Children were motivated and challenged here across a wide creative
spectrum but all endeavour served the unified purpose of bringing
together movement, mime, music and language. This is not drama,
music and language in education functioning separately, it is simply
education. Later the work was shared with other children in School
Assembly but given more direct religious significance through mime,
showing Jesus receiving the poor.

Drama and the school assembly

Some schools brought drama into their assemblies where it served both
religious and social purposes, representing joint experience and
endeavour which unites the school. The content and approaches
varied widely but the most effective and promising work seemed to be
evident where there had been little apparent loss of dramatic integrity
though inevitably some shaping for the occasion was necessary.
Generally, however, those schools which saw drama as a creative and
cumulative process were also the places in which its use for Assembly
purposes still entailed prior "building and making" involving
children, their opinions, decisions and enterprise. A number of short
examples illustrate approaches.

1   Juniors worked on a natural science theme centred on plants, seeds
and seed dispersal which "grew into a completely integrated
approach" giving scope for expressive-poetic writing and art.
Movement-drama also developed from the theme and was based upon
the parable of the sower with music composed by the children and
played by a recorder-percussion ensemble. Much co-operative
endeavour accompanied the gradual shaping and co-ordination of
both music and drama as creative activities before they were shared
with the school in assembly.

2   The children developing their Aztec work introduced aspects into
an assembly whose theme was "Experience". Two viewpoints were
represented by expressive writing; those of the dying Emperor
Montezuma and a captured Spaniard's thoughts as he was taken to be
sacrificed. These experiences were contrasted with their own in
leading to appreciation of life and living. Music for the assembly was

created by children and attempted to recall Aztec atmosphere and sounds.

3 Lower juniors developed drama from the Greek myth "The Ass's Ears" using both movement and dialogue. This formed the focal point for an assembly concerned with "Sympathy".

4 Infant children shared their "Hansel and Gretel" drama with the rest of the school in assembly. For this occasion they added suitable "props" made by themselves which included a very large cardboard sweet shop and costumes. The whole class was involved in either drama or its accompanying music.

Drama as formal presentation

At various times throughout the year drama is widened to include more general performance as a special school event and by far the greater proportion of the survey schools draw children, parents and community together in this way. Approaches range from completely scripted plays where children learn parts written for them to polished improvisations and the occasional documentary. Very few headteachers felt that imposed scripts represented an adequate challenge to children's creative abilities in drama, but they justified the use of them on a number of grounds: 1) children enjoyed performance and were motivated to co-operative endeavour by its prospect 2) staff members and different departments (in some middle schools) were given opportunity to work together on a total school project thus strengthening inter-school links and relationships 3) production standards could be maintained at a high level; organisational factors were more readily controlled 4) it was an effective means to bring school children and neighbourhood closer to each other. Probably none of the survey schools would disagree with any points included here but some had another view whose importance they stressed when presentation was considered and that was the opportunity for children to present their own creative endeavour as dramatic constructions. In addition, teachers sometimes observed that drama reaches a "presentation point" quite naturally when it becomes appropriate to share the outcome with others. Perhaps this point needs to be considered more carefully.

Again some examples will illustrate school approaches here.

1 Infant Harvest Presentation. Children used movement, mime and dialogue to express the wide variety of enterprise necessary for a full harvest. Different groups represented varied work tasks such as miners, farmers, fishermen, etc., in a presentation that was shaped yet still retained spontaneity.

2   Junior Christmas Play. "Amahl and The Night Visitors", together with the Nativity, formed a basis for a polished improvisation involving music, movement and fluent language. A village community had been established and its inhabitants and their relationships explored, so that role and interaction were convincing. Language remained free but the pattern of events and essential ideas had been decided upon and selected during a process in which drama and not presentation was important.

3   Junior Thematic Presentation. Each year the whole school takes part in a thematic production with classes contributing varying items to the total production. But within the school a lively approach to the creative arts ensures that thematic work undertaken is "first experienced on an educational level" before being shaped for presentation. Movement, mime, dialogue and music are all given scope within the themes which range from London's history to a study of America. Here scenes from Hiawatha, Columbus and his discovery, the struggle for independence, slavery, early western life and twentieth century features were major thematic areas. In this school the headmaster speaks of his difficulty in regarding drama as something separate and uses themes "to integrate all the subject areas with performance as the culmination of experience. The first priority is therefore not an end product in terms of production but getting children inside a situation and allowing them to feel and react."

4   Aztec Documentary. The drama work outlined earlier led naturally into a production which brought together the many varied dramatic activities into a unified whole and reflected an impressive historical accuracy. Shape was determined by story sequence in which language interaction and movement were bound together and supplemented through music, songs, choral speech and narrative composed by the children themselves. In this way creative work in music and writing undertaken during the drama process, together with artefacts and costume, were effectively combined with their dramatic source to give both children and audience a convincing integrated and artistic experience. There was no doubting children's enthusiasm and commitment in bringing their work together and sharing each others' endeavours while at the same time drawing school and neighbourhood into closer relationship.

Some headteachers commented on how objectives and criteria of assessment change when drama work leads into production. Both teacher and children have to consider shape more carefully when performing in public. Inevitably, theatre aspects are developed and this entails some change of roles with emphasis on how to produce, but yet retain the integrity of children and their work.

When considering all integrative work in drama we are constantly brought up against the importance of how a school organises its learning environment and the advantages or limitations that result. The most promising work observed seemed generally to come from those schools which maintained no unnecessary subject or time restrictions (other than those necessary for resource allocation) and encouraged the natural integrative force of drama through fluid and flexible learning arrangements. Examples of work have shown the wide range of activities and developments which drama may sponsor when it is allowed full scope, but frequently children need time and opportunity to develop their drama concerns in all these different ways and ideally this requires more than a weekly session in the school hall.

If individuals or groups are to reflect upon dramatic experience and deepen its quality through reading, written expression, art, craft, music making or any of the many outcomes possible, and feed those into drama interests and strengths drawn from many sources, a strong commitment seems necessary and one that builds upon interests, initiative and responsibility. This implies, of course, a global view of learning and dramatic activity that recognises its fundamental relationship with the whole curriculum and children's total development.

Reference

Drama in the English Classroom, Douglas Barnes, N.C.T.E. 1968.

The role of the teacher

The need for a rationale to guide practice

The work examined in preceding sections throws some light on the importance of drama in education and presents the main approaches through which teachers and schools are attempting to realise its values practically. Nevertheless, it would be misleading to suggest that the overall picture is one of successful practice or that drama flourishes throughout the five to eleven age range. There is certainly a good deal of productive enthusiasm and insight, but there is also much uncertainty and indifferent practice based upon varied belief and understanding. For every teacher who uses drama effectively, there are several who strive towards a better understanding of it and even more who remain unconvinced that they can use it to any extent in their work. Some have tried particular approaches and experienced difficulties from which they drew back, to rejoin those for whom drama remains a rather obscure area. These teachers often stressed that children's responses, which provide the basic substance of drama, tend to be fluid and sometimes intangible, with the result that formulation, control over the work, achievement and assessment, can become problematic.

Teachers often frankly admitted doubts about their own work in the areas considered here and referred to problems at both theoretical and practical levels. What should we be doing at various ages and stages? Is it possible or desirable to attempt a drama "programme"? How is quality of drama work improved? What sorts of material can be used effectively? What goals are appropriate in particular circumstances? The questions are numerous, not only from teachers relatively new to the field but also from those with considerable experience. Indeed they often reflected a teacher's own development and growth, accompanying comments like the following: "I established my idea of drama but then find a gap exists between the ideas and what is accomplished in practice. I need to work at it to close the gap, but then I think I move on because a new gap appears and I realise there are new possibilities. At the same time there are new problems." Continued questioning is important at any level of teacher development, and here it underlines the need to help teachers towards greater insight and role competence. Frequently teachers recognise this themselves and stress the value of knowing what others are attempting and achieving, the means by which patterns of work are built up and extended, what goals are sought and how these are assessed.

A difficult area of role to examine, yet possibly the most important, is that of why teachers offer children certain experiences in drama. What is it that underpins the decisions they make in terms of the drama they offer and their own working strategies? The reasons are not easily defined or discussed unless the teacher is aware of his own background of belief and principle which guides his practice. A composite survey statement on why schools value drama, such as that set out in Chapter One, may support belief in why drama is necessary. But such a generalised view does not reflect the considerable variation between teachers and what they think about drama in terms of values and goals, or how far they have teased out the implications for their own practice.

The main cry is for what to attempt and how to do it effectively. Ultimately, of course, the connections between what is attempted in drama work lead back to what we believe is the nature of it all and how far childrens' development and learning is enhanced as a result. Observations of fruitful work during the survey, together with discussion with teachers concerned, suggest that a guiding rationale is required, linking "why levels" and thus relating ideas and goals to effective working approaches, materials and strategies. In these circumstances it becomes clear that an effective grasp of role rests upon a teacher's fuller understanding of what drama is and its inherent educational potential. A conception of drama is required, therefore, which allows and encourages worthwhile work, one that reflects something of the comprehensive nature and functions outlined in section one, where imaginative nourishment and endeavour support shared creative opportunities.

To this end there is no doubt that a school's learning environment is important. While a facilitating environment is no guarantee that drama will flourish, it offers a background of support when teachers begin to look more closely at its value and extend their own experience in practice. Certainly, there is much evidence to suggest that in one very real sense drama means to teachers what they have experienced of it. Understanding, appreciation of possibilities and effective approaches depend to a significant extent upon what they have ventured and how their conception of drama has developed as a result. There are, of course, many sources of insight which reveal more of the field and help teachers fashion a drama rationale, but it is only by venturing and testing possibilities in their own circumstances that a deeper conception is forged – capable of supporting commitment, confidence and enterprising work.

The opposite is also true and is substantiated by some present practice. Where teachers work within a narrow conception of drama and adapt their role accordingly, a kind of circular reinforcement is set up, limiting their experience and keeping them within a restricted framework. They sometimes seem to prefer this situation because the role is comfortable, or is one they can handle confidently. While many headteachers recognise the problem and would wish to extend teacher development here, they also recognise that confidence is important in drama work and stress the need for more help at inservice and adviser levels.

We are now seeking to establish worthwhile activity that brings us up against more than the mere provision of drama opportunities. This implies that we bring ourselves as teachers and the children in our care to a recognition of the underlying responsibilities brought by dramatic ventures: commitment to an enterprise, responsiveness to situations, roles and interaction, appreciation of form where this is appropriate and a readiness to work at the unfamiliar and challenging, to be extended in any of the ways possible in drama. This means establishing various criteria within the groups we teach to encourage application, commitment, a sense of purpose and achievement, and an appreciation of where we're going and what we're doing.

Where does all this leave the teacher who uses drama for more incidental purposes, perhaps simply to illuminate a history lesson or provide an easily constructed learning situation? Here children may be given the pleasure and satisfaction inherent in dramatic activity so that interest and motivation are strengthened without a "total drama" commitment being involved. The answer seems to lie in why we undertake such approaches. If our goal is the enrichment of children's experience and learning, then any means by which this may be accomplished – including drama, raises the question of how effective they are in practice and we might then ask how much more effective they would become if we strengthened our own understanding of them.

Role of the teacher in practice

If we look more closely at the work of a number of teachers, it is possible to discern how they see their own teaching roles in terms of goals and strategies. The following examples throw light upon several important areas. It should be emphasised, however, that these are only some possible approaches and the work examined below needs to be set in the context of the whole range of work outlined earlier.

Example 1

This teacher had only recently developed an approach to drama, after attending an in-service course organised by her adviser. The work involved six year old infants whose snow rescue adventures were observed later and it occurred early in the first half of their autumn term when class and teacher were beginning to form an understanding relationship. A children's theatre group had visited the school and their play about an ogre had stimulated interest in similar themes.

The teacher aimed at using the idea of an ogre for dramatic enjoyment and learning more about how to build drama and work together. In the process she hoped to introduce simple decision making and problem solving within the drama context and to stimulate both movement and language as natural outcomes. The children worked throughout the lesson in their classroom and began by enjoying an ogre story. They then moved readily to an individual space and began to work as woodcutters with the teacher observing their actions. After a few minutes she asked them to pause and began to develop more thoughtful awareness through questions which focused attention upon qualities of effort required for cutting trees and fear that the ogre would appear. They would have to work and watch at the same time. Through narration the teacher then moved children from wood-cutting to tidying up their homes which had been upset during their absence in the woods. This represented their first problem to solve. "Think about what would need to be done in the house, then go and do it." Then she moved round the classroom observing and asking them to explain what they were doing.

Afterwards they were introduced to a second problem. Without doubt the ogre would shortly be coming, so could they organise themselves in small groups and work out some means to get the better of him? When they had discussed this fully, they chose a group spokesman and reported their idea to the listening class. Co-operation and language exchange were very effective at this point, giving satisfaction to both teacher and class.

The final part of their lesson concerned implementing the suggestion that they dig a trap. This was done in movement by the various groups with the teacher joining in role and stimulating discussion through questions: How deep has it to be? Will the sides fall in? Now the children watched from hiding places as their teacher in role as ogre slowly emerged from the wood. Some giggling here showed both enjoyment and lack of belief. Questions were asked to remedy the situation. Were they afraid of the ogre? Was he terrible? Yes. Then wouldn't they be giving away their secret? Wouldn't the ogre know something was wrong? Yes, their laughing would tell him. This particular point was taken by the class who preserved an anticipatory silence when next the ogre came and was duly trapped.

Afterwards the teacher assessed achievements. Co-operation and sensible working patterns were beginning to emerge together with confidence in language, greater sensitivity and pleasure in having problems to think about and solve. In addition, children were learning to build drama themselves through an evolving story structure.

Example 2

Sometimes dramatic activity, however carefully planned, fails to engage children's full interest and their involvement is correspondingly weak. The teacher's role is then to make quick decisions to retrieve the situation, even if this means substantially modifying original intentions. This is what happened in one thirty minute lesson involving a class of vertically grouped infants. They were used to working together in dramatic situations and implementing ideas, so it was not demands from these sources which caused the problem. What happened was simply the failure of a dramatic framework to support continuing interest.

The class teacher had recently seen a large box brought into school by another member of staff. It contained a kitten which was admired by the children and provided much stimulation for conversation, writing and art. However, before the "mysterious box" had revealed its contents, much curiosity was aroused and from this came an idea for drama which might:

1   Involve all the children in a dramatic situation where they could work with confidence.

2 Bring involvement and expression through movement and mime, but also through language.

3 Provide a planned basic framework within which children would have some degree of choice.

The lesson began with children sitting as their teacher produced two parcels and commented "O! Here comes the postman. Look what he's brought." A dramatic element was thus introduced which prompted imaginative responses to her question, "What do you think might be in here?"

Various suggestions were made by children who showed considerable interest at this stage and eagerly volunteered to open the parcels. One contained a brooch and led to the idea that these were birthday presents. Naturally, the second parcel was expected to yield something equally desirable and there was much vocal surprise when a piece of rock was found inside.

The next stage of the lesson took children into an active movement sequence. "Find a space where there is a 'box'. What are you going to put in it? Make up your minds and then put on the lid." Children worked individually or in pairs as they mimed the actions and prepared their parcels. Language was a natural outcome.

After allowing sufficient time for this phase, their teacher asked them to carry the parcels to a central point and focused attention on size and weight, so that movement quality reflected what was being carried. Further imaginative activity came with the teacher's announcement that she was coming round to see the contents of each box. Would they open them and hold their object? When she had "seen" each one, they could decide where to hide it for safety.

Up to this point, interest and involvement had been sustained, but now restlessness and loss of concentration became increasingly apparent. Clearly the original "box" idea was not going to support a full lesson as planned. Assessing the possibilities available, the teacher quickly decided to retain the "birthday element" as a basis for renewing interest. Birthdays were occasions for treats. Would they like to go somewhere special? At once, attention was revived and after many suggestions, an island adventure was chosen. What they would need to take on the journey provoked some lively discussion before they assembled at the railway station ready to leave. Train movements and noises then involved groups in recreating convincing rail travel which took them to a port of embarkation.

The final phase of their lesson included some discussion on ships and who was to be captain. Afterwards the teacher assessed developments. Her original framework had not sustained involvement and it had been necessary to look for new stimulation. Fortunately, this had succeeded and promised more scope for she could see classroom possibilities arising from ships and the sea.

Example 3

This example comes from an infant school in a small industrial town where organisation is based on year grouping with class teachers able to develop particular approaches at a curricular level, although formal teaching is undertaken where this seems desirable. Dramatic play is encouraged with younger children and is seen to offer experiences for many kinds of learning, but drama itself has been developed chiefly in her own class by the deputy headmistress who had recently attended an advanced course. Her approaches included a stress on the enjoyment and achievement gained through creative involvement, but beginning with children's interests and offering opportunities appropriate to their needs and abilities, a conviction that drama creates learning situations which also nourish confidence, decision making, responsibility and an acceptance of reality in dramatic concerns. Language possibilities and role awareness are both emphasised. Her class was a rather subdued group used to a formal mode of working; they lacked initiative and were very dependent upon their teacher who found that their questions often indicated insecurity. There as a general unwillingness to exchange ideas though the majority did have sufficient communicative ability to do so.

Her goals included the following:

1   The establishment of a happy atmosphere of mutual trust where children could grow in confidence, initiative and sense of responsibility.

2   Activities that would promote curiosity, a willingness to learn and allow scope for creative ideas.

3   A tight initial structure allowing a sense of achievement and at the same time ensuring that some of the rules were understood, i.e. drama involves talking, listening and respecting each other's ideas.

A series of short "one off" story situations was the chosen strategy and current interests were called on: "What would you like your story to be about?" A further question evoked an early sense of achievement, "Could you help me to build it?" At this stage teacher and children sat together and discussed possibilities before moving into a more active sequence. One typical example involved elephants and the teacher's heavily loaded questions, necessary at this stage, drew out essential details. Where did these elephants live? What happened to cause trouble? etc. So the story of a rogue elephant leading others into varied situations was built up, discussed and dramatised within a very controlled structure. These experiences provided enjoyment and stimulated interest, with further reading and research complementing collage pictures as follow-up activities.

This early phase had allowed ground rules, confidence and trust to be sufficiently established in a context of achievement, so that the teacher felt she could now offer a wider challenge. The way was open to extend possibilities by drawing more from life experience.

It was still necessary, however, to maintain a discipline-forming structure and this was where the idea of a primitive village was introduced, providing a wide range of options and greater role variety but still maintaining the desired framework. The teacher hoped that as a result children's thinking, feeling and initiative would be strengthened and decision-making exercised.

Discussion within the classroom began to establish a concept of community and involvement. This was an important phase in the drama, so adequate time was spent on talking over and deciding details of families, their names, occupations and needs. It was recognised that a village leader was necessary but at this stage the teacher was unsure who was ready to accept the responsibilities associated with a leader's role. Her strategy led children into conscious appraisal of leadership qualities.

Teacher	What qualities do we look for in a leader?
Child	He must be brave.
Teacher	Is that enough?
Child 1	No you need to have brains.
Child 2	You must care for people.

184

Child 3	You must be fair.
Teacher	Can we think of a test to select a leader?
Child	Fight a bear – the man who fights it best is the leader.
Teacher	That's a good idea because you need to be very brave to fight this animal. You must be clever to watch and anticipate its movements.

In all discussions one problem is always how long to continue. Younger children (and some older ones) have only a short concentration span and here the teacher noted some restlessness in the group. Action was what they wanted and so the opportunity was provided through a movement contest with an imaginary bear. Finally one boy emerged as the chosen leader and the drama was ready to move forward.

Certain roles can sometimes be demanding and children require support from their teacher. At times it is also necessary for a teacher to reduce the burden of role or to move the demands from one child to another. This occurred here when the leader, having sustained his role for several weeks, wished to change. In such circumstances it is the teacher's task to facilitate the changeover without loss of face or self-confidence. "Our leader has been wise and cared for his people. He has led us safely but now he is getting old and feels a younger man is needed to take over. Let us show our thanks for the excellent job he has done." Thanks were expressed and the villagers decided to vote for a new leader. The runner up became his assistant.

Meanwhile, the need for shelter was well recognised and families began the task of "building" a village. However, movement was poor and belief weak. Strengthening strategies appeared essential and the teacher introduced a classroom activity designed to help. They could think of their individual house, its design and the materials available to build it; subsequent drawings formed the basis for a village model. Some guidance came through the teacher's questions. "Are your houses in the village like our houses here?" and "Where would bricks and cement come from?" to one group producing a modern type dwelling.

As a result their drama village and family relationships became more of a reality so that it was possible for the teacher to introduce a new and very different problem – lack of water. In role as a villager she led

185

them to face up to the situation, assisted by her visiting course tutor, also in role as the "old man of the forest" and guardian of water. Belief was indifferent at first (the situation only became more of an exercise in social learning as the "old man" declined to consider the babble of requests for water). Through his comments in role, ideas of courtesy and politeness were conveyed implicitly, "Why have you burst into my room. I am busy writing." Eventually, mood was established and involvement deepened through a ritual where all villagers sat together and then in turn came to the old man, and sat again with toes touching the bucket . . . while he intoned in solemn and formal language. "I give you this water, fresh and clear – taste it."

Three points seem important here. First that children can be moved into challenging situations by the teacher in role who is also available to give support and guidance as participant; second, mood and belief are often deepened when the drama is "focused" – in this case through a water ritual; third, the teacher's own language served several functions – it induced mood, controlled pace and acted as a resource. When the children met "the old man of the forest" their social and linguistic responses were uncertain. This was a subject taken up later by the class when they considered how their voices could affect other people's reactions.

Child	That's why the Man of the Forest didn't want to give us water.
Teacher	Why?
Child	We didn't talk properly. We didn't have good manners.
Teacher	Is there a special way for talking to different people?

The drama offered other opportunities for encouraging linguistic awareness, and skills. In the following extract children are being led to explore the best way to conduct a village meeting. Their interest in each other's comments showed an awareness of the need for listening.

Teacher	Is there a special way of talking when a lot of people, like the villagers, are having a meeting?
Child	When one person speaks the others must listen. One person speaks at once.
Teacher	Is this necessary?

Child 1	Because if you don't, you won't know what they're doing and talking.
Child 2	You don't know what they're doing or saying in the drama.
Child 3	If everybody wants to say something they get excited and butt in.
Child 4	Then they will get punished.
Child 5	They will be sent out of the meeting and will have to make food for all the villagers' tea.
Child 6	They must give a sign ... bow your head and if the leader bows back you can speak.

This discussion shows linguistic sensibility and initiative being developed jointly as elements in children's growing dramatic and social maturity. The village began to reveal a collective character as group identity was slowly established and confirmed by events. As a result the teacher saw new possibilities for moving the children into areas of stronger thinking and feeling and was led to consider which issues raised during the drama offered suitable scope.

Opportunity came with developments following the Forest Man's gift of water. The villagers took the limited supply seriously and arranged to keep their buckets in a central place guarded by family representatives. However, not all buckets were brought and one or two families failed to provide guards. The teacher resolved to focus community attention on the concept of responsibility, at the same time deepening dramatic impact. As families came forward to receive an agreed ration she assumed a participant role and opposed giving water where responsibilities had not been met. "What about these? They didn't care about their water. Surely we are not going to allow them to share ours?" Subsequent verbal exchanges brought children up against two aspects of responsibility: the consequences arising from neglecting to safeguard their water; and the question of community responsibility posed by the teacher asking, "What about these ...?" thus focusing thought on the fact that we have water but do we share it? The extract shows how reflection was influenced by a real concern which overlooked the dramatic negligence and established sympathetic bonds. "It would be selfish not to share." "It's not fair. They are part of our village. Anyone can make a mistake." This growth in confidence allowed the teacher to plan a situation which required an individual response and so gave every member of the group an opportunity to contribute actively. She assumed the role similar to that of the "old man" who guarded the water but this time required something in return.

Villager	Excuse me, sir, we have used up all our water, could we please get some more?
Teacher in role	I am not the old man of the forest but I know him. He let's me stay here. I don't care if you have no water, all I care about is things, mind you don't break any of them.
Leader	We have clever hands. We will make things for you if you will let us get some water.
Teacher	Alright. Return to your village and make me some beautiful things but remember each one must be different.

The villagers eventually returned with gifts and formed a circle to begin the presentation. There was an atmosphere of stillness and anticipation as each one presented a gift and awaited the decision of the old woman. Afterwards the teacher concluded with discussion giving children an opportunity to clarify and refine their thinking about this strange character, her questions again channelling thinking.

Later, she emphasised her belief that a large part of a teacher's skill lies in the ability to judge when to intervene and move the drama forward and when not to intrude. This demands an understanding of the process and a heightening of sensitivity to signals from the group, so as to move the drama in a way that suits needs and challenges abilities.

Example 4

The second year juniors whose work with *Beowulf the Warrior* provided the language examples on page 93 were a mixed-ability group whose previous experience of drama had been largely movement-based.

The use of the Beowulf story as basic material presented a move into more language conscious drama. These children had reached a stage where heroic tales satisfied imaginary appetites and could form a basis for wider dramatic opportunities. The story had been greatly enjoyed and offered considerable scope for dramatisation. The teacher planned to use it as a flexible framework with emphasis upon the plight of people facing a new and challenging situation. The children were to be actively involved in building and shaping the drama. Their ideas, opinions and decisions would complement the teacher's contributions but in return they would be expected to commit themselves to the enterprise and show purposeful endeavour.

In discussions of the story from a drama perspective – the situation of the king's hall in relation to Grendel's lair, the allocation of roles – the teacher acted as chairman and used his situation to begin a process of establishing working patterns – how we sit together when talking things over, the careful listening and consideration of each other's ideas or comments, self-discipline in not interrupting each other.

Signals from the class at this point suggested eagerness to enter the drama and experience the monster Grendel's awe-provoking appearance. But certain safeguards were first necessary, so that control was established and maintained. These came through questioning: they were asleep; would everyone wake at once? Could each family agree on who would wake first among them? How clearly would they see in the gloom? What sort of reactions could follow Grendel's recognition? In this way a thoughtful backcloth of possible responses was established without imposing an over-shaped conception. Afterwards the teacher assessed qualities and problems. Children's satisfaction was evident and belief in the situation had obviously been helped by prior discussion. Nevertheless, movement was lacking in sensitivity, the king and his bodyguards had demonstrated a lack of relationship among themselves and with the people. So it was back to discussion where the points were talked over. The children themselves had noted how authority had been missing from the king's part in events and there was criticism too for bodyguards who had deserted their posts. It was also observed by some womenfolk that their husbands had left them to fend alone while they found safe places for themselves. Some time was subsequently spent on looking more closely at the points raised, in particular, how the qualities of a chosen warrior king affected his subjects' expectations, the obligations of a bodyguard to his lord and whether it was possible to deal with Grendel. As part of their classroom work children were asked to discuss those matters further and begin a self-portrait of themselves and their life in writing, using facts drawn from reference material and their own imaginations.

Meanwhile the movement quality was deepened by individual work and "family groups". Everyone tried the role of Grendel and explored the accompanying physical and mental sensations before combining in groups, each working with its own monster.

This groundwork bore fruit quite early so that when the class assembled for further work the opening discussion yielded many ideas. Some of the more interesting concerned ways of dealing with Grendel (page 93) and these were encouraged by the class teacher's questions because they provided a means of shaping and deepening the situation.

At this point the teacher intervened for the first time in role as a member of the settlement. Grendel had departed taking his victim and leaving a near silent settlement. "Are we all to die in this place? Cannot the king and his warriors save us from death?" The resultant debate was wide-ranging and alive. It revealed not only the beginning of feeling related to the drama events but also an intellectual probing into varied areas of concern. Included were references to a lack of concern for the victim; failure of the king to protect his people; failure of the bodyguards to assist; and alternative possibilities the king might have adopted.

Two areas in the discussion were particularly productive. The criticism of the king was lengthier and led to people taking sides. One boy announced that they should find a better king who was willing to stand, his statement acting as a funnel for others' thoughts and bringing the question into sharp focus. Here was authority, having failed in its obligations, open to doubt and possible transfer. Second, many ideas for dealing with Grendel were generated but risked being lost as the verbal give and take moved quickly on. By moving the interaction into a more controlled and reflective phase when the issues were still alive, the teacher hoped to encourage deeper consideration of ideas. "My lord, I think we should have a meeting and sort this out" brought the desired effect and the quality of discussion represented by the extract in section three.

Example 5

This example comes from fourth year junior work in a school where drama is established and valued. An integrated approach is encouraged so that dramatic interaction is related to many classroom activities and mutual bonds are established.

The class involved had previously undertaken some drama based upon story which they used for their own creative purposes. As a result they had built up some drama strengths and could work co-operatively in dramatic situations so that now their teacher felt they were ready for a more extended challenge. Classroom interest had focused upon journals and diaries referring to the town's history and in particular those details recorded by Bede. Accordingly the headmaster and class teacher, working jointly, planned an approach that would allow the recreation of an early Saxon community within which events and issues could be explored.

Early goals included:

1   The establishment of a Saxon community to provide opportunities for understanding early history and culture.

2   Development of children's ability to build their own drama framework and encounter more challenging situations.

3   To encourage a wide range of interrelated classroom activities with special emphasis upon language work and reading.

The drama began with classroom activity and discussions which sought to establish a basis for later hall sessions. The children needed to know something of the factual background so that roles and community could be focused upon which roles to adopt, who made up the various families, what kind of homes they had and what work was done.

A classroom resource area allowed all the relevant books and materials to be conveniently accessible, while wall space was prepared with suitable captions for information, subsequently written up and illustrated. Apart from discussions, this work was organised on a group or individual basis throughout the normal working week and thus avoided any strain on the available resources. It also provided the degree of flexibility necessary in mixed ability classes engaged upon varied tasks. From the beginning their research and discussion fed dramatic purpose so that roles, occupations, homes, implements, customs and the yearly cycle of work provided a working foundation. Part of a Saxon calendar was discovered in one book, and served to stimulate the production of a large original version which illustrated the whole Saxon year.

Hall work began by establishing a spatial conception of community so that particular spaces became significant as locations of one sort or another. This was initially achieved through questioning and discussion to allow children's contributions and to sort out priorities. Group activities followed where families explored their homes, community and work tasks, having been challenged to begin a day's activity. The factual foundation showed its value here as children moved tentatively into inter-group discussion and work sequences. This was also a period of assessment by the teacher. Activity of this kind is often an indicator of how far mood is being created and whether the group's growing maturity and insights are producing co-operation at both dramatic and social levels. Importantly too, it shows how far less confident children are finding security and an individual or group level of commitment and belief. The signs indicated that these early goals were being achieved but a long period of such activity was unnecessary; it was possible to extend the challenge in other ways. When a situation is established without a predetermined shape and sequence, some event or problem is required to bring the community together (or split it) so that a tension is created and decisions must be made against a backcloth of ideas and discussion. This is where feeling is often engendered, expressed and controlled within dramatic exchanges so that heightened awareness of self, group, and issue may extend both thought and language. The teachers were looking for community involvement in valid circumstances. The class knew from Bede's work that a monastery had been established locally and it seemed, therefore, that here was a likely source of tension. How had it come to be approved? Was there any opposition? It was felt that certain questions required attention in classroom research. How did we know about Saxon monasteries? How were decisions made in early settlements? What information was available on pre-Christian religion? How much authority did a Thegn possess?

The teachers meanwhile were looking at role possibilities in this situation. If a pagan priest and the Christian monk who sought to displace him were involved jointly in a community gathered together for decision making, then different attitudes, loyalties and preferences should at once begin to enrich proceedings. These were roles that could be tried by any of the class interested.

Renewed discussion began the next hall session. Much had been discovered from the classroom assignments and now supported dramatic shaping. The class decided with teacher as chairman that the emissary work would first seek out the Thegn and convince him privately, so that subsequently he would appear as an ally when the moot was summoned. As an inducement to the settlement, a holy relic consisting of one sacred bone would be promised as a gift for the monastery should it be built.

At this stage the teachers saw these possibilities:

1 The moot would create a formal situation with its own atmosphere and dramatic control, affecting language-style and role awareness. Tension would spring from a number of factors; the pagan priest and what he could find to say, the monk's contribution and their Thegn's lack of impartiality as one in authority. Adding to the issues would be those demands made on the settlement by a new monastery and disquiet about change in religion.

3 The sacred relic would provide an interesting symbolic challenge. How far would these children accept or justify it as "treasure"?

In fact the moot did provide a valuable drama experience with all the possibilities explored to some degree. At several points teacher intervention was necessary in order to deepen or focus thought, or stimulate reaction. This was always done from a role stance as member of the settlement but without directing or exerting a distorting influence. Subsequent discussion readily brought out the children's own appraisal and topics for consideration. Things had been talked over but not from one idea to another too quickly. The monk had been very un-Christian in his attitudes towards the pagan priest and over generous in what he promised as rewards for changing religion. Understanding of the holy relic's symbolic nature had not been strong.

At this point priorities had to be decided because time was running out. After brief examination of the ideas expressed in the moot, "family" groups were asked to discuss these further in class and clarify their own minds. Some attention was then given to the monk's role, attitudes, belief, etc. and helpful comments were made on which he could draw subsequently. He was also allocated a group of "supporters" to work with him in discussion and establish more thoroughly those important areas of concern. A similar arrangement was made for the pagan priest. Finally, the children were asked to devise some dramatic means of giving more significance to their holy relic. In these ways the whole class was given opportunity to think round events and shape their drama as it progressed.

The teachers were prepared to spend drama time over one or two weeks for this deepening process because it added substantially to commitment, belief and the total quality of experience. If the drama had faltered then plans would necessarily have been revised, but it happened that a growing interest developed mutually with greater insights.

Events moved forward in time when the monastery was "built" in movement and its holy relic brought in procession. This was a natural opportunity for dramatic intervention by the pagan priest who refused to go into the new church, but instead harangued families as they prepared for the occasion. Small group interaction like this was seen as a further way to give varied opportunities for dramatic scope within a class situation.

Classroom activities meanwhile continued to build up a comprehensive picture of contemporary life and stimulate varied language forms. Diaries were kept and letters written; one example is given here:

St. Hild's Monastery 707: To Father Bede, We are in great need of a new dormitory as we are getting rather crowded in here at the moment. We thought the near left wing would be a good place. A small fire broke out behind the kitchen yesterday through hot ashes but there was no damage done apart from some scorching. The church is coming along well. We have not yet finished the notes you gave us to write up but we shall soon. I think I should ask you about the second leaf. It does not state what you are talking about. Is it the raid or the trial? That is all now. Peace be with you, Brother Wellram.

P.S.   I have enclosed the plans for the new dormitory.

The situation of the pagan priest was considered in discussion because it contained important elements. How do people react to loss of face, status and power? What feelings would be aroused among the people, sympathy, derision, indifference or something else? From this interchange of views came the suggestion that he would not willingly accept his new diminished role but would seek an opportunity to turn the tables on those who had displaced him. There is seldom any shortage of ideas in these circumstances and the teacher's role is concerned with encouraging those possibilities offering most scope. So the notion of disaster in the settlement for which the monks could be blamed and pilloried was developed. Valuable oxen were found drowned and the granary was empty, thus provoking a confrontation between pagan priest and people who were asked to propitiate the gods by a secret blood-letting ceremony, at the sacred tree. The scapegoat was to be the granary keeper.

This gave an opportunity to use some material seen on television which had shown an ancient fertility rite enacted each year in a nearby village. The priest, his assistant and several others were given the task of devising their own ritual, while masks, robes and other essential props were prepared for them in class. From the outset, details of the ritual were kept secret as part of dramatic interest so that mood and atmosphere were more effectively evoked. Children's own music on recorders had been added here by the group responsible and a symbolic dance devised.

At this point the teachers looked ahead at possibilities. Underlying these events were basic issues like justice, authority and responsibility. With care these could be brought to the surface for recognition and consideration in a dramatic context that might yield wider conceptual understanding. So at a judicious point in the ritual a suggestion made quietly took news of the event to both monk and Thegn with consequent intervention. The result was two committed and opposing groups, two sources of authority and one man as the point of focus or concern. It led almost inevitably to challenge and the acceptance by the community of trial by ordeal for the accused man, but not before much feeling and thought had been generated. Through careful comments in role the teacher focused attention upon a number of significant areas, acting as guide but not determining outcomes; rather, allowing children time to explore and savour issues at their own level of understanding. This was a situation in which children faced up to the significance of events, clarified their own responses and organised what they felt and thought through giving it expression – here chiefly in language. Interesting areas examined included the following:

(a) Questions of authority and obligation. The Thegn was law upholder and had obligations both as community judge and friend of the accused man. Here the pro-christian group had to recognise how his formal position distanced him from theirs.

(b) The pagan priest now represented an alternative source of authority based upon his supporters' renewed belief. The two conflicting positions and attitudes served as reference points and produced some oscillation of thought as comments originating in one group were picked up and answered by the other. As a result thinking levels were deepened.

(c) Friendship, loyalty and responsibility were all given some attention, not in conceptual terms but through the experience and thoughts being discussed.

This development provided some useful language possibilities within the classroom with children able to draw upon their role experience and write from within the situation. This was not narrative but represented a personal commentary on events that allowed reflection in role. One example is given here.

Outcast
"How could all my friends betray me over something that has not been found to be true. My husband never in his life had let down any of the villagers. Just because their friends say he's guilty they all go on their side and Thegn, I'm sure he is the cause for most of this business. He has the key for the granary so I don't know why they don't blame him. But I suppose they are frightened of him. Carl must have something evil in him. He just has to mention this trial and everyone agrees to go on with it and I'm sure they wouldn't like it happening to them. But just think what my poor husband must feel like locked up in that cold dark hut and being accused of taking something he didn't take. We have looked after this granary since this settlement started. Our grandfathers and grandmothers looked after it before we did and no one ever blamed them. That man guarding the door is very unfaithful. Not even letting me see my husband and after we had helped him. Now he won't even let me have a favour back from him. After all, no one would know anything about it. But he said he was obeying the Thegn's orders and he was not going to betray the Thegn. I just don't know what has come over all these people, once all gay and laughing, now unfriendly and evil. I'm beginning to wonder if it could be the monk's fault for upsetting the village."

Related background research also stimulated the following contribution.

Trial by Ordeal
If a man was accused of a crime he had to find oath helpers who would come forward and stand for him. If he could not find enough oath helpers he would be judged by ordeal, the Judgement of God.

Ordeal by Fire
This would take place in a church with the priest there. The accused man had to hold a piece of red-hot iron in his bare hands

and walk three paces. Then his hands were bandaged up by the priest. At the end of three days if his hand was healing properly he was innocent. They thought this was a sign from God but if his hand was festering he was guilty.

Ordeal by Water
In ordeal by water the man would have to pull out a stone from a cauldron of boiling water. Then his hand would be bandaged by the priest to see if it healed properly in three days. Also he could be thrown into a pond or river. If he floated he was guilty but if he sank he would be rescued and was innocent.

This drama was still very much alive when other class events necessitated a change of emphasis.

Assessing needs and possibilities

Discussions with teachers underlined the importance they attached to some form of preliminary assessment of what should be offered, which underpins the practical work introduced and developed. It represents an essential part of any approach to planning and affects both long and short term intentions. There appear to be five main components.

1 Children's past experience and present interests. As children move through school they build up drama strengths, attitudes and consciousness according to their own capacities and the opportunities provided for them. In any combination of teacher and group past experience affects what is possible and influences decisions on new work. So it is not surprising that in different circumstances a teacher maybe concerned with basic approaches that, "show children what drama is about and how they can work in it," while she leads another group towards language challenge, role awareness or deeper understanding of a relevant issue. However, the underlying intention in all cases is to increase children's experience and further their development. But very often, teachers find difficulty in knowing where this development lies and the following problems are not uncommon.

Drama stays at an unchallenging level. There are many activities and skills to develop, but they often continue merely as the staple diet.

Many possibilities are not recognised and goals are consequently more limited.

Some goals are sought but not attained because strategies and quality of experience are lacking. Language objectives are particularly vulnerable here.

2   The Social tone of the group. An important role function is gauging the capabilities of a class and whether it is strong enough to support specific drama ventures. This implies the constructive attitudes, willingness to venture and sensible working habits that support the drama process in discussion, interaction or any related outcomes. The strength or weakness of these qualities significantly determines how children can be moved into drama and the kinds of situations and strategies that are adopted. One teacher, commenting on an inner city class of ten year olds who wanted to be cops and robbers without commitment or thoughtful application said, "they thought it was a soft option and required no effort". Since she believed in building on children's interest she accepted the theme but obliged the class to determine what kind of robbery it was, what sort of people and goods were involved and how it was to be planned and executed.

3   The relationship between teacher and children. Teachers are normally aware that in drama their relationship with the group is a crucial factor in establishing response and enterprising work. We show children that their ideas, opinions and suggestions are valued but in return it allows us to ask for commitment and application. A great deal hinges upon this aspect of teacher expectation. Until good relationships are strengthened.and sustained there will always be difficulties in moving children towards the kind of work we believe they can undertake.

4   Where the teacher stands in drama. It must become evident from work observed that preliminary assessment must include the teacher's own readiness to begin or extend dramatic ventures. What is possible in drama may be crucially determined by how we see ourselves in relation to the ventures we feel able to make. There is considerable evidence from the survey that many teachers do assess themselves in this way and plan much of their drama approaches accordingly.

We need to look at our own role within the drama; when to offer support and guidance, act as a catalyst or introduce a new challenge. It is important to be aware of necessary resources and how these may be deployed, including here the teacher himself and the children, to know when individual, group or full class involvement will best serve intentions and needs.

5   Implications of what is proposed. What has been discussed so far represents the underlying factors influencing choice of approach and structure when planning drama experiences for children. Within this preliminary assessment process, the teacher has always to consider the implications of what is proposed and the kinds of demands likely to be made on both the children and himself. A dramatic approach that is too clear cut or constraining will make few demands, though there may be sound reasons why an initial venture of this sort is desirable. On the other hand, a situation which is too vague and loose can lead to uncertainty, shapelessness and loss of confidence. Some teachers stress the balance they seek between giving scope for constructive trying out and a structure which ensures a satisfying and fruitful experience. Whatever the final choice, it can be examined with specific questions in mind. What kind of dramatic situation will be set up and how are children to be taken into it? What will be the range of dramatic tasks found there? Will role and interaction be important elements? Is there scope for language challenges, and opportunities for discussion? What will be the dramatic issues likely to foster feeling and thought? What resources will be required? How might it relate to classroom work? It is not suggested that all the answers can be found, but promising work observed in the survey schools indicate that these are questions – along with others – familiar to perceptive teachers.

Longer-term planning

All that has just been outlined affects teachers in their role as long-term strategists seeking well-conceived programmes of drama work and helps to clarify why "programme planning" is usually undertaken on an individual basis. The teacher's own goal formulation is fundamental here. Additionally, we have to consider that drama has many different functions and may be employed in various ways within a school or class. Where an organisational approach encourages drama linked to themes then planning requirements will not be the same as those concerned with separate, half-hour weekly lessons. Indeed, the degree of curricular integration encouraged may affect drama intentions considerably, by extending the basic experience and consequently setting new goals for future work. Moreover, since the amount of drama undertaken within or between schools, differs according to interest, resources and provision, it is difficult to formulate what may be regarded as a common background experience for any particular age group.

At an individual school level, guidance is sometimes attempted within the framework of supportive schemes which offer suggestions for approaches and activities. The teacher's own role is then to adapt these for his own particular purposes and goals. But again it must be stressed how individual this process is in practice so that achievements for any class or teacher will often be peculiarly "their own".

The most helpful suggestion seems to be that of again stressing those "developmental factors" outlined in section two as points of reference for longer-term planning.

Where children stand in relation to these reference points will help determine longer-term goals. One teacher remarked when asked about his own intentions here, "I have to see what a group makes of an experience before planning ahead in detail. If they can work within a story framework perhaps it is time to challenge them with an improvisation they build up themselves; or if 'black and white' characteristics have been encountered, perhaps they are ready for something which brings them up against being more discriminating." Comment from another experienced teacher emphasised an alternative approach. "When I've finished this historical work, I'll probably take the class into a movement form or perhaps an everyday situation. I like to keep a balance and within that develop all the qualities we can."

In effect, both teachers stress the blend of factors involved in taking children forward dramatically, and reiterate that we are not simply concerned with straightforward linear progression. What is really at stake, however, is how effectively teachers can involve children at appropriate levels in relevant and challenging activities. Planning along these lines gives at least some guidelines for assessing what might or should be attempted.

Control in drama

Teachers of all age groups between five and eleven tend to be concerned with aspects of control in drama and see this as a major role responsibility. Consequently the structures they introduce are usually influenced by their assessment of children's development and their own working modes. Crucial here is whether they recognise that, along with its emotional and intellectual potential, drama also provides a possible discipline-forming framework which supports responsibility, initiative and co-operation.

Three levels of control then have to be considered:

1   The teacher's own control over how children are introduced to drama and their subsequent activities together at a level of sensible working relationships and behaviour.

2   The control ceded to children so that they have opportunities for active sharing and the developments this may bring.

3   The control exercised by the teacher to guide children in their dramatic concerns so that potential experience and learning are enriched whenever possible.

The examples of work examined clearly illustrate a considerable variation in how teachers approach their role here. As we have seen, many prefer a movement-centred activity which offers children security and shape until they have developed sufficient confidence to begin more challenging work. However, in some cases the movement form remains the preferred framework at the expense of other possibilities. The same comment holds true for dramatic exercises and games which are used effectively by a number of teachers to induce concentration, group awareness or response. They can become a substitute for drama itself and limit experience for both teacher and children. What is needed are ways for teachers to build up children's confidence and initiative gradually, until the control levels maintain growing social and dramatic abilities.

Children's age and development affect the methods used and with infants in particular (though also with some older children). As a number of lessons have illustrated, there is often a necessity to work within tight structures at first so that security and ground rules can be established. Sometimes this is achieved through movement but several infant teachers were observed using a story approach which was shaped as the drama proceeded. Acting as narrator when new developments had been decided, they were able to employ their voice as a hidden structure controlling pace, making suggestions, encouraging co-operation and importantly, bringing children up against dramatic learning opportunities. The narrator's role is easily changed to one allowing direct participation and further scope for controlling events and children. For example, one young six year old brave who was determined to arrange everything for his tribe met this remark from his teacher in role. "Wait a minute, you've just come into this tribe. We want to hear what the other braves have to say." These are early lessons in control, when children learn that teacher is a partner but there are firm rules which govern what we do together. Some rules are peculiar to particular situations or approaches; the spatial arrangement for a village, how much noise is permitted for mill machinery, or the way in which a contest will take place. Often, however, they can represent steps on the way to increasing maturity and competence, especially when they have been jointly produced and agreed through discussion, so that children have a stake in how their work is guided.

Talking together like this is often an effective means to achieve control of the work at any level and it is potentially more productive when linked with careful initial planning. Despite the fact that some teachers prefer to retain a completely loose framework, fruitful drama for most others seems to grow more from a careful consideration of possibilities, where children can be appropriately involved in discussing their drama, how it might go and its necessary preliminary shaping or organisation. We then increase the opportunities for children's creativity and control, by bringing their own ideas and sense of purpose into a working relationship with the teacher's goals.

Control of this kind is extremely variable among teachers; in essence they must bring children up against an appropriate dramatic challenge which is sufficiently focused for them to deal with. It implies some awareness of possibilities and an ability to guide children towards productive learning points within the situations encountered, then to ensure that pace is suitable and detracting issues avoided.

Very often the teacher's organisation of his own work reflects a concern for control which takes him from a class-centred approach into individual and small group tasks. Indeed one of the patterns for children's development noted earlier and practised in many schools is the progression from individual to pairs to small group. There is no doubt that many teachers find this kind of organisation suitable for their own particular approaches and build up working patterns round it which lead children into a variety of dramatic experiences. Its one major drawback when used exclusively seems to be in a relative loss of the central purpose and focus which can unite teacher and class. Indeed if employed continuously it really raises the basic question, "How do we see drama?" Yet there is no reason why any dichotomy should exist. There will always be occasions when some forms of organisation are preferable to others for sound dramatic reasons; there will always be times when a class needs the particular challenges and experiences of working as individuals or groups; and there may well be teachers who feel more comfortable with group activities. Nevertheless, much promising work seen during the survey indicates that a conception of drama constantly limited by group organisation will lose many learning possibilities.

Commitment and belief

Control in drama is closely linked to children's own commitment and belief. "I want them to understand what we're about, to believe in the situation and become involved. If they're grimacing, then nine times out of ten they're not involved and not giving much." Commitment is likely to grow according to how much children have at stake in the drama and how much it has encouraged their initiative and decision making or giving opportunity for role, relationships, events and issues to strengthen attitudes and convictions at a dramatic level. Belief is closely related to commitment and means to most teachers an attitude or quality made possible in the first place through "willing suspension of disbelief", but supported by a situation or role children can accept as possible for them. Both commitment and belief exist at personal and group levels in drama, but teachers are not always confident about how far strengthening strategies are necessary or which are effective. Nevertheless, one thing is certain; these difficulties experienced when commitment and belief are lacking counteract teacher intentions and prevent the realisation of some dramatic possibilities.

Teachers use varied means to encourage development. The infant teacher allowing her six year old children to build their own drama assumed the role of ogre falling into an agreed trap (pages 181–182). But when they giggled and were noisy she let it be seen that the ogre was consequently warned and thus challenged their group belief. As a result the ambushers were more serious and so succeeded. In contrast, the "Old Man of the Forest" (page 186), also working with upper infants, introduced a slow-moving ritual when faced with villagers whose quest for water was characterised by indifference and some lack of appropriate dramatic behaviour. The water-giving ceremony induced a mood which strengthened their belief in the drama. Of course, commitment and belief are always variable, so flexibility in approaches or intentions is often necessary. Nevertheless, when the time seems right for children to be given scope for a greater range of imaginative ventures, roles, situations and co-operative endeavour, they need help in building up the necessary degree of involvement to support their achievements and growth.

At times, teachers merely observe and offer support through comments or questions. The wrong tone or an inappropriate comment can quickly bring down a dramatic edifice, especially where early building is taking place. Where teachers use the tentative question, "Will the captain overlook this man's rudeness?" or perhaps the narrator's voice, "And the brave laid his kill before the totem", belief is likely to be strengthened rather than shaken. Whatever the comment, however, and no matter what the circumstances it remains true that a teacher's voice is one of his most valuable resources. The examples just quoted above demonstrate that brief participation or even interjections in role could be strikingly effective when adopted to serve the needs of the moment, and this is true also for older children's drama.

Discussion gives everyone an opportunity to contribute, but surprisingly many teachers do not fully exploit this potential. Sitting together and reviewing events to date or planning further development gives the teacher unrivalled opportunity for strengthening attitudes, willingness and confidence. In this respect, as in all others, the quality of the teacher's own questions and contributions to discussion makes for achievement.

There is a firm belief by teachers in schools which maintain strong curricular links that the essential disciplines and commitment supporting drama often owe much to the integrated learning environment. There was an occasion during the survey when a fourth year junior boy, having finished a jewelled clay dagger for Pharaoh's tomb, went to place it by the sarcophagus. "It has to be just right; they believed it had one special place." With such a background perhaps it is not surprising that this group's discussion on choice of Pharaoh reflected a factual belief which richly supported their drama tasks and echoes the view that the strength and nature of a curricular relationship can greatly effect commitment and enterprise. Many infants' teachers already see how effectively this relationship functions, but relatively fewer teachers working with the older age-ranges capitalise on possibilities to the same extent and perhaps should look more closely at their own work here.

Some teachers stress their wish to deepen commitment and belief in the early stages of any work to establish a convincing framework. This is exemplified by the "space drama" undertaken with third-year juniors to give them an experience of a scientific perspective. After preliminary discussion of their concepts of space,

space vehicle building, life and support systems, they were organised into groups and asked to plan a space venture.

It quickly became apparent, however, that things were not going well and the teacher diagnosed some aimlessness, a lack of specific purpose and consequently a weakened commitment and belief in the tasks being undertaken. The children were re-assembled, chairs were set out in rows and they were invited to a formal meeting as scientists called together by the government to advise on a proposed space probe. There was a serious tone to the whole business as their teacher, in government agent role, explained that advice and planning were required for the proposed space venture. During this meeting various "heads of department" were chosen on the basis of leadership and knowledge. The drama session came to an end here, having largely achieved its objectives; children were beginning to think as scientists within a dramatic situation with commitment and belief. Further planning and preparation by their teacher before subsequent work continued ensured that shape and purpose were strengthened even more. Sheets listing "requirements" were prepared and made available for choice by the various groups.

A large master chart was made for wall display, listing these tasks, providing sections for entries when decisions had been made, e.g. materials to be used, energy sources, choice of symbols, total weight, etc. Here the "what if" nature of drama was encouraging scientific hypotheses and careful work, sustained by a motivating commitment, all greatly helped by the teacher's preparation and thought. Where does this leave belief and commitment in respect of those enterprises which are initially very tentative? The upturned chairs which create the surface of a strange planet for juniors or the story which evolves as younger children construct drama together? The experience must still remain meaningful, cannot develop without points of contact and has quite soon in most cases to face implications of relationships, situations, roles and issues.

Movement is also important as a means to establish or strengthen belief. Teachers often stress how they capitalise on the mood it can so quickly create and which absorbs children so fully when the challenge is right, taking them effectively into a dramatic frame of mind. The young infants described earlier digging traps for an unfriendly ogre became caught up at once in a task which was real and produced a natural language flow as questions from their teacher prompted expression of accompanying thoughts. Similarly, the movement that represented a pre-Christian Saxon ritual to appease betrayed gods, or the Aztec dances symbolising Montezuma's dreams as Cortez approached with his soldiers induced moods of involvement and strong belief. Of course, not all movement concerns are so dramatically "weighty" as the latter examples, but nevertheless they serve the same process: other children created belief through stalking prey, experimenting as nineteenth century agricultural workers or mill-hands and toiling as poorly-fed sailors.

Examples like these suggested that here movement was contributing naturally to the total drama fabric and was not being unnecessarily separated from reflective concerns where problems were faced and solved as part of group enterprise. This whole area is one where teacher intentions need to be more clearly defined in terms of dramatic purposes and not just because a movement approach or one more verbally active is always considered appropriate. Children's speech and movement qualities combine so naturally in early dramatic play, yet often they seem to be unduly separated by later drama. When this occurs the reflective language element may be the chief casualty.

Feeling, thought and learning

At the centre of children's dramatic experiences lie the feeling and thought engendered as a result of involvement. Teachers will often refer to how children enjoy what it feels like to be someone else and enter those situations which give scope for experience of different kinds of feeling. This is seen as one of the great strengths of drama and a strong motivational force. Nevertheless, teachers sometimes express uncertainty about the place of feeling in the total drama process. To say that dramatic ventures allow children opportunities for exploring feeling in a controlled situation is undoubtedly true, yet it can mean so little at a practical level without further amplification. Hence the value of those examples previously examined which draw attention to fundamental links between feeling and role awareness, group experience, language development and which illustrate in practice the way feeling stimulates immediate thinking, as well as the more reflective processes of later discussion, writing and art.

Having acknowledged this it must also be recognised that what seems appropriate or possible for different age groups in terms of feeling in drama, requires careful thought and suitable methods. Perhaps we need to know more about its developmental characteristics than is the case at present.

Some infants' work shows how younger children can be taken into drama situations where feeling is effectively realised at their own level and contributes fully to sense of purpose and thoughtful outcomes. The groups of five year old infants who created and explored a world of Bogglybogs or enjoyed the discovery and exhilaration of being puppets manifested a strong feeling component in both drama activity and subsequent related art.

As children move through the age range a greater consciousness of feeling becomes available during drama if teachers are able to find approaches and situations offering appropriate scope. Sometimes feeling is desultory because children are being asked to engage their energies on material which makes little dramatic impact and underestimates capacities. On the other hand some drama excites strong feeling yet fails to progress from this level and achieve more sensitivity. It is not the strength of feeling that mars drama here but rather its undifferentiated nature and lack of dramatic purpose or focus.

Almost imperceptibly, discussion of feeling in a drama context also begins to involve related thinking and for some teachers the latter is a basic goal. Of course, some thinking in drama may be divorced from a strong feeling component; planning is one example, together with rule formulation or critical appraisal. In each of these areas teachers may seek relatively objective viewpoints and suggestions. Perhaps we should also note those differences discernable when active drama gives way to a complementary reflective phase. Each is important for what it contributes to the total process; the experience of being involved directly in dramatic activity so that children feel and think on their feet as participants. Though feeling and thought are not normally separated in the reflective process there may be varied threads teased out according to interest or intention.

It seems important that more teachers should recognise the range of thought drama can foster and how this also extends to the younger age groups. Those six year old infants troubled by a monster threatening their school faced up to the problem thoughtfully and considered various solutions. Though fastening its mouth with sellotape or throwing water inside to put out the fire may not be solutions nine year old juniors would advance, they are not so far removed from the older children's suggestions for dealing with Grendel which included digging a pit and crushing him with boulders. The older children went on to consider their situation in greater depth but the basic process was similar in each case – a problem requiring solution and the stimulation of varied ideas to achieve this end.

Drama often brings children (and the teacher) up against the necessity to make decisions at a dramatic level. Some teachers emphasise the great variety of problem situations available through drama and how relevant these are to "creative thinking" being encouraged in such circumstances, because the problems are open-ended and invite a range of solutions. Such views are undoubtedly justified, but they should not detract from the full scope of dramatic thought. It is often possible in drama to consider a number of possibilities and acknowledge alternative solutions, but the fundamental process involved may sometimes be a narrowing down to one possibility or outcome. So Grendel's threat began a process of open-ended divergence in thinking, as many ideas were provoked but eventually led to agreement as these ideas were appraised and eliminated one by one.

Basically what we need to achieve as teachers when considering drama, is how children can be moved into areas of significance where they will encounter appropriate challenges to learning. This does not detract from their own part in shaping events and indeed often builds on it.

When upper infants were faced with the rescue of their captured Indian chief, one outcome was a group assignment to formulate selection tests for suitable braves. In effect the task paralleled that of the older juniors choosing their new Pharaoh but here it was seven year old children creating their mental construction and giving conceptions of rescue qualities some thoughtful shape. The essential concern of the teacher in these circumstances is judging how far children have reached a stage where they can profitably undertake group tasks defined for them. Young Indian selectors required careful support which helped to control group interaction and focus thought, without providing solutions or inhibiting imaginations. Teachers sometimes move children into areas of significance more directly by adopting roles themselves or through comment. It is not unusual for both aspects to be used in a single lesson, though some teachers often make no interventions when children are working, except at a control level.

Sometimes the intention is to channel thought more effectively and slow the pace so that children have time to consider things more carefully. Where such approaches are regularly adopted, a drama discipline can emerge which builds upon the balance established between what children themselves would do and a teacher's concept of the possibilities. The two aspects should be compatible and encourage positive attitudes towards drama so that sound working habits are established.

Experienced teachers who use discussion as part of their drama approaches are normally aware that it serves varied functions. They differ in how often their children will be called together for talking things through, their own role at the time, and whether the process carries over into related classroom activities. But on two points they are generally agreed; the quality of a teacher's questions in discussion is often important for ensuring productive exchange; and there are many occasions when children need opportunity for talking things over among themselves. One teacher expressed his view in these words, "There are times when having seen them into the situation we make ourselves redundant for the moment".

Assessment

Most teachers involved in the survey believe it is necessary to assess drama activities and they accept this task as a basic component of their teaching role. They frequently emphasised its importance as essential feedback which helps determine how and when to intervene in the work, what has been achieved and those areas of difficulty requiring attention. Nevertheless, practical assessment is not without its share of problems and many teachers would welcome help in this area. The following factors offer some explanation of why difficulties may be encountered.

(a)   In drama, personal and unique responses may be evoked, reflecting the influence of children's subjective lives and worlds. Even though it is shared activity, the individual and his development is fundamentally important.

(b)   How teachers approach assessment will normally be influenced by how they see drama and what it does in terms of their own practice. It therefore involves teachers looking at their own strategies and methods as well as appraising children's endeavours.

(c)   The kinds of activity undertaken may often focus attention upon different dramatic elements and outcomes. For example, where drama stimulates reflective discussion or related language work, etc., there will probably be additional material to assess.

(d) A drama experience is more than the sum of its parts and requires an empathetic response from the teacher as well as more objective assessment.

Several teachers stressed the intuitive responses they sometimes make in drama and which do not seem to rest upon considered decisions. One experienced teacher said, "Quite a lot of work is by guess". Further teacher comments will add usefully to the discussion here.

"Teachers feel they can assess spelling or a piece of written work but assessing drama is different. A lot (in drama) depends upon what people think education is. We can learn so much about children, their real attitudes, and much of how they cope depends upon what we want them to do or be like in drama. Quality comes from children's reactions. If they're still buzzing about it after the lesson and talking, etc., as if they're still part of it, then it means involvement, therefore success. I've deepened their thinking about something or other. This is a key factor."

"I'm always happy to see children getting deeply involved on a personal basis and getting the balance between that and other aspects. My assessment looks at control of space, their own ideas, quality of discussion, role awareness, language and absorption. I include conscious appraisal by children. And we should assess the teacher's role."

"I look for a reality and children being able to see this, honesty of emotion and some thinking and bringing together of experience. I look for an appreciation of outcomes by children in the drama, that they can see consequences of events. Language is important and I look to see how it encourages children. But much depends on the situation and movement can be important too."

These comments indicate that some teachers recognise various levels of activity within drama and the fact that assessment is possible at these levels, which can be:

Level of the individual
Level of a group
Level of situation/action
Level of skills

Level of feeling and thought
Level of teacher's goals and strategies

It is not suggested that these are unrelated (indeed the contrary is true) or that they form a hierarchy. But they do represent angles from which to focus upon experience that is both individual and social and which may contain a number of different features, e.g. role-playing characters, group co-operation, language interaction, decision-making, thinking, etc. This is not to suggest that such features neatly co-exist for analysis; in drama children often move from one mode to another, sometimes working at a personal level, sometimes at a group level; discovering new skills or exercising old ones.

The view was often expressed during visits that teachers have priorities based upon their particular circumstances. Much of the work examined earlier shows how this affects their approaches and what is assessed before, during and after a lesson or period of dramatic activity. In play, the teacher's prime goal may be to encourage social co-operation or possibly stimulate role-taking and this is likely to focus his or her attention more upon these outcomes than others.

There are sufficient examples from the survey material to indicate that a number of teachers are aware of difficulties in assessment and have gone some way towards satisfactorily resolving the problems for themselves. Others, however, seem mainly conscious of the difficulties (and then not always entirely) but "persevere" without an effective rationale. Establishing such a rationale therefore seems important, although perhaps individually adapted in view of differing practices and goals so that teachers gain greater insights into possibilities, options and effective working strategies.

Within the levels previously outlined, teachers have stressed a number of factors which aid their assessment.

1 Achievement of an individual teacher's specific goals.

2 How effectively children moved into the drama situation.

3 Individual or group commitment and belief.

4 Degree of group co-operation, integration and awareness (at social and dramatic levels).

5 Grasp of movement, vocabulary, movement, gesture, sensitivity.

6 Ability to use and respond to verbal and non-verbal signals.

7 Overall mood or "emotional grip".

8 Quality of listening.

9 Ability of children to take initiative, shape, order, exploit and develop (at both planning and dramatic levels).

10 Structure and pace of the situation.

11 Awareness of space.

12 Quality of role-taking and role-making.

13 Feeling, thought and imaginative power generated.

14 Appropriateness and relevance of material or situation.

15 Use of music, special effects, etc.

16 Capacity of children to assess their work.

17 Success of teacher's own role-planning and teaching role.

18 Usefulness and quality of discussion (at all levels).

19 Children's continuing or fading interest.

20 Degree of enjoyment and self or group satisfaction.

21 Quality and range of related outcomes.

22 The relationship between teacher and children.

23 The extent to which all children found the work appealing and challenging.

24 What might follow in subsequent drama.

Two areas are often specifically emphasised:

1 Non-verbal language. Any age group must have some experience and awareness of movement and have achieved appropriate skill and sensitivity before they can communicate feeling and imaginative ideas, whether these are individual or collective. Teacher experience, insight and sensitivity build up a "standard" against which drama work can be judged. This includes gesture, mime and the "reading" of non-verbal signals within a drama lesson.

2 Verbal language. Andrew Wilkinson draws attention to the motivating force of language produced in expressive and communicative acts and stresses the value and significance when this is rich, varied and real. Through the sentence "Who says what to whom;

how, why and on which occasion", he offers a guide to some elements in the process for teachers engaged in assessing drama through its verbal (and non-verbal) language. Allowing for the age and stage of children's development, we could regard it in the following way:

Who?	Role taker. His status, knowledge and sphere of authority; his kind of language, register, attitudes and values.
What?	Reflects ongoing content/focus of the drama. The interactive content, the search for meaning awareness, understanding.
To whom?	Social relationship role; in the drama situation, he too has status, knowledge, language, attitudes, values, etc.
How?	Strength or paucity of language, nuance, shade of expression/statement, symbolic gesture, silence or action.
Why?	Motive, commitment and consequence.
On which occasion?	In drama, as in real life, what we feel, think, say and do is heavily influenced by the occasion. The unexpectedness of the appropriate, or the tension of the unexpected.

What we are assessing from language is how children grow in confidence and fluency, relating to each other role, situation and the challenge of ensuing development. How they may move from uncertainty, tentativeness and lack of experience towards a developing awareness, insight and understanding centred on people in the drama and the issues at stake. We are given evidence of whether the drama is alive, and perhaps are able to gauge the feeling and thought being generated.

Discussion proves its value again and may be regarded here as an assessment process related to many aspects of activity, critical awareness, feeling, commitment, role strength, reflection, etc. The fact that it feeds into and from the drama makes it quality significant. It represents a useful assessment tool when handled perceptively and sensitively. Certainly, though discussion children themselves may be given scope to develop their own assessment abilities.

Written language may be a further help. Most children seem capable of moving from interaction in drama to forms of written expression.

Reflected in the many different kinds of writing possible is the many-sided nature of drama and its assessment; narrative, comment, criticism, reflection, stories, letters, songs, poetry, ceremony, may all contain experiential content and be motivated and shaped in varying degrees by the involvement in drama or its planning.

Without the feedback provided by effective assessment, teachers may be handicapped in their teaching roles. Knowing how or when to move children on, why certain strategies seem desirable and what will enrich the drama process, are so often dependent upon assessment that is focused and purposeful within the frameworks created by teacher and children. It is equally necessary also for looking forward to further activities appropriate to children's developing abilities.

Footnote

The whole area of the teaching and assessment of drama has been researched and documented by Lynn McGregor's team. See *Learning Through Drama*. An Enquiry by the Schools Council Project: Drama 10–16. Lynn McGregor, Ken Robinson, Maggie Tate. Pub. Heinemann.

Reference

The Foundations of Language, A. Wilkinson, O.U.P. 1971.

Staff and resources

School resources

The drama observed during the survey and the related discussions indicate that its provision is rated highly by some schools. This is acknowledged wherever formal arrangements are made and time is allocated for drama activities. This said, a definitive summary of drama provision is difficult to compile, because there is considerable variety in how schools organise their approaches. Not only may it be regarded differently in terms of function and purpose, but staff commitment, expertise and other available resources also vary. In the younger age groups drama may not be formally separated as a curricular activity and this is also so with several junior schools even where an integrated approach is practised. Sometimes, terms are used interchangeably so that movement may be classified as drama and vice versa. Perhaps the most useful way to approach this area is through basic models of provision and organisation, looking first at the primary sector and considering middle schools separately.

Altogether 57 schools are represented. Infants' Schools 11, First Schools 5, Primary Schools 19, Junior Schools 14, Middle Schools 8.

Model 1

Infant/First Schools 12 (out of 16), Primary/Junior Schools 19 (out of 33). Class teachers are responsible for their own drama work and have hall periods allocated each week in addition to any classroom time employed. This arrangement may be timetabled as drama or movement, but sometimes it represents allocation of space and time which can be used for other purposes at the teacher's discretion, e.g. P.E., music, etc. There are many individual school variations.

(a)   Hall periods differ widely in terms of number and total time allocated. Often this is determined by how many classes there are in the school and the extent to which the hall is used for other purposes. Some schools vary the allocation for older children and give fewer, longer periods.

(b)   The B.B.C. Movement and Mime radio programmes are often used especially by younger age groups. Here time allocation is normally fixed but recording the programmes may give more flexibility.

(c) Allocation of hall time does not necessarily mean that drama will be undertaken by all teachers, and often the individual teacher's own interests and attitudes seem to be the deciding factors, though movement in this context is affected less than other forms of drama. Headteachers normally emphasise their reluctance to change this pattern when teachers are not confident about drama approaches generally.

(d) Very wide variations exist in how far drama organised in this way is an integrative feature of classroom work. Again, much depends upon the teachers and how they see drama in terms of its relationship with the curriculum and potential learning possibilities.

(e) In some schools drama arrangements are allowed to be incidental or flexible, notwithstanding any timetable formalities. Occasionally some hall periods are purposely left free for incidental use.

Model 2

Infant/First Schools 2 (out of 16), Primary/Junior Schools 6 (out of 33). These are schools organised on a class basis but have a specialist teacher for drama whose time is allocated to different classes.

Basically, the work involves a time-tabled commitment, together with necessary planning, preparation and teaching, though some advisory functions within the school are sometimes undertaken and these may influence arrangements, e.g. length of hall periods, follow up work etc.

Individual school variations:

(a) In one primary school the headmaster and two members of staff share all hall drama activities and sometimes any necessary classroom preparation. Work evolves chiefly from classroom centres of interest and related studies which lead into drama, so that integrated and thematic patterns are stressed. Co-operation between all the teachers concerned ensures that objectives and approaches are well-planned. In addition, class teachers observe their own children's drama and as a result are able to discuss developments and plan follow-up work effectively. Infant classes in the school are vertically grouped, but for hall periods upper and lower age groups work separately.

(b) The headmistress of a recently reorganised junior school used a specialist teacher to work alongside each class teacher on a regular weekly basis during one year. Thereafter specialist teaching was limited but the teacher was available for advice and consultation.

(c) An infants' school timetables its classes for drama during afternoon sessions and one teacher is responsible for the work. Normally each class will have one period a week.

Model 3

First Schools 1 (out of 16), Primary/Junior Schools 4 (out of 33). General school work is organised on a year-group or unit basis and normally, though not always, this arrangement operates in an Open Plan building. There is a hall area available, allocated to each year-group or unit at certain times during the week for drama activities. A team teaching approach is usual and drama becomes the responsibility of each team. Where it forms part of a co-operative arrangement like this, it is likely that drama will relate to those interests and themes being pursued in the school and often these provide stimulating material for dramatic exploration. Additionally, all teachers become involved to some extent in the drama work, planning approaches, sharing hall periods and encouraging subsequent outcomes. Teachers often mention the discussion necessary for co-operative work, which ranges widely over possibilities, including drama ventures.

Model 4

Primary Schools 4 (out of 33). Represented here are those schools with no hall available and consequently drama is a classroom or corridor activity. Several small schools are included in this category and normally there is some vertical grouping so that the five to eleven age range is split into three bands, separated at upper infant and middle junior points.

Individual school variations:

(a) One school uses its largest room for movement activities and to avoid unnecessary disruption this is arranged on an afternoon basis. Each class has one session during the week and teachers are responsible for their own work.

(b) A "studio" has been created in one classroom. This is an area approximately four yards square, carpeted and partially screened from the remainder of the room. Children in "family groups", i.e. several infants and juniors working together, are allocated thirty minute drama-play periods here and may work on their own or suggested themes. During selected afternoons this room is cleared and used for larger groups which are age related, thus allowing appropriate work to be undertaken. Each teacher shares in the school's drama approaches.

(c)   The headmaster is responsible for drama himself and uses it when circumstances seem opportune. Therefore no formal allocation of time is necessary. He uses the largest room and works only with the oldest children, chiefly on themes deriving from classroom studies. Dramatic play provision is available for infants and younger children in a well equipped corridor area.

Model 5

Play. The children are taught in their own classrooms where there is some provision for dramatic play (blocks, helmets, hats, dolls, etc.) and a degree of choice is permitted according to time, numbers involved and other learning tasks requiring attention. In a corner of the cloakroom a larger play area is equipped with dressing-up clothes and stimulating "props". Teachers may be helped by an assistant with N.N.E.B. qualification and they structure play situations, intervening at judicious moments with suggestions or support for the children's activities.

Individual school variations:

The extent of play provision varies widely. Some schools have completely equipped rooms while others have only small classroom areas. The amount of time allocated for play also varies. It is usually greatest for five year old children and younger but can tail off at six and seven as more formalised learning increases. A few schools allow their children to continue with dramatic play into the junior years, but provision beyond seven or eight is not extensive as a rule.

How much drama takes place?

These outlines illustrate how schools set about providing and organising drama for their pupils and in this respect they indicate needs and purposes. Yet while showing that drama is accepted as a recognised curricular activity in the schools concerned, they do not necessarily indicate the actual extent of drama practice. In several respects, of course, we are not always dealing with something measurable, even though a time table may be a very objective organisational instrument. Dramatic play in infant situations has very blurred boundaries and so has drama with more extended curricular links. But if these considerations are excluded for the moment, what can be said about the amount of dramatic activity undertaken? First, that there are schools where all children experience drama on a regular basis and build up related skills, attitudes and abilities. Second, this situation is not general, for even when formal provision is made it does not follow that facilities will be utilised; time and space may be available but much may depend upon the enthusiasm and interests of particular teachers. Third, drama is often intermittent and may either be strongly in evidence or largely absent.

The reasons why drama sometimes becomes intermittent are varied and have different roots. Often it relates to the availability of interested teachers in a school. Three schools visited were currently experiencing a fall-back in drama because valued staff members had taken up appointments elsewhere, and this situation highlights the difficulties which may be experienced when one teacher largely sustains the work and influences school attitudes. In many cases they represent a reservoir of experience, but ideally this needs to be shared with others in the school so that common strengths can be built up.

Resources required for drama

Even if these models do not represent a definitive statement of drama provision in the schools concerned, they at least indicate that different conceptions of its functions and values will greatly influence organisation and resource allocation. A willingness to foster dramatic ventures and make available the necessary resources depends upon commitment within the school, and how far this is underpinned by belief in drama's potential educational advantages. In this context the requirements for an activity which is limited to one thirty minute period a week are rather different from drama seen as an integrated part of the school's total approach to learning. There are also age factors, and differences in provision and organisation become apparent when the needs of younger and older children are considered. Perhaps these could be examined separately.

Infant classes

The infants' headmistress who stated "I can't see where drama begins and where it ends" was speaking in the context of an integrated approach to learning and the natural play world of young children. To some extent it is true of every infants' class – that drama provision has an incidental and opportunist basis for coping with the possibilities and challenges found there. Nevertheless, some formal pattern is required if only to allocate resources and indicate priorities. Consequently hall periods are normally allocated for activities including drama but are kept relatively brief, although they are available more frequently throughout the week. In this way the shorter concentration spans of younger children are recognised while at the same time opportunity is given to introduce those varying drama activities examined earlier.

These larger spaces do produce their own problems, however, and the creation of a satisfactory atmosphere and mood are often influenced by more intimate surroundings. One infants' teacher remarked, "The hall can be so overpowering to younger children and affects them in all sorts of ways. It seems to make them uneasy or fidgety and unless we're doing movement with percussion or music so that they are caught up, it's hard to get concentration." Perhaps this is one reason why, although the hall allocation is welcomed, some teachers develop aspects of drama in the classroom even when children are old enough to have gained greater confidence and suitable working habits. The infants' own room often has an immediacy of purpose and an atmosphere conducive to settling down for collective enterprise whether this be story, discussion or actual dramatic enactment. Examples of work examined in previous sections show how enterprising work can be achieved quite effectively within such an environment. In addition, of course, the classroom functions as a resource area for subsequent drama outcomes – further discussion, reading, writing, painting or making, so allowing teachers to utilise the whole of their normal resources effectively.

These extended approaches usually require approval from the school and often reflect a policy initiated by headteachers or evolving from staff discussions. Certainly a degree of staff consensus seems to be one significant feature in those schools where dramatic activities are generally apparent and allowed fuller scope. At the same time a good deal of what is attempted hinges upon the individual teacher's personal commitment and insights, so that both particular approaches and the time allowed for them reflects how far needs and goals are recognised. Flexibility is often important here, a feature emphasised by another headmistress. "I think it's necessary for teachers to have the courage and insight to drop the daily plan when opportunities appear or when drama needs more time."

The same remark could equally apply to play provision where children engage in dramatic activities of their own making. Differences in the arrangements made for play in schools underline the fact that its values and functions are not always recognised equally. Where provision is well maintained the following elements are normally included:

(a) Time for play. Teachers stress that absorption in play is common as children become immersed in a process where learning and understanding are fostered but often require a child's time rate. Many schools allow a degree of choice for these activities, especially when younger children are involved, and are flexible regarding time. Others allocate specific periods for various groups in order to ensure equal sharing of available resources.

(b) Space. Much depends on the school's layout and size. Several examples of ingenious adaptation were seen; a dramatic play area established under stairs, cloakroom areas screened off and corners utilised. Similarly, careful consideration of play provision in classrooms can make small areas available when furniture is suitably arranged.

(c) Stimulating props. These range from the imitative and realistic objects often required by younger children (or those who develop more slowly) to pieces of cloth, dresses, etc., which may extend imaginative play ventures. Selected props are often the means chosen to structure play situations or provide thematic approaches for extended work.

(d) Language and experience. The provision and organisation of dramatic play has direct implications for language and experience. Children coming together bring their own resources in addition to their individual interests and some schools capitalise by purposefully seeking a "cross-fertilisation" of interests, ideas, experience and language in play groupings. Specific examples of these arrangements were referred to in earlier sections and they have particular significance perhaps for S.P.A. of mixed ethnic areas. Back-up resources for play are also important elements in the total process. A good library for story and reference material, stimulating displays of pictures and objects, materials for related art or craft activities and visits to outside environments, have all been stressed by teachers who consider dramatic play and its provision from a wider learning perspective.

(e) Adult availability. There is no doubt that much dramatic play takes place relatively independently of teachers or their nursery assistants. However, careful structuring or intervention which offers support and guidance without diminishing children's own scope seems to be influencing more play situations. In these circumstances the availability of a sympathetic and perceptive adult is held to be desirable and advantageous.

Junior classes

It has been observed earlier that transfer into junior classes is accompanied by a change in dramatic environment for many children. There is a move away from the natural play-drama world of their infant years and a "settling in" period begins during which drama may become largely movement centred. However, some survey examples illustrate that awareness of language needs and possibilities, together with related learning and development need not be overlooked in the early junior years. There are schools where a balanced approach challenges, extends and satisfies the individuals, groups or classes concerned, without unnecessarily creating arbitrary distinctions.

When resources are discussed with junior teachers they often emphasise that adequate space is necessary to properly organise and sustain drama. There is no doubt that difficulties may occur when this is lacking, but even so drama activities have been observed in a variety of locations, including classrooms, corridors and school corners. The juniors in a village school who brought Norman lord and Saxon serfs into dramatic confrontation did so within the confines of their modest-sized classroom with some group discussion taking place in a small library area. Nevertheless, time was lost and inconvenience incurred as desks had to be stacked and rearranged. There is also some dramatic loss in these circumstances and when the headteacher's own notes of this venture are read (page 52) it can be seen that improving the listening and spatial awareness proved to be problematic when an entire "village community" had so little space for meeting. Other limitations are apparent; it would be difficult to create any sort of dramatic environment that depended upon large spaces or achieve expansive movement sequences which involved a whole class. At the same time it should be stressed that enterprising and fruitful work in junior classrooms can be undertaken where the teacher's commitment is strong enough to overcome the disadvantages.

It is clear, however, that in addition to any smaller spaces utilised, most teachers prefer allocation of larger areas for some drama work.

Not only does this allow them to develop children's drama competence more fully, but it provides an environment capable of allowing many possibilities requiring a lot of space. One or two survey schools were especially fortunate in having a large area available other than the main school hall, so that interruptions and background noises from kitchens etc. were not endured. Generally, however, the school hall does provide the main area for drama activities and most are equipped with rostra blocks, record players and tape recorders. Occasionally efforts are made by a particular school to improve the dramatic environment. One hall had been provided with curtains which could be drawn to cover large glass doors, while in another school three differently coloured spotlights arranged on the hall walls created various lighting effects. The majority of halls, however, are not readily transformed but remain as the typical multi-purpose activity spaces for large groups, not sound proofed, and often a through route within the building.

Time allocation

Sometimes the allocation of a short period of hall time to each younger class, often about thirty minutes, is maintained for the older children. The reason is usually timetabling; a certain number of classes need time and only one hall is normally available. As the number increases so does the problem. Yet most children become capable of sustaining drama for longer periods in the junior years and require time to discuss and develop their attempts. It is interesting, therefore, that some schools attempt to overcome the problem by allocating fewer but longer periods where the age group and drama approaches suggest this is desirable. Where flexibility is sought, it is occasionally achieved by reserving a limited amount of time in the hall for spontaneous drama use, but in many schools this is impossible.

It is not possible for a survey of this kind to draw firm conclusions about the effects on drama of team teaching or year group organisation, though outstanding work was seen in some schools employing these features. Much obviously depends upon commitment, expertise and some organisational skill. Where these exist then team discussions seem to extend possibilities and ensure adequate planning so that drama may be effectively realised.

Specialist teaching

Apart from children themselves, teachers form the most important resource for drama provision. Without their interest, commitment and insight no school can effectively develop drama approaches or build on children's natural capacities for dramatic activity. Visits to schools show how crucially goals, methods and achievements are bound up with having teachers on the staff who recognise possibilities and possess adequate working strategies.

Some schools attempt to ensure drama provision through specialist teachers but this is not common. When the middle schools are excluded only eight of the survey schools maintain a system whereby drama is the general teaching responsibility of specific staff members. Even in these schools the pattern varies and normally the specialism is shared by two or three teachers so that drama is only part of their total work. Of course, in many schools the occasional exchange of class occurs but this is generally confined to movement lessons, whose content may not always be drama centred.

The nature of the specialist teaching varies. In one infants' school the deputy headmistress takes all classes for drama during the week and sometimes this is related to classroom or school themes but at other times it is an independent activity. Elsewhere, an infants' headmistress gives time to fostering drama with her older children and again this may pick up a current interest or begin a new classroom theme. A further example comes from the First School whose headmaster shares drama teaching with two other colleagues and they relate the work to thematic approaches, especially in the older age groups. This pattern is also followed by a junior school headmaster who likes to see drama as an integral part of his school's learning and shares teaching with two colleagues. On the other hand a few specialist teachers work alone in junior schools and often prefer a system of "one-off" activities because they find it possible to organise approaches more effectively this way.

What are the views of those teachers who undertake specialist work? Generally they seem to enjoy the challenge and the opportunity of working in an area which engages their personal interest and expertise. Very often, however, their comments indicate that satisfaction comes from the linking of drama with other curricular areas; they are still teachers in the broad primary school sense.

Headteachers in the primary sector were generally reluctant to view specialism as a means of building up their own school drama strengths. The views expressed cover several points.

1 Specialist teaching meant attracting staff with specific expertise. They doubted whether these were available, and emphasised that even teachers coming with main course drama training from Colleges often needed considerable school experience before they were ready for any extended responsibility.

2 Specialism usually implied a responsibility allowance and an absence of normal classroom teaching duties. But in primary schools, staff resources were limited and there were many areas of priority. It was unlikely that the school could afford to have one teacher solely for drama concerns and would therefore be responsible for other duties. In these circumstances the most likely designation would be for language development or creative activities, and this would allow drama to be represented, though probably not taught as a specialism.

3 The heart of most primary approaches lay in a class-teacher or group-teacher relationship, which facilitated an overall view of learning and gave the opportunity to relate activities where desirable. Even in co-operative teaching these bonds seemed important. Therefore in most cases there was a need for every teacher to be aware of drama possibilities and improve their own expertise.

4 Nevertheless, headteacher views on drama varied and this was reflected in the kind of expertise they hoped teachers would possess. Everyone looked for sound general teaching ability, but where drama was viewed as a mode of learning then approaches were emphasised which would achieve this objective. Consequently hall periods taken by a specialist and isolated from other school work would have limited value only.

Helping the non-specialists

These views bring into perspective the problems faced in those schools which seek a stronger drama commitment and where perhaps potential benefits are recognised but not achieved. Obviously much depends upon the willingness of teachers to venture and their own desire for more effective teaching strategies using drama. In this context attitudes and insights often move together, a feature noted by several headteachers in their comments.

> "You can't legislate here; so much depends on attitudes and what they think drama can do. They need to find this out and see the value themselves. Yet the experience is needed for this to happen and if they're not convinced then they won't seek the experience."

There is much in the survey to support these comments and suggest that outside the ranks of teachers committed to drama are many others who see it as a frill, as play production, or an activity making over-heavy demands upon them. So what can be done? Some forms of in-service work will be examined briefly in the next section but here the focus is upon the school itself. How do schools influence this pattern?

Without doubt the headteacher's role is crucial. Because drama is often not a specific requirement in the normal day to day teaching, it may be neglected or narrowly conceived. By emphasising its values and effecting organisational strategies to increase both drama provision and staff insights, headteachers can improve the situation in their own schools. The models of provision outlined earlier illustrate how this was achieved in specific cases through teachers working together, either directly on dramatic hall activities, or co-operatively planning thematic approaches which used drama and involved staff teams as joint partners. Together with a willingness to make the necessary resources available, share ideas and possibly maintain some degree of flexibility, these approaches may encourage staff involvement. Certainly a head that suggests there is more to drama than formal plays or productions would be one significant step towards improving some attitudes and conceptions. The following examples represent some ways in which sharing took place on specific occasions.

(a) One teacher without drama experience planned an environmental studies theme for his class, based upon an area of the town. By arranging for additional teaching (one hour weekly) from the member of staff with most drama experience, the headteacher was able to introduce this feature into the study. Discussion between the two teachers established that a particular period of town history should be illuminated through drama. As a result the class teacher had an opportunity to integrate hall and classroom activities.

(b) New members of staff were given an hour each week when they worked alongside an experienced teacher who discussed approaches and outcomes with them. In this way it was hoped that they would build up their own strengths and insights. The period of co-operation lasted for one term so that a variety of work was involved.

(c) A team group of teachers discussed a thematic approach for the term. Between them and with the headteacher's co-operation they established a central resource area with books, pictures, objects etc., and supplemented this with children's own work as the theme developed. Regular discussion took place so that progress and possibilities were continually assessed.

(d) In one primary school an experienced teacher with responsibility for drama met with interested members of staff after school. They were not sure at this stage how to lead into dramatic activities and wanted guidance. Everyone who attended was asked to bring ideas, stories, poems or themes which could possibly be used, and these were discussed from the viewpoint of beginning drama and linking this with writing, art, etc. The teacher concerned emphasised that the biggest hurdles seemed to be confidence for starting, the recognition of how varied material could feed into drama and possessing enough working strategies to ensure satisfying work. As well as discussing approaches, staff members also attempted some simple role play situations themselves.

(e) A video recording of ongoing drama work was available for staff showing and discussion. In the same school the headteacher arranged for local T.I.E. members to work with the staff for short periods after school when the discussion was school biased.

(f) Often, work was shared in school assemblies and it was possible for other members of staff and children to see how drama was being used. This was especially the case when relevant written work (sometimes read) and art were presented at the same time.

(g) In several schools there were stimulating displays of work related to drama and these were set up in suitable areas. Consequently, attention was focused upon some of the wider learning opportunities and curricular links which were fostered.

It is difficult to estimate how far a school may be moved on through any of these methods but there is little doubt that they do help in building up drama awareness and insights among teachers. Also important is that they influence attitudes and perhaps bring a more thoughtful appreciation of drama functions. One teacher who was able to share in the work of another had this to say:

> "I can't say that drama had any appeal to me. But I was fortunate to work with a colleague who used drama a good deal. That's how I found that history comes to life in a way that's difficult to achieve normally. The children wanted to research; they wanted increased awareness of people and things because they were involved. My classroom also came to life that way. I see drama as one of the strongest tools in the teacher's toolbox for motivation or work. My attitude to drama now is what I can see it doing in the classroom, not just for the bright children but also for the less average. They think and question in drama and you can see imaginations being stirred."

Provision in areas of social difficulty

A final point concerns the social environment in which schools are set. How far does it affect the provision of drama and teacher views on its usefulness? The survey considered work undertaken in ten S.P.A. schools and drama was found to be recognised as a basis for exercising linguistic and social skills. It would not be true to say that the skills were developed for their own sake; the reflective and creative nature of drama was also emphasised. But there is little doubt that the total process was welcomed and acknowledged by those teachers concerned. Perhaps more schools in difficult areas could provide drama opportunities that promote reflective elements and take advantage of curricular links.

Some schools refer to the problems posed by mixed ethnic groups and how this can affect both drama provision and teacher requirements. One headmaster in an urban environment saw his situation in these terms:

"We have a very mixed ethnic intake and this provides many problems but drama is one means for all children to find security, achievement, skills and the chance to be creative. That's why I arrange for it and need keen dedicated teachers. Here we have a responsibility post for the work and some specialism."

Teachers themselves sometimes echo these thoughts but point out that difficulties are not easily overcome. There are often different degrees of response and varying background situations to cope with. "You have to be very careful if you intend to try social drama" was one comment. It was also pointed out that differences in language ability can mean that movement approaches are favoured, though often this stimulates subsequent language and art. Nevertheless, in some schools where these difficulties are experienced, challenging drama is attempted and provides situations for creative endeavour and varied learning. One additional point here concerns the use of incidental drama for specific learning purposes in mixed ethnic schools. From discussions it would seem that simple role playing and short dramatisation activities in class are used by teachers to give children experience of the everyday world and its language requirements. These approaches capitalise on the dramatic play element involved, the personalising of varied situations and an enhanced motivational interest.

Middle schools

Provision for drama was found in all eight middle schools visited though its extent and organisation varied. Three models illustrate some of these variations.

Model 1

Six schools (out of 8). The school is organised on a year group basis but accommodated in separate classrooms. Consequently there is some teacher–class relationship and organisation but also some specialism in various subjects. Drama is served by two specialist teachers who are responsible for the lower and upper age groups respectively. The first year intake is allocated one drama period each week (thirty-five minutes). In the second year, allocation remains unchanged except that sometimes two periods are taken weekly over part of the school year. An empty annexe classroom provides the main drama space for these age groups but tables and chairs are available for incidental use. Individual school variations:

(a) Some schools are accommodated in new open plan buildings where year groups are organised in their own areas and are the responsibility of a teaching team. Integrated approaches are then possible that parallel similar junior arrangements.

(b) Facilities vary widely; often there is a large hall available and some schools possess specific drama areas.

(c) Time allocation can range up to one hour weekly.

(d) Specialism varies; sometimes drama is taken by the teachers responsible for daily classroom work but there may be specialist provision for main drama work undertaken.

Model 2

One school (out of 8). Each year group is divided into four sub-groups and two of these are given drama facilities for one double period (an hour) weekly. After a four week cycle the facilities are made available to the remainder of each year group and a new cycle begins. In addition to the main drama space (hall) one classroom is also used – primarily for language concerns that relate to dramatic activities. Two teachers share the drama work and one holds general school responsibility for the subject in association with history. Curricular links are sometimes fostered through Related Studies (History and Geography) but require detailed discussions with other staff members to be fruitful. Consequently much of the drama is planned and organised as a four week unit especially in the first two years (nine to eleven) with thematic approaches normally being kept for the older groups. At the same time the drama staff are anxious to forge productive links within the school and their position is summarised thus:

> "The drama team will work on central themes agreed at the half-termly meetings, the total efforts being brought together for discussion and/or 'showing' at the end of a given period of time. Some team teaching is also envisaged, when one member of the staff will provide the initial stimulus and others act as supports, guiding the various group activities which ensue. It is hoped that the drama staff will offer their services to other departments so that children can explore in drama any ideas arising from other fields of study. We envisage particularly close links with the English, Related Studies and R.E. departments."

Model 3

One school (out of 8). Drama is organised together with Music and Art as an Expressive Arts approach. Within each year-group children are allowed to choose between the three areas, and time-table arrangements allocate one hour for the selected activity.

Three members of staff share the drama work, one holding general responsibility for the department and co-ordinating what is being undertaken. The headmaster is also keenly interested and teaches a good deal. He wishes to draw curricular activities together and he has linked drama purposely with the other arts but feels that stronger bonds should also exist with English, History, Geography and Religious Education. Theatre Arts are also included in the curriculum but this activity is timetabled separately so that drama and production do not become synonymous.

There is no general pattern of drama provision apparent when the middle schools are considered together. Nor do their activities reflect any significant consensus on common approaches appropriate to the middle years. This is illustrated by those main drama activities ongoing in age groups up to eleven years, when visits took place. While it is not suggested that these give a comprehensive picture of work undertaken in any individual school, they do serve to indicate how widely approaches vary and the different forms involved.

Each school is listed separately.

1 Expressive movement activities, close to P.E. but containing a dramatic element.

2 Improvisations based upon children's own suggestions and story.

3 Improvisation based upon a cave disaster and associated role play. Group activities combining movement and language. (A theme on "routes" had just been completed with improvisation, movement and related classroom work.)

4 Improvisation based upon a space theme.

5 A production based upon actual adventures at a school camp had recently involved children in contributing ideas and helping to shape the drama.

6 Group movement work.

7 Group and class movement work.

8 Group and class improvisation based upon a "relationships" theme.

As in some junior schools the extent of drama provision and the nature of the dramatic enterprise are often influenced by curricular organisation. Where schools maintain a year-group arrangement and team teaching approaches, it is possible that drama relates more closely to studies or themes being undertaken. One headmaster with this form of organisation stated, "I simply timetable my hall and drama studio for the varied year groups. They plan their own timetable within that to suit what they're doing and how much drama they want. It can take any form; mime, movement or picking up work interests." At the same time thematic interests can be developed in other circumstances along with more independent forms of drama. But sometimes specialist teachers wishing to engage in more extended work expressed the view that it is not always easy to arrange links between themselves and other teacher groups or departments; consequently much drama is "self supportive" and is planned as such. Of course, where a teacher–class relationship and organisation exists, work can be of any form within the constraints of available facilities and time. Similarly, the use of drama as an incidental feature of normal school studies often depends solely on a teacher's own propensity for assisting learning in this way.

One feature of middle school drama which does provide a common problem is that associated with first year intakes. Here the variable nature of children's past experiences and present strengths pose questions and often affect the provision required. A headmaster's comment summarises the position. "I have seven schools feeding into this building but only in one of these is there any systematic drama done. We have to create a basis for all our work in the first year." Achieving creative response, positive attitudes and co-operative working skills thus becomes a fundamental goal and influences patterns of work, perhaps to an extent where the exciting projects and themes sometimes seen in later middle years are not always considered appropriate for younger age levels.

Space

Space and other general resources for drama in middle schools are generally good, though one or two places had little more available than the average primary school – one large hall to be shared between all age groups. However, in most of the newer buildings designed for middle year intakes, careful thought had obviously been given to drama provision. Here purpose built studios or working areas enabled classes of thirty children to work comfortably and provided varied facilities that often included lighting, audio–visual equipment, adequate storage space and assorted rostra blocks for differing levels and acting arrangements. Teachers working here generally agreed that these facilities allowed atmosphere and mood to be created more effectively, helped children's attitudes (teachers' also) and avoided disturbances or interruptions. The existence of resources intended specifically for drama is an obvious inducement where provision is concerned, and it becomes possible for a school to organise on the basis that they are available for each full day if required, thus avoiding many interruptions and the claims of other activities on hall space. In addition, of course, any hall time available is a useful bonus.

Staffing

This remains a key factor governing drama provision in middle schools and is repeatedly emphasised by headteachers. If no specialism exists the situation often parallels that in junior schools where drama depends for its scope and quality upon the enthusiasm and expertise of non-specialist staff. There will always be teachers willing to use its incidental nature or undertake occasional ventures, and these are undoubtedly valuable for children's experience and learning. Yet some headteachers wish for much more and depend for this upon the organisational arrangements they make and how effectively their staffs can stimulate and employ dramatic forms. In one large school visited only a single teacher, newly equipped from in-service training, worked on drama regularly with her class, though movement and P.E. activities were undertaken on a time-tabled basis.

Specialist drama teaching is regarded by several schools as one solution to the problem and the models illustrate how this functions in varied ways depending upon the availability of teachers and the organisation of the time-table. Nevertheless, several headteachers using this approach hoped that specialism would encourage and not restrict the drama activities of other staff members. They saw specialists as a source of advice, guidance and enthusiasm for the school generally, in addition to providing drama experiences directly through their own teaching activities. However, sharing enthusiasm and expertise is usually more easily said than done, and here the middle schools face a problem met by others in the primary sector.

Headteachers of all schools serving the five to eleven age range have some concerns in common. How to maintain drama commitment and insight in the school sufficient for children's needs and capacities; the forms of organisation which seem best suited to the building, staffing resources and educational requirements; how to consider any specific curricular emphasis in the light of a particular social environment and the school's broader learning objectives; ways to encourage inter-staff enthusiasms, discussions, co-operation. One essential difference lies in the middle school span; that at eleven years children are only half way through this particular educational journey and have reached a stage where developing intellectual abilities, recognisable feeling and increasing social maturation may find in drama a useful medium for challenge, creative endeavour, expression, communication and learning.

Outside resources

Advisory services

Many of the geographical areas covered by the survey are served by specialist advisory staff who influence drama in their schools. Certainly the support and guidance they can give is welcomed by the great majority of those survey teachers who have gained from adviser involvement in their own teaching situations, either directly or through in-service courses. Perhaps the service is spread too thinly at the level of practical help but this is a problem not easily overcome when the number of schools is large and resources are limited. Nevertheless, where schools have benefited from advisory support there is usually evidence of purposeful awareness in the dramatic work undertaken.

Observations in schools suggest that the following issues seem currently important in this context.

1   The need to develop stronger interest and commitment in schools towards drama in education.

2   How to take teachers from the "springboard" stage to establish an effective rationale and work in depth.

3   Support for teachers newly using and developing drama.

4   Encouraging schools to make the best use of available resources.

In-service courses appear to provide one effective means of help and their usefulness is often stressed. However, much seems to depend upon how they are structured with the problems and needs of teachers in mind. What seems to be required ideally are frameworks within which teachers can grow in confidence and develop further insights. Perhaps this is achieved more effectively when in-service work extends over a period and supports on-going school activities. In these circumstances, opportunities for discussing problems and achievements are increased so that teachers often gain deeper drama understanding.

Several local authorities whose schools were visited during the survey have supplemented their advisory services with Teacher Advisers or Drama Advisory Teams. Their function is primarily to help with the in-service training of teachers, particularly non-specialists: sometimes they organise or contribute to courses but chiefly their time is spent assisting teachers in schools. Here they want to introduce drama and its potential benefits through working with children and building up dramatic response and disciplines whilst at the same time helping teachers gain some understanding of the medium and a knowledge of useful strategies. Two significant advantages were observed; how occasionally all staff would be involved, thus making a whole school drama conscious; and the possibilities for a productive one-to-one relationship with teachers. However, there were differences to be noted. For example, one Drama Team regarded themselves as a resource for all subject advisers, to be drawn on when appropriate, but elsewhere Teacher Advisers for drama worked exclusively in their own field. The patterns of time allocated to schools also varied and depended upon whether a concentrated effort or an extended period of support was preferred.

During the survey many teachers referred to their own relative isolation regarding drama. They wished to know more of what was happening in other schools and their approaches. In one county area the Senior Adviser for drama had attempted to meet this need at the secondary level by commissioning a series of video tapes which illustrated varied dramatic work in her schools. Accompanying the tapes was a detailed handbook offering comment and suggestions. There seems to be considerable value in this kind of approach because it supplies a visual component which is often lacking when teachers come together for courses or discussions. Furthermore, the resource represented by the tapes is capable of being used in many different circumstances and might be particularly useful for in-service purposes within single schools where staff are keen to gain further insights.

In the same area, advisory staff organised "drama days" when one school hosted children from several others and each group showed something of its own drama work. Though the polishing required for such occasions was recognised, it was felt that they offered schools an opportunity to see varied approaches and share in an enjoyable collective enterprise. Several other areas visited had similar events taking place at intervals – perhaps once a year – and the advisers hoped to strengthen appreciation of dramatic possibilities as a result.

A variation of this approach was the annual "Drama Week" instituted in another survey authority. Here children from different schools were brought together to work in drama on a common predetermined theme and one example will illustrate what was involved. The classes concerned worked for six weeks in their own schools on aspects of the theme prior to their common "workshop sessions". Meanwhile, their teachers met with advisory staff at intervals for discussion and planning. During this period children from the participating schools were in active contact with each other and used tape recordings, video and writing for this purpose.

The knowledge that they were to meet within a common framework provided a focus for the work carried out in the individual schools.

Drama centres

In several areas, schools and teachers are served by Drama Centres, often housed in converted older school buildings. Sometimes a full-time warden organises or co-ordinates their activities but drama advisory staff may also undertake this function. Teachers generally welcomed centres as a useful resource offering a variety of services. This view is reinforced by the staff who often provide a wide range of services.

(a)   The provision of a central meeting point and facilities for teachers wishing to improve their drama expertise. The value of meeting together like this was mentioned in several schools and seems to be particularly valued because it allowed discussion of ideas and experiences.

(b)   Facilities for in-service courses are often extensive. There is normally a large, well-equipped space where practical work can be undertaken, and smaller rooms for group activities. These workshop facilities offer interested teachers many opportunities to explore aspects of dramatic work and build up their own strategic resources. One warden commented, "We try to involve teachers and help them in ways they will find useful. For example, we look at how ideas can be approached from different angles and from different levels. Then we look at the practical problems concerned with how ideas may be introduced or presented. We hope to serve all teachers because we believe that they are looking for a useful grounding in drama."

(c)   The Centres sometimes act as resource pools, making equipment or other material available on loan or for reference. A source library containing drama books, stories, poems and other useful material is also occasionally built up. In one Centre display facilities allowed teachers to see something of work undertaken in other schools. Writing, art and craft, perhaps with photographs, then illustrate curricular links and serve a dissemination process. Elsewhere, an exhibition of costume encouraged children's interest and involvement by allowing items to be tried on as stimulus for imaginative work.

(d)   Provision for children to attend the Centres and engage in dramatic activities is a further service offered in some places. This may involve evenings or weekend arrangements but there are authorities where children attend during the normal working day. Advisory staff usually teach on these occasions with class teachers observing and perhaps developing work or outcomes in their own classrooms. One possible disadvantage associated with this arrangement is the idea that drama is something special or different which needs an outside agency. There is, of course, obvious value in the experiences offered to children through such visits but, ideally, perhaps the schools themselves should seek to blend these with an appreciation of drama in ordinary teaching circumstances.

Theatre in education

Schools are sometimes served by T.I.E. teams who use a combination of teaching and acting skills to structure "dramatic programmes" for children. Although these occasions often involve theatre elements, the basic intention is to stress learning rather than entertainment. Normally, schools and teachers are consulted beforehand so that chosen themes provide situations of interest to the age groups concerned and characters with whom they can readily identify in a process of dramatic exploration. The drama can take varied forms but it engages children directly as participants, allows them to share in its development and creates scope for subsequent classroom activities. Often, the theatre group concentrates effort on one or two classes in a school, perhaps visiting them weekly over an agreed period and in this way working relationships are established. Of course, the T.I.E. approach differs from typical school drama because it lacks the normal teacher–class relationship and assessment of specific needs in particular circumstances. It may also be less flexible than the work initiated and developed by teachers. Even so, T.I.E. can offer useful ways into drama and provide learning experiences which also encourage dramatic strengths and insights.

One example will illustrate how T.I.E. may function in practice. Here a programme was devised "to assist in the development of language and imagination, particularly among children in disadvantaged areas and provide experiences and opportunities for children to participate, through which their verbal and expressive skills can be stimulated and improved." Drama situations evolved from a "time machine" idea which took children into adventures with a scientific professor and his amiable assistant.

Subsequently, teachers and T.I.E. team came together for a review session when achievements and problems were discussed. This allowed exchange of ideas and appraisal of further possibilities. It represented an important part of the total process where drama provided a means for learning within structured situations and allowed teachers to use it as motivating and enriching experience.

Acknowledgements

I wish to acknowledge with gratitude the help received from the survey schools and their L.E.A.'s. They willingly gave permission to incorporate material into the text. In addition, Miss E. Foreman and Mr. G. Davies allowed access to their own studies of dramatic work and Mrs. Janet Watson made available video and film recordings. Other material came from Mrs. D. Mills, Mrs. M. Robson and Mr. K. V. Hutchinson. The project Consultative Committee gave much encouragement and support throughout the survey period.

Project consultative committee members

G. Hodgson English Adviser, Cleveland.

Miss M. E. Aspinall Head, St. Hild's School, Durham.

J. W. Bright Department of Drama, New College of Education, Durham.

J. Claypole Headmaster, Ingol Primary School, Preston, Lancs.

Miss E. Foreman Headmistress, Consett Roman Catholic Infants School, Consett, Co. Durham.

G. Gould Adviser, English and Drama, Oxfordshire.

R. Hancock Drama Adviser, Newcastle upon Tyne.

A. D. Jackson County Education Officer, Cleveland.

Mrs. L. McGregor Director, Schools Council Project; Drama Teaching 10–16.

Miss A. D. Sutton Headmistress, Stebon Primary School, I.L.E.A.

R. E. Walker Headmaster, Mount Pleasant Junior School, Darlington, Co. Durham.

Mrs. J. Watson Headmistress, Brindley Heath Junior School, Kinver, Staffordshire.

Mrs. E. Weir Headmistress, Fieldsend Primary School, Hemel Hempstead, Herts.

Miss Helen Carter Schools Council, 160 Great Portland Street, London, W1N 6LL

Miss Diana Matias Schools Council, 160 Great Portland Street, London, W1N 6LL

Mr. Murray Ward Schools Council, 160 Great Portland Street, London, W1N 6LL

Schools included in the survey

Brambles Infants' School, Middlesbrough, Cleveland.
Castletown Infants' School, Castletown, Sunderland.
Consett R.C. Infants' School, Consett, Co. Durham.
Ellerslie Infants' School, I.L.E.A.
Hedworthfield Infants' School, Jarrow, South Tyneside.
Ocean Road Infants' School, South Shields, South Tyneside.
Rossmere Infants' School, Hartlepool, Cleveland.
Western Springs Infants' School, Rugeley, Staffordshire.
Wharrior Street Infants' School, Newcastle upon Tyne.
Whickham Fellside Infants' School, Gateshead.
World's End Infants' School, Birmingham.

Dinnington First School, Dinnington Village, Newcastle upon Tync.
Greenbank First School, Rochdale, Lancs.
South Beach First School, Blyth, Northumberland.
South Wellfield First School, Whitley Bay, North Tyneside.
Turnfurlong First School, Aylesbury, Buckinghamshire.

Addison Primary School, I.L.E.A.
California Primary School, Eston, Cleveland.
Cliddesden Primary School, Basingstoke, Hampshire.
Clifford Bridge Primary School, Binley, Coventry.
Clothier Street Primary School, Willenhall, Walsall.
Combe Primary School, Combe, Oxfordshire.
Cowgate Primary School, Newcastle upon Tyne.
Dolan Primary School, Llanharan, Mid-Glamorgan.
Hart Primary School, Hart Village, Hartlepool, Cleveland.
Highfields Primary School, Sandwell, W. Midlands.
Kenmont Primary School, I.L.E.A.
Kenton Bar Primary School, Newcastle upon Tyne.
Kingsley Primary School, Hartlepool, Cleveland.
Marley Hill Primary School, Gateshead.

Mount Pleasant Primary School, Darlington, Co. Durham.
Rollright Primary School, Great Rollright, Oxfordshire.
Springlands Primary School, Sudbury, Suffolk.
St. Josephs R.C. Combined Primary School, Sutton Coldfield, Birmingham.
Stourton Primary School, Stourton, Leeds.
Walshaw Primary School, Walshaw, Bury.

Brandhall Junior School, Warley, Sandwell, W. Midlands.
Brindley Heath Junior School, Kinver, Staffordshire.
Bucksin Junior School, Basingstoke, Hampshire.
Deighton Gates Junior School, Wetherby, Leeds.
Five Elms Junior School, Dagenham, Barking.
Manton Junior School, Manton, Nottinghamshire.
Oakfield Junior School, Cwmbran, Gwent.
Oatfields Junior School, Harrogate, North Yorkshire.
Sacriston Junior School, Sacriston, Co. Durham.
Throston Junior School, Hartlepool, Cleveland.
Towers Junior School, Hornchurch, Havering.
West Boldon Junior School, West Boldon, South Tyneside.
Wharrior Street Junior School, Newcastle upon Tyne.

Blackwood Middle School, Streetly, Walsall.
Byewell Middle School, Dewsbury, Kirklees.
Fir Tree Middle School, Leeds.
Gosforth Middle School, Newcastle upon Tyne.
Harehills Middle School, Leeds.
Hayden Middle School, Aylesbury, Buckinghamshire.
Horringer Court Middle School, Bury St. Edmunds, Suffolk.
Redbrook Middle School, Rochdale.